After Council Housing

Also by the authors

Bramley, G., Munro, M. and Pawson, H., *Key Issues in Housing: Policies and Markets in 21st -Century Britain*

Mullins, D. and Murie, A., *Housing Policy in the UK*

Pawson, H. and Mullins, D., *Allocating Social Housing: Law and Practice in the Management of Social Housing*

After Council Housing
Britain's New Social Landlords

**Hal Pawson
and
David Mullins**

with
Tony Gilmour

First published 2010 by
PALGRAVE MACMILLAN

Palgrave Macmillan in the UK is an imprint of Macmillan Publishers Limited, registered in England, company number 785998, of Houndmills, Basingstoke, Hampshire RG21 6XS.

Palgrave Macmillan in the US is a division of St Martin's Press LLC, 175 Fifth Avenue, New York, NY 10010.

Palgrave Macmillan is the global academic imprint of the above companies and has companies and representatives throughout the world.

Palgrave® and Macmillan® are registered trademarks in the United States, the United Kingdom, Europe and other countries.

ISBN 978–1–4039–3514–4   hardback
ISBN 978–1–4039–3515–1   paperback

This book is printed on paper suitable for recycling and made from fully managed and sustained forest sources. Logging, pulping and manufacturing processes are expected to conform to the environmental regulations of the country of origin.

A catalogue record for this book is available from the British Library.

A catalog record for this book is available from the Library of Congress.

10 9 8 7 6 5 4 3 2 1
19 18 17 16 15 14 13 12 11 10

Printed in China

Contents

List of Tables

List of Figures

List of Boxes

List of Abbreviations

ALMO	Arms Length Management Organizations, England
BME	Black and minority ethnic
CBHA	Community-based housing association
CIH	Chartered Institute of Housing
CLG	Department for Communities and Local Government, England (from 2006)
DCH	Defend Council Housing
DETR	Department of the Environment, Transport and the Regions
DoE	Department of the Environment
ERCF	Estates Renewal Challenge Fund
GGFD	General Government Financial Deficit
HAT	Housing Action Trust
HRA	Housing Revenue Account
LHC	Local Housing Company
LSVT	Large Scale Voluntary Transfer
NFA	National Federation of ALMOs
NHF	National Housing Federation
ODPM	Office of the Deputy Prime Minister, England (to 2006)
PFI	Private Finance Initiative
PSBR	Public Sector Borrowing Requirement
PSNB	Public Sector Net Borrowing
RPI	Retail Price Index
RSL	Registered Social Landlord
SSHA	Scottish Special Housing Association
TMO	Tenant Management Organization
TUPE	Transfer of Undertakings, Protection of Employment

Acknowledgements

We are enormously grateful to the Joseph Rowntree Foundation and the Communities and Local Government Department (and its predecessors) which funded or commissioned our research for a number of studies on which our text draws. We would also thank the numerous people who contributed to these projects as research participants or Advisory Group members and to the many officials in Government departments, the former Housing Corporation, local authorities and the new landlords who provided access to data and tacit knowledge to enrich our account.

We would also like to acknowledge the help of various colleagues who provided invaluable expert advice on drafting certain chapters – especially John Perry and Steve Wilcox, as well as the intellectual stimulus provided by Peter Malpass which runs throughout the book.

Finally, as the two lead authors, Hal Pawson and David Mullins, are especially grateful for the input of Dr Tony Gilmour, who led on the drafting of Chapter 8 (ALMOs) and contributed to other chapters as well as managing referencing and indexing for the entire text.

HAL PAWSON
DAVID MULLINS

Acknowledgments

Chapter 1

Modernizing Social Housing

' . . . putting New Labour values into action . . . buried for good the old ideological split between the public and the private sector' (Tony Blair 1999: 2).

'As social housing moves to organisations that are legally independent of the state those organisations are increasingly instruments of policy, delivering a national programme that is specified in much more detail than was ever the case in the past' (Malpass 2005: 206).

This book examines a process that, over the past two decades, has seen the transfer of more than a third of Britain's council homes from local authority ownership, management and control to the independent non-profit housing sector, generally known as the housing association sector. By 2009, in almost half of municipalities in England and Wales 'council housing' was a thing of the past. As the quotes above indicate this change process has been subject to many interpretations. For some it is seen as part of an ideological project, for others it is seen as a pragmatic response to meeting tenants' aspirations as the following quote from the Labour Government's first Housing Minister indicates: 'I have no ideological objection to, nor ideological obsession with, the transfer of local authority housing. If it works, and it's what tenants want, transfer may be the appropriate option. What matters is what works' (Armstrong 1998: 4). What is not in doubt is that there has been a massive switch of ownership and management of former council housing to third sector housing associations. What this means in terms of the role of the state and the market, or the ability of government to steer policy delivery, has been the subject of wide ranging debates.

This process is usually referred to as stock transfer. Its common elements are the sale of large parcels of tenanted housing stock by local authorities to registered housing associations following a positive test of tenant opinion (usually by ballot), approval by the Secretary of State, and private borrowing by the new landlord to finance the purchase and repair of the property portfolio.

The process has several variants regarding the proportion of an authority's housing portfolio that is encompassed by the transaction and the nature of the receiving organization. Most frequently the entire stock is transferred to a single newly-established registered housing association; however, in some cases transfers have been to more than one new landlord, to specially created subsidiaries of existing registered housing associations, or direct into an existing association. From 2000, in England, two alternative options were introduced for local authorities to attract funding to upgrade their housing stock. These options – Arms Length Management Organizations (ALMO) and Private Finance Initiative (PFI) – also transfer management and investment responsibilities from local authorities to third parties but preserve long-term council ownership. A fourth option of enabling authorities to borrow to improve their homes without transfer of functions has been much discussed, but has so far been confined to 'prudential borrowing' against income streams rather than against the asset value of the housing stock.

The greatest overall impact of these changes has been felt in England. However, our title 'Britain's New Social Landlords' means that we have been keen to recognize the distinctive national dimension of stock transfer in Scotland, where there has been a longer tradition of small-scale transfers to community-based housing associations, and Wales, where until recently there has been more limited transfer activity (see Chapter 2). After 2000, take-up of the new ALMO option gathered pace in England, with almost a quarter of social housing under ALMO management by 2008, alongside a similar proportion accounted for by stock transfer housing associations (see Figure 1.1). We therefore include an account (see Chapter 8) of the experience of ALMOs in managing council housing at arm's length without taking transfer of the asset or moving outside of the public sector accounts, incorporate emerging evidence (Reid et al. 2007).

The nature of the transfer process is underpinned by a number of contingent political and financial factors. National politics have been important in setting the context and regulations for transfer in different periods, local politics have affected the extent of support for transfer, the formation of opposition campaigns and emerging and changing relationships between the local authority and new landlord in the years after transfer (see Chapter 4).

Meanwhile there can be no escaping the fact that the primary driver for transfer has almost always been financial, as a means to secure the resources required to remedy the backlog of council housing disrepair. The transaction at the centre of the transfer process is the purchase of the housing stock from the local authority funded by a large private loan. The valuation of the stock, the terms of the loan and the robustness of the business plan against which the money is borrowed, and whether there is 'overhanging debt' are all crucial factors that have affected the scope for transfer and the prospects of the new organizations set up to manage the acquired asset (see Chapter 3). Meanwhile, the ways in which the new organization is governed and accounts to external stakeholders (see Chapter 5) and its internal organizational culture (see Chapter 6) are key elements to understanding some of the differentiation that has emerged among Britain's new social landlords.

The quantitative significance of these changes for the ways in which social housing is provided in different parts of Britain is discussed in detail in Chapter 2. Transfer has been equally important as a route to de-municipalization (where in recent years it has overtaken the right to buy as the main mechanism for erosion of council stock), and in expanding the housing association sector (where, post-1997, it became considerably more important than new building in increasing associations' asset holdings).

The impact of transfer on de-municipalization of housing is its most widely recognized quantitative impact. Since 1988 more than half of all local authorities in England, Scotland and Wales have transferred all or part of their housing stock to registered housing associations. Over 180 have ceased to be landlords altogether as a result of whole stock transfers to one or more housing associations (see Table 2.2). Central government sought to counter the perception held by some early transfer authorities that this ended their housing role altogether (see Chapter 9). Rather, Ministers argued that the *separation* of strategic from operational housing functions was beneficial in itself. There has been increasing expectation that authorities should develop an effective housing strategy role after transfer. Extensive guidance has been produced to support this, and Audit Commission inspections have stimulated increased emphasis on the strategic role of post-transfer authorities in England. Nevertheless, the loss of housing management has had major implications for the size and structure of these authorities and raised issues for managers of central services previously supported by a large client department.

The political implications have also been substantial with councillors losing the possibility of clientelist relationships with tenants and housing trade unions, whereby in some cases they perceived an ability to influence lettings and housing management and to support public sector jobs (e.g. in direct labour organizations). Some councillors have experienced difficulties in coming to terms with the different expectations placed on them as housing association board members or simply as ward councillors in areas with significant stocks of social housing now outside the authority's direct control. Councillors' desire to retain greater influence was one of the drivers for the local housing company model of transfer in the mid- 1990s and the development of ALMOs as an alternative to transfer after 2000. In the case of ALMOs, local authorities continue to own the asset, but with an institutionalized separation of operations from strategy and governance vested in autonomous boards with minority local authority membership.

The impact of stock transfer on the composition of the housing association sector has also been substantial, particularly in England where over 50 per cent of the largest stock-holding associations in 2007 had their origins in the stock transfer process. The entry of these large-scale landlords posed particular challenges for the key institutions operating in the housing association sector. For the Housing Corporation, which between 1964 and 2008 was the funder and regulator of housing associations in England, there was the challenge of registering and regulating significant numbers of new associations, with risk profiles associated with high ratios of debt to assets and relatively inexperienced boards and senior management teams. For the National Housing Federation (NHF), the housing association trade body in England, there was the challenge of maintaining a unified non-profit housing sector by balancing the interests of traditional and stock transfer associations.

Both these challenges have been met with fairly high levels of success. While some English transfer landlords have encountered episodes of Housing Corporation intervention and supervision and lessons have been learned (Ashby 1999, Ashby and Dudman 2003, Tickell and Phethan 2006), most transfer associations have avoided major regulatory problems. The NHF has successfully absorbed the new members, who are well represented in its committees and activities; for example, peer mentoring for chairs of newly established transfer associations.

Here we can summarize these impacts by looking at how the make-up of social renting has changed since 1981 – see Figures 1.1–1.3. Figure 1.1 shows that, by 2008, stock managed by transfer landlords and ALMOs together accounted for almost half of all social housing in England. While the ALMO model has not been made available in Wales or Scotland, Figures 1.2 and 1.3 illustrate how transfer housing associations have also come to account for a sizeable share of all social housing in each jurisdiction.

If these trends continued the expectation would have been the end of *directly managed* council housing by 2015. However, the 2007 Housing Green Paper published shortly after Gordon Brown's succession as Labour leader indicated renewed Ministerial support for local authorities in a housing provider role (CLG 2007a: 38). Subsequently, albeit on a modest scale, central government funding for new council-house building has been made available in both England and Scotland. These moves

FIGURE 1.1   English social housing restructuring, 1981–2008

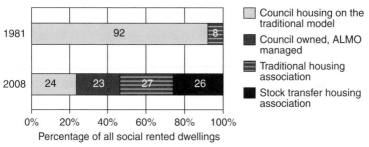

Sources: Wilcox (2009), Housing Corporation RSR data, National Federation of ALMOs.

FIGURE 1.2   Welsh social housing restructuring, 1981–2008

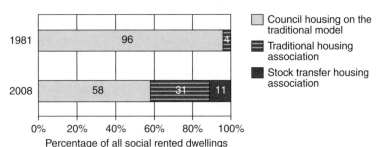

*Source*s: Welsh Assembly Government (2008); unpublished WAG figures on stock transfers.

FIGURE 1.3   Scottish social housing restructuring, 1981–2008

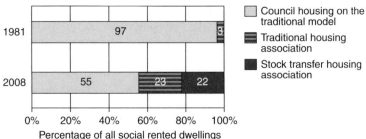

Sources: Scottish Government website; Scottish Housing Regulator website.

have been perceived by defenders of council housing as heralding a significant shift in Government policy (see Chapter 4).

More fundamental changes to the drivers for transfer emerged in 2009 when a long awaited review of the local authority Housing Revenue Account (HRA) system was completed, changing some of the incentive structures that had stimulated the long-term trend to transfer (see Chapters 3, 8 and 10). At the same time, the scale of public debt arising from the credit crisis, falling income tax revenues and bank rescues of 2008 had created a fundamentally changed environment for public expenditure. One key consequence was the prospect of an end to government financial support in cases where the anticipated transfer receipt was insufficient to repay a local authority's outstanding housing debt.

As further discussed in Chapter 10, the credit crisis also changed the environment for private finance of stock transfers. From 2008 interest rate margins on new loans rose, and more aggressive banking practices created the potential for negative impacts on the rates for overall loan portfolios of existing housing associations taking on new stock transfer subsidiaries. There was also a change in the ways in which funders viewed risk associated with property, and an increased use by housing associations of alternative funding mechanisms such as bond issues. The decline in land and property asset values, as well as the prospect of more general deflation, also impacted on valuations and business plans for stock transfers. Finally, the credit crisis challenged some of the underlying assumptions on which the expansion of third sector housing through stock transfer had been based. For example, there was speculation that the advantages of housing associations in borrowing outside of public expenditure could perversely become less significant in the context of a situation where overall government debt had, in any case, ballooned well beyond previously accepted limits (Joseph 2009). Taken together these factors led some housing press commentators to ask 'Is Stock Transfer Dead?' (Stothart 2009) – a question to which we return in Chapter 10.

Broader context

Our core argument is that these trends in social housing ownership and management are not just of statistical interest, but represent significant changes in the role of the state, the management of public services and the incorporation of the third sector that need to be considered in a broader context than housing policy. Seen in this way, stock transfer is not just about replacing one set of managers with another but may be one of the most significant shifts in the UK welfare state since the Second World War.

The constitutional and financial status of housing associations as third sector non-profit bodies delivering public services using a mix of public and private funding places them at the centre of current thinking about the modernization of public services. While subject to government regulation, these bodies are constitutionally independent, can raise private finance and bear financial risk. The process through which growing numbers of local authority homes have been transferred to these bodies could be seen as a prime example of exposure of public services to commercial disciplines. Given their non-profit distributing status and long-term commitment to the provision of affordable homes, associations occupy a distinctive position between the state and the market. This position is reinforced by their independent governance by boards made up of a mix of local authority persons, service users and independent experts. Recent promotion of the potential role of the third sector and social enterprise in service delivery has referred to the positive model provided by housing associations in this respect. Significantly, the definition of third sector organizations goes out of its way to emphasize the example of housing associations:

> The Government defines the third sector as non-governmental organisations that are value driven and which principally reinvest their surpluses to further social, environmental or cultural objectives. It includes voluntary and community organisations, charities, social enterprises, cooperatives and mutuals. We also include housing associations within the third sector. (CLG 2009d)

This raises questions about comparability between countries and between sectors. Has stock transfer led to a degree of convergence with most other European countries where social housing is already mostly provided by independent landlords? In some cases – such as the Netherlands and Sweden – these landlords operate on a non-profit basis; in others – such as Germany – they may distribute profits and have a shorter-term contractual commitment to a social housing role. Is the transfer of social housing to the non-profit sector a reflection of wider changes in the welfare regime, an advanced guard of the recent drive to incorporate third sector, voluntary, community and non-profit organizations as delivery agents for other public services? If so, what lessons can be learned from stock transfers that are relevant to other sectors?

This leads us to raise two types of questions that we try to address in the remainder of the book. The first set of questions concern the relative importance of top-down (vertical) influences on policy and practice (such as regulation and funding) and of bottom-up (horizontal) influences in which local actors and their organizations are involved directly in determining the direction of change. The second set of questions concerns the interpretation, meaning and impact of these changes. There are important debates about the local impacts of stock transfer on democracy and accountability – has the process created a democratic deficit, and what levers remain available to local authorities to fulfil rising expectations for their housing strategy and enabling role (the latter questions are addressed in Chapters 5 and 9)?

Housing and the welfare state

Malpass (2005) provides a comprehensive analysis of the relationship between housing and the welfare state in Britain since 1945. Contesting the view that housing was a core element of the post-war welfare settlement which was picked off by the neo-liberal tide of Thatcherism, Malpass argues that although housing was a key part of reconstruction plans it was not part of the innovation associated with the welfare state during and after the Second World War. Rather than a radical new approach to housing, there was a temporarily enhanced role for local authorities with more generous exchequer subsidies until the major shortages occasioned by war were over. At that point, the role of the market would increase. In practice, this is largely what happened, although the scale of the housing stock controlled by municipal authorities continued to grow until 1979.

In his analysis of the post-1979 period, Malpass highlights the emergence of the non-municipal alternative to council housing: 'Public funding brought housing associations towards the centre of housing policy . . . but at a price in terms of lost independence' (ibid: 115–16). Following the advent of stock transfer from 1988, the transition from municipal to non-municipal dominance of social renting was complete, leading to what Malpass terms 'a new organizational settlement of the welfare state implicit in New Labour references to the modernization of public services' (ibid: 185). In this new settlement, network forms of co-ordination between fragmented delivery organizations supplant the vertically integrated functional departments of government. Referring to Foucault (1977), Malpass argues that while such organizations are notionally

independent of government they are heavily managed and regulated and subject to 'technologies of control'. Housing is seen
as illustrating the moving frontiers of the welfare state and
stock transfer of council housing is seen as 'showing what can
happen to apparently entrenched public services in a relatively
short run of years' (ibid: 216). And yet Malpass is not convinced by the privatization critique of transfer since 'returns to
investors in RSLs are not proportionate to the performance of
the organisation. All surpluses are retained and can only be
spent on developing the service' (ibid: 194).

We return to the question of whether stock transfer can be
fairly depicted as a simple case of privatization in Chapter 4.
Here, we simply note the divided views of writers on the implications of stock transfer for our understanding of the welfare
state. Ginsburg (2005) introduces the idea of a staged transformation within the context of neo-liberalism and retreat from
the welfare state model, reflecting that 'the notion of universally accessible, comprehensive, affordable and democratically
accountable rented housing as a public service is disappearing'
(ibid: 133). He accepts that, in the short term, transfer can be
interpreted as 'a new form of the public realm in housing' combining tenant empowerment with non-profit status 'to provide
common ground between stock transfer associations and longer
established voluntary organisations which provide space for
expressions of civil society between state and market' (Mullins
1998: 146). In the longer term, however, Ginsburg argues that
this accommodation will be hard to sustain. Consequently, his
preferred interpretation is that transfer 'marks a decisive shift
towards monopolistic private landlordism, with public control
and accountability fading away over time – a true privatisation'
(Ginsburg 2005: 132).

Public policy reforms

Another interpretation of stock transfer associated with the
notion of a 'new organizational settlement' is the working out
of agendas of managerialism in the administration and delivery
of public services. Clarke and Newman (1997) have argued
that managerialism was implanted into public services in
Britain as the basis of a new organizational settlement, shifting

power from professionals to managers. Managerialism emphasized management models derived from the private sector and
gave priority to efficiency and performance over more qualitative aspects of public services. Newman defined managerialism
as 'a discourse which sets out the necessity of change; a set of
tools to drive up performance; and a means through which an
organisation can transform itself to deliver a modernised
notion of public purpose to a modern conception of "the
people"' (Newman 2000: 58). Managerialism is a key feature
of what has come to be known as 'new public management'.
Hood (1995) identified seven main elements of the new public
management: disaggregation, competition, private sector management, economy, hands-on top management, performance
measurement and the measurement of outputs.

Stock transfer could be said to exemplify several of these
aspects of the new public management in terms of separating
operations from strategy, disaggregating large-scale monopolies
into smaller units (although in this case there has been a degree
of subsequent re-aggregation), introducing competition and
financial incentives and a more businesslike culture, and performance based external regulation. Walker (2001) detected considerable evidence of new managerialism within the housing
association sector, with private borrowing the key driver for
the adoption of private sector management ideas, efficiency
drives, de-layering and performance management. He pointed
to a refocusing of stock transfer and other associations on core
property-related functions and argued that it is 'unlikely that
they will develop as welfare or people-based organisations that
commentators and politicians desire' (ibid: 693). More specific
studies of stock transfer associations by Mullins et al. (1992,
1995), Pollitt et al. (1998), Pawson and Fancy (2003) and
Pawson et al. (2004) have provided opportunities for further
exploration, often confounding or at least contextualizing the
impact of reforms associated with the new public management.

Mullins et al. (1992, 1995) reviewed some of the earliest
stock transfers over their first few years of operation. While
this research was not specifically framed as being about new
public management, it found some organizational changes
fitting this paradigm. For example, national policies on size
limits to the amount of stock that could be included in a single
transfer (initially 5,000 but then increased to accommodate the

first London transfer of 12,000 homes in Bromley in 1992) and regulations preventing transfer of adjacent authorities stock to the same landlord could be directly related to the idea of disaggregating management into smaller units and promoting competition. However, both these constraints were later removed in the interests of promoting larger transfers and the potential efficiency of the growing housing association sector.

Internally, as revealed by this early research, stock transfer associations were becoming 'more businesslike', had adopted strong performance cultures focused on meeting business plan targets and Housing Corporation regulatory requirements, had a stronger customer focus than their predecessor authorities and were pursuing growth and diversification strategies such as new development, geographical expansion, providing advice to new stock transfers and housing management services to other landlords.

External influences on these associations included the need to adapt to Housing Corporation regulation and to the requirements of lenders. There was often an ambition to 'become true housing associations rather than agencies set up to manage former council housing stock' (Mullins et al. 1995: 68). 'We do not want ourselves, nor other local authority-sponsored housing associations, to be seen as a separate breed. We seek integration with the existing housing association movement' (former Chief Executive of 1990 transfer association cited in Pawson and Fancy (2003: 39)). This suggests the relevance of institutional theory, which stresses the need of managers for legitimacy (Pollitt et al. 1998) which may be derived as much from the symbolic as from rational actions (Meyer and Rowan 1977). DiMaggio and Powell's (1983) concept of isomorphism explaining how organizations in a particular field come to resemble one another as much for symbolic as for functional reasons seems to be quite relevant to the stock transfer field.

Transfer associations' need to conform to regulation can be seen as a form of coercive isomorphism in which officially sanctioned organizational models and practices had to be adopted. A more hidden form of isomorphism resulted from the dominance of a few housing consultancies in advising local authorities and new landlords on organizational models and policies. This could be interpreted as 'mimetic isomorphism' in which associations voluntarily acceded to a limited menu of models sanctioned by these consultants and copied from their earlier commissions.

The desire to become 'true housing associations' suggests a more normative type of isomorphism in which transfer associations began to adopt the cultural beliefs and values of the wider housing association sector, completing their transition from local authority departments to independent social landlords (Mullins and Riseborough 1997). While a common strategy was to present the new association as the least change option, *'what you have now only better'* (Mullins et al. 1992: 42), and Transfer of Undertakings, Protection of Employment (TUPE) requirements meant that stock acquiring associations initially took on most relevant local authority housing staff, it was common for associations to make changes a few years after transfer, particularly in response to business plan challenges. These reforms generally moved them in a more businesslike direction. In one case study the new association had initially adopted a 'business as usual' stance, but had underestimated the changes needed to adapt to the housing association world. After a business plan shortfall and a Housing Corporation supervision episode, managers restructured the association's finances and staffing, recognized the different requirements of the housing association sector and promoted a new organizational culture with a greater emphasis on staff, committee and tenant participation.

Pollitt et al. (1998) explored four early transfers in a comparative study of decentralization of public service management alongside examples from health and education. They used the term decentralization to refer to elements of management reform programmes pursued by UK governments involving the 'spreading of formal authority from a smaller to a larger number of actors' (ibid: 6). Three paired types of decentralization were identified – see Table 1.1.

TABLE 1.1   *Paired forms of decentralization*

Political	Administrative
Competitive	Non-competitive
Internal Decentralization	Devolution

Source: Based on Politt, Birchall and Putnam (1998) Figure 2.1.

Pollitt and colleagues characterized elements of both adminis-trative and political decentralization within stock transfer. Political decentralization was seen as the more important dimension involving reduced formal authority for local council-lors. Administrative decentralization was less marked since transfer was seen as 'to a body that essentially consists of the same group of managers and front-line staff, doing much the same tasks and dealing with the same group of tenants' (ibid: 154). The decentralization process was deemed to be non-com-petitive since at that time there was no opportunity for tenants to choose between competing new landlords, simply to decide collectively whether to accept the offer from the new landlord or to remain with the local authority, and because the new landlords showed little appetite for exposing their core func-tions to outsourcing.

The asset base secured by the acquiring association is a dis-tinctive feature of housing transfers, compared with decentral-ization in health and education, because it provides the basis for independent agency and potential for reduced dependence on vertical links with government. The potential of asset-holding as a basis for independence is well illustrated by the strength of the Dutch housing association sector which has operated independently of Government following the transfer of assets and historic subsidies from government in 1995 fol-lowed by ten years of asset appreciation in a rising property market. Similarly, asset transfer strategies are forming an important element of the English Office of the Third Sector in seeking to build the capacity of third sector organizations in delivering public services and empowering communities. An example is the 2007 Community Assets Programme stimulated by the Quirk (2007) review.

Having defined stock transfer as constituting political and administrative, non-competitive decentralization and devolu-tion, Pollitt and colleagues reached much more equivocal con-clusions on whether the new organizations exhibited the key features expected of decentralization reforms in terms of collec-tive action and rational choice, institutional theory and rhetor-ical analysis. For example, they found that 'the rhetoric of transfer almost completely ignored the vocabulary of the new managerialism', with 'the language of housing management and development overlaid with some more general jargon related to customer care' (ibid: 160). They were unconvinced that external regulation was a stronger driver for transfer associations than for predecessor local authorities and found it 'difficult to discern more than a superficial commitment to a performance culture' (ibid: 148). However, their research did confirm the strong attention paid to the business plan and tensions between some transfer associations and home local authorities over plans for geographical expansion. The professionals interviewed generally welcomed the reduced influence of local politicians and some argued in a similar vein to the Conservative Minister Waldegrave that, rather than leading to a democratic deficit, stock transfer had stimulated greater accountability to residents.

Several years later, the 'Maturing Assets' study based on a more recent cohort of transfer associations reached somewhat different conclusions to Pollitt et al. in relation to consumerism and the performance culture. They found evidence of staff ownership of transfer objectives, a more consumerist ethic *'let's find a reason to say yes rather than no'* (Pawson and Fancy 2003: 23) and customer focused approach to housing management and also more united and businesslike boards. However, changes were more modest than anticipated in relation to 'private sector' managerial frameworks such as performance-related pay and associated salary differentials.

The Maturing Assets research reported that transfer associations tended to adopt flatter, leaner staff structures in reviews conducted a while after the initial TUPE-based transfers. While, as Mullins et al. had earlier suggested, this sometimes resulted from budgetary pressures unanticipated in original business plans, it was also found that notional staff savings tend to be factored into business plans from, say, the third year to eliminate 'excess costs perhaps owing to a need to accommodate local authority sensibilities in advance of transfer' (Pawson and Fancy 2003: 14).

Like Pollitt et al., Pawson and Fancy identified growth strategies among transfer landlords and went on to explore organizational implications such as the establishment of group structures to facilitate scale economies and accommodate diversification. Additionally, the research highlighted some tensions arising from restructuring of some smaller transfer associations initially set up as subsidiaries of larger housing association groups to provide for a measure of local accountability. Subsequent amalgamations of some of these subsidiaries with their parent associations were 'generally presented as efficiency measures required to meet business plan targets . . . [however] transfer housing association staff . . . may see such moves as betraying pre-ballot promises of local autonomy. The often acute nature of such tensions may help to explain what appears to be a relatively high level of turnover among subsidiary housing association chief officers' (ibid: 18).

Modernizing social housing delivery

The fit of stock transfer with the 'modernization' focus of Tony Blair's Labour governments over a decade (1997–2007) is also a close one. Daly et al. (2005) refer to a further driver for stock transfer that linked New Labour with its predecessor Conservative government, the view that council housing was a 'redundant project' characterized by falling demand, poor quality stock, unresponsive services and poor management and requiring significant rebranding.

Newman (2001) saw Blair's modernization project as combining new public management approaches such as managerialism and decentralization with a new emphasis on social inclusion, joined-up government and positive outcomes for communities. This also entailed the promotion of choice and responsibility, and the creation of a mixed economy of welfare with an important role for disaggregation processes such as stock transfer. This became the favoured option for attacking problems of poor social housing in urban areas which had generally resisted the tide towards transfers under the Conservatives. But, as discussed in Chapter 5, this required changes to the stock transfer model to accommodate aspirations for greater democratic input amongst many urban authorities, to adapt to the significantly worse housing conditions and higher debt levels in urban areas, to respond to the wider social and community regeneration needs of many urban housing estates and to overcome the limitations of the earlier decentralization model of 'single purpose' agencies.

Table 1.2 summarizes some of the key changes to the stock transfer model that can be seen as congruent with the New

TABLE 1.2   *Modernization of transfer model to extend reach to urban areas from mid-late 1990s*

Problem	Solution
Limited democratic input	Local Housing Company model enabled by 1996 Act for 1/3 local authority, 1/3 tenant and 1/3 independent representation on boards
Rundown inner city estates	Estates Renewal Challenge Fund to stimulate small-scale urban transfers
Overhanging debt (see Chapter 3)	Local authority housing debt write-off to facilitate transfers where the capital receipt is insufficient to achieve this
Negative valuation (see Chapter 3)	Government 'gap funding' subsidy to underpin transfer association business plans
Wider community needs	Wider community regeneration expectations for transfers
Limitations of single purpose housing remit	Expectation for transfer landlords to take wider role and form partnerships with other local agencies to promote community regeneration

Labour modernization project. While some of these changes were developed towards the end of the Conservative administration, they were avidly taken up as part of the Blairite modernization project.

The tension between markets and communities as drivers of modernization is writ large in housing policy. Public finance considerations dictated that the Blair Government of 1997 would not depart from starving 'unreformed' local authorities of the investment needed to modernize their housing stock. Social and community aspirations dictated that minimum standards would be set that all social housing should meet. In 2000, a Green Paper introduced the Decent Homes Standard as the mechanism that would be used to resolve this tension, with all English local authorities required to undertake option appraisals to identify how they would attract the resources to meet this standard for all their housing stock by 2010. It was at this time that the new options of ALMOs and PFI were introduced to provide some alternatives to stock transfer that might appeal to urban authorities and provide an impression of choice.

However, the limits to choice were particularly exposed by consistent failure by the Blair Government to accede to pressures from trade union and tenant activists for a 'fourth option' that would enable all local authorities to retain ownership and management of local authority housing and to secure the resources necessary for modernization to meet the Decent Homes Standard (Centre for Public Services 2004). Limits to choice were particularly apparent for authorities such as Birmingham, which had failed to secure tenant support in a transfer ballot (in 2002) and which found itself in a situation where 'we have clearly ruled out whole stock transfer: partials could be an option but one of the risks is that you lose your best stock; PFI is very cumbersome and complex, and ALMOs if we are realistic, we are a zero-rated authority and by the time we have a re-inspection the investment will not really be available' (Assistant Director of Housing Strategy quoted in Inside Housing and reproduced in Centre for Public Services 2004: 10). Ginsburg (2005) comments that 'the most glaring injustice is that done to the many continuing local authority tenants who remain in less than decent homes because of the government's punitive approach to the local authorities and tenants who have not followed the privatisation route' (ibid: 132). Relevant here is our account of how three authorities proposed to fund quality standard compliance following tenant 'no votes' – see Chapter 4.

Another continuity between new public management and modernization was the support for adoption of a performance-based culture. The modernization process replaced hierarchies within organizations with sets of hierarchical relations between organizations, as government sought to retain control over a more diverse set of delivery agencies. On the one hand, stock transfer landlords were cast as independent organizations free to make the most of their assets, but at same time they are subject to an intensive system of regulation and inspection, with their ability to access grant funding for new development dependent on meeting regulatory standards. Clarke et al.

(2000) have described how this emphasis on regulatory compliance shifts organizational focus and resources from 'doing' to 'accounting for doing'. Had Pollitt et al. returned to stock transfer organizations at the turn of the millennium, they would have found the rhetoric of the new managerialism and performance culture in abundance.

In more recent writing, Malpass and Victory (2010, forthcoming) develop the concept of 'modernisation' beyond its usual association with the New Labour reform project after 1997 to embrace a longer-term process of change which arguably extends back to the 1970s. They use the term 'modernisation' to retrospectively make sense of a series of policy developments relating to social housing: its provision, consumption and its role in the wider housing system over this extended period. This usage parallels earlier work on 'modernisation of tenure' (Malpass and Murie 1994) which had been used to make sense of a long-term process of tenure change from one based predominantly on private landlordism in the early twentieth century to one based on a split between home ownership and council housing in the second half of the twentieth century.

For Malpass and Victory (2010, forthcoming), the key elements of the more recent 'modernisation of social housing' changes from a 'public housing model' to a 'social housing model' were a set of linked developments in the role, ownership, procurement, governance, organizational culture and finance of social housing. From this perspective it can be seen that stock transfer has been an important driver of 'modernisation'; for example, by facilitating the introduction of new owners/providers, new governance models, a shift in organizational cultures and business models towards private funding. This approach to understanding modernization emphasizes system evolution, recognizing that while the present state may be 'a dynamic mixed economy of providers, there is every reason to believe that the mix will be different in years to come' (11). This recognizes that the direction and outcomes of modernization are contested, between for example the migration of social housing away from the public sector towards the private sector on the one hand or to a more permanent establishment of a mixed economy with a strong non-profit sector in the other. These contradictory pressures are played out in the business cultures and incentive structures available to stock transfer landlords, demonstrating the value of studies reported in this book of these emerging and changing cultures. As we note in Chapter 10, continued research is necessary to track the longer-term implications of transfer for the operation of the housing system both locally and nationally.

International dimensions

Ownership transfer of state housing to other social landlords has not been a uniquely British phenomenon. True, Britain is fairly unusual in that, historically, its non-market housing was developed mainly by the state rather than by third sector bodies as in many other parts of Europe (Kleinman 1993). Nevertheless, there are a number of other countries where the greater part of the social rented stock remains in public owner-ship – among them Australia, United States, Ireland and New Zealand (Whitehead and Scanlon 2007, Fitzpatrick and Stephens 2007). A variety of examples of stock transfer have emerged in different contexts and we may distinguish between wholesale transfers and smaller more experimental approaches, between transfer of existing stock or of new development, transfers to the third sector or the private sector and transfers that have significantly eroded or replaced state housing and those that have retained a significant state role in social housing provision.

The most complete case of transfer has occurred in the Netherlands where third sector providers were already domi-nant. While much of the Dutch housing association stock had been historically part-financed by government loans, these loans were cancelled in 1995 when the sector was 'floated free' to exploit and manage its assets, on condition that there would be no further subsidy (Ouwehand and van Daalen 2002). In this context, the Dutch have moved from a 'mixed economy' approach in which municipal housing companies had existed alongside housing associations towards almost total monopoly provision by associations. This transfer process began as long ago as 1980 since when virtually all of the municipal housing companies established as major social housing providers in the post-war period have transferred their assets or transformed their status into housing associations. A White Paper in the early 1980s aimed to eliminate all municipal housing companies by 1996. In practice there were still 213 in 1990, falling to 23 by 2000 (Ouwehand and van Daalen 2002). Like stock transfer in England, this was sometimes a contested process with some municipalities opposing transfer in order to retain a safety net of municipal housing. There were also some financial problems associated with the transfer of municipal stock of some companies in large cities (Stephens et al. 2008, Haffner 2002). Today, only a few acquired and residual housing stocks remain with Dutch municipal authorities.

In the Republic of Ireland, by contrast, local authorities have long played the dominant role in the construction, management (and sale) of social housing, with housing associations accounting for only a very small share of social housing provision. While the growth of associations was officially promoted from the late 1990s, this was alongside continued investment in local authority housing, and housing association investment continued to be mainly publicly funded with an income based rental system providing very limited capacity to generate surpluses or to raise private funding (Mullins et al. 2003). A recent review of policy for voluntary and co-operative housing noted that 'from a funding perspective there is little to distinguish the voluntary and co-operative sector from housing authorities' (Grant Thornton and Centre for Housing Research 2009: 58). Future funding proposals set out in the same report included the sourcing of commercial lending from banks, credit unions and pension funds. Mortgage and lease options and association participation in commercial property ventures and public–private partnerships were also recommended as ways of harnessing the asset base of around 4 billion Euros in the housing association stock. However, despite these potential moves in a similar direction to the British and Dutch sectors, the report made only a passing reference to stock transfer and pointedly omitted transfer among policy options advocated for consideration within the Irish context.

Nevertheless, a number of estate-based transfers from local housing authorities to associations have in fact taken place in Ireland, usually involving 'vacant or highly problematic estates' (Cluid Housing Association 2009: 6). Cluid housing association, one of the largest third sector housing providers with

3,000 properties country-wide has been involved in several of these small-scale transfers including projects in North Dublin and Longford. In a 'stock transfer and regeneration' guide based on this successful experience Cluid provides an indication of why larger-scale transfers were not favoured in the wider policy review outlined above: 'the attempt by one large local authority to encourage the idea of a broader policy of stock transfer has attracted a relatively high level of opposition to the idea; the main protestors citing the fear of local authorities abdicating their responsibilities towards persons in housing need and disposing of valuable public assets' (Cluid Housing Association 2009: 6). It therefore seems likely that, in the short term, transfers in Ireland will continue to be linked to area-based regeneration and to 'fast tracking the regeneration or refurbishment process' rather than to accessing private finance on a larger scale.

A very different context and transfer experience has been evident in Northern Ireland, motivated by quite different considerations. In 1972 all council housing in Northern Ireland was transferred from the municipalities to the Northern Ireland Housing Executive, a non-departmental public body set up in the wake of the troubles to 'take politics out of housing'. While new development was transferred to housing associations from the mid-1990s for similar reasons to England, there was at that time no serious consideration of disaggregating the largest municipal landlord in Europe into smaller management units. However, the option of moving the Executive wholesale outside of the public accounts in a Large Scale Voluntary Transfer (LSVT) style transaction was under active consideration as part of a wider commission on future housing policy in the devolved administration under way in 2009 (Varney 2008, Story 2009).

In Australia, although housing advocates and researchers (for example Bisset 2000) have long advocated transfers from the large state-run public housing authorities to housing associations, few transfers have as yet taken place. For example, in Victoria, the second largest Australian state, ownership of only a few hundred properties has been transferred from the state to the housing associations who had previously managed the properties on the state's behalf. In 2009 over 63,000 properties, equivalent to 86 per cent of Victoria's entire social housing stock, continued to be directly controlled by the public housing authority. This makes the state's public housing authority thirty times the size of the country's largest housing association (Gilmour 2009a). In the largest Australian State, New South Wales, the target is to transfer 3,000 properties to housing associations over the next three years from a total portfolio of just under 130,000 units (NSW Department of Housing 2007).

Debate about the potential benefits of larger-scale transfer has continued in Australia, although remains contested (Jacobs et al. 2004). A more comprehensive re-shaping of public housing is said to be under consideration by state governments, with supporters maintaining that 'reform of the public housing authorities is warranted. They could be broken up into smaller companies, each with an adequate portfolio mass to maintain management efficiencies . . . the aim would be to float off or re-assign these companies into the not-for-dividend sector' (Spiller and Lennon 2009). However, with just five per cent of Australian housing in the social sector, the main drive of the national Labor government elected in 2007 has been the overall expansion of affordable housing stock. The majority of new properties constructed under the post-2007 National Rental Affordability Scheme are being provided by housing associations not state authorities. Therefore, even without large-scale transfers, the proportion of Australian social housing managed by the third sector is increasing – albeit only slowly.

New Zealand saw an instance of state housing being transferred to a community trust with interests in retail properties (Murphy 2006). A larger transaction, somewhat contrary to international experience, involved Auckland City Council's decision to sell its 1,800 rented homes to the Crown (Badcock 2008). This was a 'protective' move on the part of central government, seeing the move as a means of ensuring that the properties remained available as affordable housing.

In the US, public housing is managed by 3,300 Public Housing Authorities financed centrally by the Washington-based Department of Housing and Urban Development (HUD). These Authorities operate independently of State or City control. For the last 25 years, new approaches to, and finance for, social housing have used market mechanisms with property ownership in the private and non-profit sectors. In particular, the Low-Income Housing Tax Credit introduced in 1986 has helped fund over one-and-a-half million new affordable units. In the last two decades, numbers of tax-credit-funded homes have overtaken the 1.2 million public housing units, despite the latter scheme operating since 1937 (HUD 2009).

Although there have been no stock transfers from Public Housing Authorities to non-profit providers in the US, owner-ship may change as a result of regeneration projects. Launched in 1992, the HOPE VI initiative has used public–private–non-profit partnerships to regenerate problematic public housing estates. Typically, these schemes have involved demolishing badly designed, often high-rise mono-tenure public housing 'projects' and transforming them to mixed-tenure develop-ments. Property ownership moves out of the public sector, though in terms of UK terminology the resulting structure is more akin to a PFI incorporating non-profit agency partners. HOPE VI was an expensive scheme and is no longer funded. Cost limited the extent of redevelopment with, for example, only five of San Francisco's 55 public housing estates trans-formed through this means (Gilmour 2009b). In the US, as in Australia, therefore, the public housing sector has remained largely intact while contracting as a proportion of total social housing. The expansion of non-profit providers has taken place more via organic growth than through stock transfers.

A different type of hybrid model has been emerging in Ontario, Canada as a result of recent reforms described by Pomeroy (2009). Here, a form of stock transfer has involved dwellings formerly owned by local housing authorities being handed over to subsidiary non-profit housing corporations set up by city administrations to own and operate non-profit housing. Subsequently, some of these ALMO-style bodies were merged or absorbed as municipal departments. Some munici-palities have, however, retained subsidiary non-profit corpora-tions (either with council functioning as the board or with a mix of council and community board members). Toronto Community Housing Corporation remains the single largest landlord in the country with 59,000 units as a result of merging three formerly separate corporations (ibid: 4).

Particularly in a world where stated adherence to evidence-based policy continues to grow, and where trans-national policy learning is becoming familiar, Britain's stock transfer story is of considerable potential interest. However, there is a need for careful consideration of the context, definition of policy problem and conceptual equivalence (Oxley 2001, Hantrais 2009) before meaningful analysis of policy transfer can take place. We hope that this volume provides a useful starting point for such an endeavour by providing a nuanced and detailed account of the varying drivers, evolution, forms, processes and outcomes of stock transfer applying at different times in different parts of Britain. In this way, more specific types of policy problems and instruments can be identified for comparisons within the bundle of approaches taken to stock transfer at different times in these contrasting jurisdictions.

What real difference does transfer make?

This chapter has introduced a number of different perspectives on transfer that are considered in more detail elsewhere in the book. In this concluding section of our introduction we focus on two main dimensions that underpin some of the differences of view we have found. Table 1.3 summarizes these two dimensions as the extent of change involved in transfer (minimal or transformational) and the extent to which such change is viewed as positive or negative.

On the one hand, there is the minimal change perspective which suggests that transfer is simply a new way of packaging and delivering existing services.

A benign version of the minimal change interpretation was found in early transfer ballot campaigns which stressed the advantages of sticking with the existing staff, remaining local and avoiding the various financial and policy constraints that would otherwise lead to deterioration in the existing housing services.

A more negative 'emperor's new clothes' perspective is provided by some critics of transfer who suggest that it is simply a financial manoeuvre to take advantage of public accounting rules but does little to tackle to underlying problems that have beset social housing as it has become increasingly the resort of the poorest, residualized and in need of re-branding.

In contrast to the above two categories, many commentators emphasize the disjuncture that transfer represents for social

TABLE 1.3   *Interpretations of the difference that transfer has made*

Change	Positive	Negative
Minimal	• Remain local • Ability to deliver the service local authorities had always wanted to • Trust with existing staff retained • Influence of local stakeholders retained	• Emperor's new clothes • Only real change is financial • Same staff, same practices • No real impact on underlying problems of residualization and poor image of social housing
Transformational	• Better resourced • Better, more customer-focused operational practice • More effective management of limited resources • Empowered staff • Independent from political control and leakage of funds to other departments • More responsive to residents • Focus for local regeneration partnerships	• Financially dominated • More commercially motivated – downgrading of welfare role • Growth orientated: diversify and expand out of area • Erosion of tenants rights • Less accountable to residents and local government

housing from the past. A key feature of most critiques of transfer is to emphasize the extent of change involved; for example, through 'privatization', erosion of tenure rights, increased financial drivers of the new landlords, erosion of local democracy. Proponents of the 'privatization' view would suggest that transfer landlords will adopt a harder nosed business culture and will be less inclined to house those with known behavioural problems and to evict those with rent arrears or exhibiting anti-social behaviour.

More positively, many commentators have stressed the disjuncture between 'the council housing department' and the locally-based housing association as an opportunity to meet customer and community needs and to operate in a more businesslike way. Alternatively, they may stress improved management, better resources, financial independence, the impact of new stakeholders, opportunities for staff to operate more entrepreneurially, to enjoy enhanced access to training and promotion opportunities and for tenants to become more engaged. Indeed, this appears to have been the view taken by successive governments to transfers and ALMOs, the latter having additional pressures for improvement through needing to achieve an 'excellent' inspection rating in order to access funding.

On balance, we conclude that there are few grounds for claims that stock transfer has a minimal impact and is simply a financial manoeuvre. However, within the substantial change perspectives there is a need to probe the evidence base to tease out the circumstances in which some of the more positive and the more negative outcomes outlined above have emerged in practice – or may do so in the future.

Structure of the book

We have set out to do two main things in this book. Firstly, we have sought to provide a framework in which readers can make sense of the process and outcomes of stock transfer and the different interpretations to which it has been subjected. We do this by taking a fairly broad view of the relevant theory and literature that is necessary to consider in interpreting these changes. Secondly, we have brought together empirical evidence on the process and outcomes of stock transfer to begin to test the relevance of competing ideas from academic and policy debates.

Our evidence base comprises secondary sources including published, unpublished reports and studies and specially commissioned national aggregate data and primary research involving case studies and surveys from each stage of the transfer process drawing on national research commissioned by government (Mullins et al. 1992, 1995; Pawson et al. 2005a) and supported by the Joseph Rowntree Foundation (Pawson and Fancy 2003, Pawson et al. 2009). The recent JRF research has the further advantage of including the experience of stock transfer in Scotland and in Wales along with 'second generation' urban transfers in England. This unique time series of case study based research complements other primary research we have undertaken in which stock transfer figured large (Mullins and Riseborough 1997, 2000, Mullins 2006, Pawson and Mullins 2003, Pawson et al. 2004). All this places the authors in a strong position to address some of the questions raised by the perspectives discussed in this introductory chapter.

Drawing mainly on empirical material from our own research we seek to illustrate some of our arguments with case study examples relating to specific local scenarios. In particular, the Glasgow City Council 2003 transfer is used to exemplify a number of points at various stages through the book (see, especially, Boxes 3.3, 4.4 and 5.3). Given its unparalleled scale, the turbulent story of this enterprise is arguably a particularly important one in its own right. It is also, in many ways, unique. At the same time, however, a number of aspects of the Glasgow experience can be seen as highlighting – albeit in especially sharp relief – issues relevant to many other transfer contexts.

The book is divided into three main sections, following this introduction and preceding a concluding chapter. The first section (Chapters 2–4) sets the context for stock transfer by providing a historical overview of the process, by exploring the motivations and financial dimensions of transfer and by considering the political context at national and local levels. The second section (Chapters 5–7) probes a number of more specific aspects and outcomes of transfer including the governance and accountability of transfer landlords, organizational and cultural change after transfer and the impact of stock transfer on housing conditions, tenants and communities. The third section (Chapters 8 and 9) considers ALMOs and local government. Chapter 8 explores the experience and impact of ALMOs, as the other main grouping of social landlords emerging in Britain 'after council housing', with Chapter 9 looking at the implications of transfer for the role of local authorities in local housing systems. A concluding chapter returns to the questions set out in this chapter, considers the prospects for further stock transfers and reflects on the extent to which social housing has been transformed by the transfer of ownership to housing associations and of management to ALMOs.

Chapter 2

Tracking Stock Transfers

A small district council centred on the commuter settlement of Amersham may seem an unlikely site for the start of arguably the most fundamental restructuring of British social housing since the Second World War. Yet the December 1988 handover of Chiltern Council's housing stock to Chiltern Hundreds Housing Association is generally seen as marking the beginning of the stock transfer revolution. In fact, Chiltern was only one among a sizeable body of councils drawn to the transfer option in the housing policy ferment of the late 1980s. Earlier in 1988 it had been reported that 30 local authorities across England and Wales were 'seriously developing transfer plans' and that up to 200 had made transfer-related enquiries to central government (Platt 1988).

The trigger for this activity was probably the third term election victory of the Thatcher government in April 1987 – or, perhaps, the pre-election publication of the Conservative Party manifesto laying out far-reaching plans for the reshaping of British housing. This was followed by consultation papers signalling the government's intention to wrest control of housing away from local authorities through a variety of measures. In particular, the proposal to enable 'hostile takeovers' of council stock (as further discussed below) had raised alarm throughout council officialdom and the tenants' movement. For many in these constituencies, the 'voluntary transfer' option was seen, first and foremost, as a protective response to this perceived threat.

Understanding the context for the start of the stock transfer process, however, demands a broader appreciation of the development of housing policy under successive Conservative administrations during the 1980s. This chapter therefore briefly reviews some of the most significant policy themes of this era, highlighting the importance of certain key Thatcherite legislation. We then go on to discuss the different manifestations of stock transfers since 1988 and the changing shape of stock transfer as the process unfolded during the 1990s and into the new millennium. Finally, we take a preliminary descriptive look at the question – who are Britain's new social landlords (in each phase of the process), a topic we will return to in a more summative way in Chapter 10. First, though, the chapter looks at some of the key characteristics of British social housing circa 1988, and at the policy origins and antecedents of what has become known as stock transfer on the Large Scale Voluntary Transfer – LSVT – model.

Social housing in 1988

The phrase 'social housing' was barely coined in 1988. This can be seen, in part, as a testament to the contemporary dominance of council housing in the 'non-profit rental' field (see Table 2.1). While, by 2008, associations were managing almost as many dwellings as local authorities, the ratio in 1986 had been 13:1 (see Figures 1.1–1.3 and Table 2.1). However, although council landlords remained numerically dominant at this time their primacy was clearly being eroded. Large-scale local authority house-building had been quickly wound down after 1979 and sitting tenant sales under the Right to Buy were swiftly reducing council property portfolios from 1980 onwards. Sales were also making an important qualitative impact on local authority housing, with more popular properties – particularly larger houses on more desirable estates – being disproportionately stripped out of local authority portfolios. This can be seen from the fact that, during the ten years to 1989, one-bedroom flats (a generally less popular category) increased from 17 to 21 per cent of the national local authority stock (Mullins et al. 1992). Increasingly, housing remaining in Council ownership was therefore being seen as 'residual', with the whole sector subject to rapid 'residualization'.

These developments were something of a demoralizing shock for a sector which had known only growth in its previous 60 year history. Even during the 1970s, for example, half a million properties were added to Council housing and, with a growth rate similar to that of the private sector, local authorities maintained their share of dwellings, nationally (at 30–31 per cent). At the same time, with the ageing of the stock, increasingly

TABLE 2.1 *Tenure structure, Great Britain, 1981–2006*

Year	Owner-occupied %	Private rented %	Housing assoc %	Local authority %	Total %
1981	58	11	2	29	100
1986	62	10	2	26	100
1991	66	9	3	22	100
1996	67	10	5	18	100
2001	69	10	7	14	100
2006	70	12	8	10	100

Source: Data from Live Tables, Communities and Local Government website Table 102.

restricted maintenance funding and a weak asset management culture, local authority landlords were facing growing problems of disrepair. By 1986, nearly seven per cent of English council housing was classed as legally unfit for habitation (Wilcox 2003).

Partly reflecting growing disrepair and partly as a reaction to unsuitable design and management, some local authority landlords were also beginning to face serious problems of unpopular housing and the emergence of 'difficult to let' stock (DoE 1981). This compounded the dent to the morale of a sector which, for generations, had become conditioned to a market situation of perpetual shortage where its vacancies were always in demand.

At the same time, many local authorities faced growing pressures from the rising incidence of homelessness with the number of households annually classed by English local authorities as 'priority homeless' (and therefore enjoying a statutory right to social housing) more than doubling between 1980 and 1990. This had to be reconciled with the shrinking council housing stock (though it was only in some regions that the flow of vacancies fell proportionally to the contraction of the stock).

In their style of housing management, council landlords typically remained locked into a bureaucratic and paternalistic approach, as reflected by their governance structures and the use of discretionary power primarily to serve provider interests

(CDP 1977). As emphasized by Merrett (1979), power and control remained firmly in the hands of Elected Members and their appointed officials. Only in isolated cases were serious attempts made to engage with tenants' and residents' representatives in relation to strategic and managerial decision-making. Most housing department staff received little training and few were professionally qualified. Rather, new staff were 'typically "shown the ropes" by longer serving officers [with the result that] attitudes and behaviour [were] handed down from one generation to another with little thought about the wider implications of particular activities and action' (Merrett 1979: 208).

Housing associations had enjoyed something of a revival with their emergence as standard bearers for inner city regeneration under the Housing Act 1974. Under the 1974–79 Labour government associations had been 'draw[n] . . . within the boundaries of the public sector' (Malpass 2000: 171). This had provided access to generous public funding and this had seen them building and renovating 185,000 homes over this period. By 1979, associations' national stock, at nearly 400,000, had doubled since 1970.

In the years immediately following the change of government in 1979, associations fell somewhat out of favour under a Conservative government with other immediate housing policy pre-occupations (see below). At the same time, however, it was clear that ministers saw associations as substantially preferable to council landlords: '[housing associations have] . . . great expertise, and a generally good reputation in managing rented housing [whilst] . . . too many council tenants are justifiably discontented with the . . . standards of service they get' (William Waldegrave, Housing Minister, speech to Institute of Housing Annual Conference, 19.6.87).

The mid-1980s saw associations remaining as largely niche operators, with their role generally seen as specialist provision for groups such as older people and people with disabilities (i.e. those needing specially designed or supported accommodation) or for groups typically neglected by councils (e.g. single people of working age), and also played an important role in acquiring and improving properties in association with area improvement strategies (Housing Action Areas and General Improvement Areas). With much of their stock having been relatively recently built or renovated (although not always to the highest standards), association dwellings were typically in fairly good condition and, with their general exemption from the Right to Buy, were free from the erosive pressures experienced by council landlords.

From an association perspective, the post-1974 funding system was 'to all intents and purposes risk free' since grant payments paid on scheme completion were adjusted to cover agreed cost overruns (Randolph 1993: 49). This encouraged a perception of associations as somewhat cosseted organizations, insulated from economic pressures and disinclined to adopt businesslike approaches. Increasingly, Conservative Party thinking was inclining to the view that associations were 'absorbing unacceptably large amounts of public expenditure' (Malpass 2000: 172).

The charitable roots of housing associations were at this time exemplified by the term 'voluntary housing movement' by which HAs liked to be known. In this respect, association culture was far removed from that of council landlords. Nevertheless, as Malpass (2000) records, they attracted similar criticism in terms of their remoteness from tenants 'in terms of both housing management practices and the conduct of committee business' (ibid: 170).

Housing policy and legislation in the 1980s

As noted by Mullins et al. (1992) two major themes ran through British housing policy in the 1980s: the promotion of home-ownership and the control of public expenditure. The first of these found expression in the Right to Buy for local authority tenants, certainly the single most significant housing policy of the past 30 years. Under this measure, created by the Housing Act 1980, more than a million council tenants bought their homes during the 1980s – a figure equivalent to more than a fifth of 1979 tenancies.

Throughout the 1980s, capital spending controls severely restricted councils' ability to re-invest receipts generated through sales, though a temporary relaxation in the 1987–90 period encouraged receipts to be spent on repairs to remaining council dwellings. By 1990/91, overall housing capital investment had (in real terms) fallen by more than half of its level a decade earlier (Wilcox 1995).

The Conservative Party's 1987 'third term' general election manifesto once more placed housing reform at centre stage. The White Paper and Housing Bill which swiftly followed the Party's ballot victory set out a number of key aims including:

- the continued promotion of home ownership
- putting new life into the 'independent rented sector' by (a) de-regulating private landlords, and (b) restructuring housing associations to enable them to access private finance
- reshaping local authorities' housing activities by enhancing their 'enabling' role at the expense of their landlord role and giving tenants a greater say in housing provision.

The main instrument for the enactment of these reforms was the Housing Act 1988. This statute (and its sister legislation for Scotland) created a new financial regime for housing associations where, crucially, capital investment funded through borrowing was defined as 'off balance sheet' for public expenditure accounting purposes and the repayment of such loans financed through rents.

More directly relevant to local authorities were the Act's provisions to facilitate the ownership transfer of local authority housing under the 'Tenants' Choice' and 'Housing Action Trust' (HAT) provisions. HATs were to be corporations set up to take over large run-down local authority housing estates to 'secure the repair and improvement' and to secure its 'proper and effective management and use' (Karn 1991). The refurbished housing was to be passed on to a successor landlord (possibly, as it was later conceded, handed back to the predecessor local authority) at scheme completion. The impact of HATs is further discussed below.

The Tenants' Choice mechanism was seen as a more broadly targeted device for facilitating the removal of local authority housing from municipal control. Under the Tenants' Choice provisions, tenants acquired the right to choose an 'alternative landlord'. While prospective successor stockholders would need to be 'approved' by the Housing Corporation, it was for a time unclear what this would involve. Moreover, the transfer mechanism could be triggered not only by a group of tenants wishing to 'escape council control', but also by a prospective landlord expressing an interest in a given estate. And, although Tenants' Choice transfers were to require ballot endorsement by the residents of the specified area or estate, proposals would fall at this stage only where *a majority of eligible tenants voted against* (abstentions being counted as pro-transfer). At the same time, however, where a transfer went ahead, those who had voted against would have their homes leased back to the local authority.

Importantly, the 1988 legislation was followed by the Local Government and Housing Act 1989 (though this was limited to England and Wales rather than also encompassing Scotland). This latter statute ushered in a new financial regime for local authority housing, tightening the constraints affecting council landlords. Key components included:

- the obligation to use 75 per cent of capital receipts to repay debt (ending the opportunity for recycling 100 per cent of receipts into housing repairs)
- the ring-fencing of local authorities' Housing Revenue Accounts and other measures to strengthen ministerial powers to push up council rents
- the incorporation of rent rebates within housing subsidy calculations such that, in councils with housing revenue accounts deemed to be 'in surplus', housing benefit payments would be financed from other tenants' rents.

As Mullins et al. (1992) observed, 'Local authorities soon came to realise this Act posed an even greater challenge to the continuation of their traditional role in providing affordable housing than either the Right to Buy or Tenants' Choice' (ibid: 7).

While the 1988 and 1989 Acts were crucial in kick-starting the stock transfer process, the legal provisions under which transfers take place were largely created by the Housing Act 1985 (as amended by the Housing and Planning Act 1986). In the sense that this was legislation enabling local authorities to opt for tenanted stock disposals, it gave birth to the 'voluntary' tag in the subsequently adopted term 'large scale voluntary transfer' or LSVT. The standard form of 'LSVT valuation' is explained in Chapter 3. Under ss32–34 and 43 of the 1985 Act local authorities may dispose of land or dwellings held for housing purposes subject to the consent of the Secretary of State. Section 132 of the Housing Act 1988 itemized considerations to be weighed by the Secretary of State in determining whether to endorse a stock transfer proposal. These included:

- the influence of the local authority making the disposal
- 'the extent to which the intending purchaser would become a majority or substantial landlord of rented accommodation in the area'
- the terms of the proposed disposal.

Although this legislation (in contrast with Scotland) does not stipulate that a tenant ballot must demonstrate majority support for a transfer proposal, custom and practice dictates that this is, in fact, a requirement for obtaining Ministerial consent.

Stock transfer policy origins and antecedents

While the Chiltern District Council transfer cited above tends to be seen as the start of the process, ownership handovers of state housing have some earlier antecedents. A basic distinction may be drawn here between the ownership handover of tenanted and of vacant housing partly because – irrespective of legal obligations – the proposed transfer of occupied homes clearly implies the need for consultation and negotiation with the residents concerned. Tenanted transfers imply the continued utilization of dwellings as rented homes – at least in the short and medium term. Vacant possession transfers present a potentially wider range of post-transfer options – including the possibility of outright privatization (in the sense of open-market sale).

Early tenanted transfers

One of the earliest examples of tenanted stock transfer on an appreciable scale – and one that arguably prefigured post-1988 developments – involved Knowsley Council's disposal of the Cantril Farm Estate in 1983. Here, 3,000 dwellings were handed over to the specially-created Stockbridge Village Trust, a body charged with raising finance to overhaul the stock and improve the area – subsequently renamed Villages Housing Association (Murie and Nevin 2001).

In a larger, but more drawn out programme, much of the housing built and managed for rent by English New Town Development Corporations was being handed over to new owners through tenanted transfers during the 1970s and 1980s. In England, this programme involved New Town tenants being given a choice of the local authority or a Corporation-selected housing association as their new landlord. In the final tranche of English New Town transfers (1987–93), for example, outcomes were decided on an 'individual choice' basis, with each tenant having their home handed over to the successor landlord of their choice (Goodlad and Scott, 1996). Vacant properties and those occupied by tenants failing to vote were allocated in line with good housing management practice. Sheltered housing schemes were, however, treated differently, with these being handed over to a single landlord on a majority vote. In most instances, the process described here led to the relevant local authority inheriting most of the stock concerned.

The mechanisms used in the English New Town transfers programme were described by Goodlad and Scott (1996) as important in piloting the tenant voting procedure and in laying the basis for the 'individual choice' approach adopted for Tenants' Choice in the Housing Act 1988 (see above).

In an arguably closer antecedent for the post-1988 local authority stock transfer phenomenon, Glasgow City Council launched a programme of tenanted transfers of run-down estates in the mid-1980s. Coming several years ahead of the Chiltern scheme, some see this initiative as the true starting point for stock transfer as the term is now understood (Taylor 1999). The Glasgow transfers created a cohort of community-based housing associations (or CBHAs), a model subsequently adopted by a number of other Scottish local authorities and generating a total of around 50 CBHAs across Scotland by the mid-1990s (the CBHA model and its influence is further discussed in Chapter 5).

Like many of the later whole stock transfers (see Chapter 3), the main aim of the CBHA handovers was to facilitate housing investment (Taylor 1998). In the main, however, such investment was publicly funded Housing Association Grant rather than private finance. This follows from the fact that the majority of the CBHA transfers took place before the creation of the new financial regime for housing associations under the Housing Act 1988. Importantly, therefore, the landlords created under this programme were primarily grant-funded rather than debt-funded. In this sense, they did not exploit one of the key features of later transfers, namely the use of private finance outside of the Public Sector Borrowing Requirement and this would be a strong argument for treating such transfers as *forerunners*, rather than early exponents, of stock transfer as we now know it.

Preceding any of the initiatives described above, the Northern Ireland Housing Executive's 1972 acquisition of all Northern Ireland municipal housing could, perhaps, be portrayed as the largest 'whole stock transfer' of them all; a process of aggregation rather than disaggregation. Only recently, however, has there been any subsequent move equivalent to the Scottish Homes transfer programme to break up this portfolio (Story 2009).

Vacant possession transfers

More distinct from, though perhaps still relevant to, post-1988 tenanted stock transfers were a generation of local authority vacant possession housing disposals carried through in the 1980s and into the 1990s. At least tacitly encouraged by central government post-1979, the number of local authorities contemplating and/or undertaking transfers of this type grew quickly as the 1980s progressed (Duncan 1991). By 1986 the Department of the Environment reported that there were 'a total of 40 such schemes under way' (Glendinning et al., 1989). According to Usher (1988) 'more than 60 local authorities . . . sold over 150 council estates involving 30,000 dwellings in the period 1981–87' (1), while Duncan (1991) found that 24 of the (then) 56 Scottish local authorities had been involved in stock disposal schemes between 1979 and 1990.

Vacant possession block or estate handovers of this era were often aimed at redressing the unpopularity and/or poor physical condition of the dwellings concerned. In some cases, the purchaser was a housing association intent on refurbishing or clearing and replacing the transferred buildings to create new or improved housing for rent. Initiatives of this type became increasingly significant during the early 1990s and it was found that housing associations invested in 26,000 properties on (former) local authority estates in England in the period 1991/92–1993/94 (Crook et al. 1996). The prospect of generating substantial capital receipts for investment elsewhere in the locality was also a prime motivation for some of the earlier disposals of this type (Usher 1988).

The promotion of low-cost home ownership was the main motivation for some vacant possession block or estate transfers during the 1980s and into the 1990s (Rosenburg 1995). Such transfers were encouraged by central government. Through City Grant in England (Malpass and Murie 1994) and GRO-Grants in Scotland (Scottish Homes 1994), central government also directly pump-primed the process in some localities.

Typically, low cost home ownership-inspired disposals involved the local authority re-housing tenants from the project area with the (vacant) stock then being transferred to a private developer agreeing to refurbish the buildings to a specified standard. Subsequently, the homes would be marketed for sale, perhaps with priority being given to local authority housing waiting list applicants or other potential first time buyers. In some instances housing associations played the 'developer' role (Rosenburg 1995).

Finally, while such instances were probably relatively rare, it was alleged that certain authorities effecting block or estate transfers into private ownership during the 1980s were primarily motivated by a wish to alter the make-up of the local population to secure electoral advantage for the ruling administration (Usher 1988). An aspect of Westminster City Council's 'homes for votes' scandal involved the Council in targeting a vacant possession sales programme in a politically motivated attempt to manipulate the electoral balance in certain 'key marginal' wards (Weaver 2001).

Housing Action Trusts and Tenants' Choice transfers

Running in parallel to early LSVT stock transfers were the ownership handovers of council housing triggered under the Housing Action Trust (HAT) and Tenants' Choice provisions of the Housing Act 1988 (see above). In all of the six areas initially designated for HATs by central government, the proposals were opposed and ultimately defeated by local authorities and tenants. While HATs offered the prospect of substantial public investment in run-down estates, the combative council response was perhaps predictable given the ministerial presentation of the mechanism as 'a way of rescuing tenants from incompetent local authorities' (Karn 1991: 75). For tenants' part, anxieties over privatization and loss of democratic accountability overshadowed the prospect of physical renewal.

A second round of HATs, developed according to a substantially less confrontational model and accepting the need for tenant endorsement, proceeded with greater success in the early 1990s. Under 20,000 properties were transferred in all, with the subsequent regeneration programmes seen as having secured substantial improvements albeit at a relatively high cost met entirely through public funds. Given that the six HATs consumed £1.1 billion – a unit cost of between £50,000 and £100,000 – it is perhaps unsurprising that there were no subsequent designations. In several instances (including Castle Vale in Birmingham, Tower Hamlets and Waltham Forest) housing stock improved under HAT auspices was subsequently transferred into housing association ownership (see Box 5.2, Chapter 5).

Concerns sparked by the Tenants' Choice scheme were, as noted above, important in sparking initial interest in LSVT transfers. Tenants' Choice itself, however, was, by any standards, a policy failure. Not only were council tenants found to be largely hostile to the scheme, but interest in playing the role of 'successor landlord' was also found to be thin on the ground. 'Government expectations that private landlords would [be interested in taking] over council estates proved unfounded, and housing associations who were more obvious candidates were concerned to avoid damaging their relationship with local authorities' (Malpass and Mullins, 2002: 676). Regulatory expectations such as equal opportunities and tenant involvement that were unfamiliar to private landlords at the time proved a significant barrier to market entry (Mullins 1990). Moreover, Tenants' Choice, whilst an apparently simple concept, turned out to involve complex procedures making proposed TC transfers both highly costly and vulnerable to delay. A failed attempt to use Tenants' Choice to take over Torbay Council's housing in 1995 cost the Housing Corporation £1.87 million in irrecoverable support for legal advice and other costs (Tulloch 2000).

Consequently, by the time the legislation was repealed, Tenants' Choice had facilitated the transfer of only 1,470 homes in England (Tulloch 2000). Well over a third of these were accounted for by the innovative and contested use of the legislation by Walterton and Elgin Community Homes to transfer from Westminster City Council (see Box 4.1, Chapter 4). The device was slightly more effective in Scotland where it led to the ownership handover of 2,100 properties – though again in this instance three quarters of these were to a single landlord – Grampian Housing Association.

Forms of stock transfer

Overview

By 2008, some 1.4 million tenanted dwellings had been handed to new landlords under the stock transfer process (see Table 2.2). This is equivalent to over a quarter of total council housing stock as at 1989. Across Britain, twenty years later, 183 councils had transferred their entire housing stock – hence ceasing to operate as landlords. In England, such post-transfer councils by 2008 accounted for 47 per cent of all local authorities; in Wales and Scotland, the equivalent figures were 40 per cent* and 22 per cent, respectively.

Up until 2008 over 50 authorities had undertaken 'partial transfers' – i.e. the handover of individual estates or groups of estates – usually selected as those particularly in need of investment. Allowing for the fact that a few of the partial transfers involved councils which subsequently handed over all their remaining housing, the number participating in the transfer process since 1989 totals around 236 – well over half of the 398 local authority districts in the three jurisdictions.

Figure 2.1 illustrates trends in transfer activity in England in

---

* As in Table 2.2 this figure includes three authorities' planning transfers in 2009/10.

TABLE 2.2 *Stock transfers by transfer type, Great Britain, 1988–2008*

	LA whole stock		LA partial transfers		Scottish Homes	New Towns
	No of LAs	Dwellings transferred	No of LAs	Dwellings transferred	Dwellings transferred	Dwellings transferred
England	167	1,006,000	34	134,000	NR	NA
Scotland	7	118,000	18	23,000	52,000	4,000
Wales	9	55,000	1	500	NR	0
Total	183	1,179,000	53	157,500	52,000	4,000

Notes: 1. A small number of LAs enumerated in cols 1 and 3 have subsequently been amalgamated with others under local government reorganization. 2. NR = not relevant; NA = not available.

Sources: Data from: England – stock transfers table (CLG, 2009); Scotland – Taylor (1998); Communities Scotland transfers dataset; Taylor (2001); Gibb et al. (2005); Audit Scotland (2006); Wales – unpublished figures provided by Welsh Assembly Government – includes 3 authorities planning to transfer in 2009/10.

FIGURE 2.1 Stock transfer transactions in England, 1988–2008

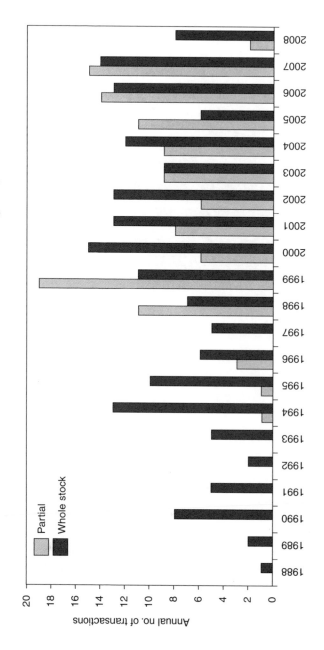

Sources: CLG stock transfers dataset.

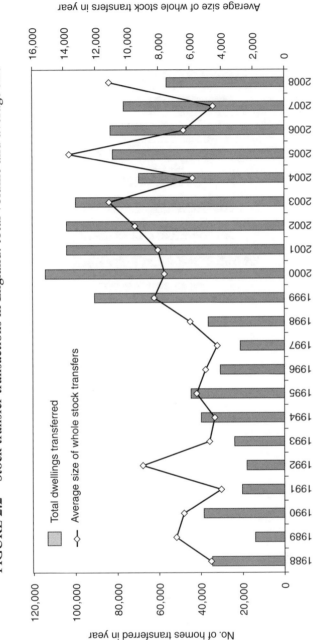

FIGURE 2.2 Stock transfer transactions in England: total volume and average size

Note: 'split transfers' treated as sungle transactions in calculation of average.

Source: CLG stock transfers dataset.

terms of the numbers of individual transactions taking place each year. Increased activity after 1997 largely reflects more full-blooded Ministerial promotion of the policy – see discussion below and in Chapter 3. Figure 2.2 illustrates the pattern of activity in terms of the number of homes changing hands – rather than the numbers of transfer packages. Presented in this way the impact of increased activity post-1997 is slightly sharper, reflecting the typically larger size of participating local authorities (as also shown in the graphic). Notably, while Ministerial encouragement saw the annual number of homes transferred topping 100,000 from 2000–02, the figure never approached the 200,000 per annum official target set in 2000 (DETR, 2000c). The apparent tailing-off in the volume of transfers in recent years is probably attributable to two main factors. First, the impetus created by the establishment of the Decent Homes target in 2002 has gradually worked through the system. Second, a large proportion of councils potentially benefiting from transfer without the need for government subsidy had already done so by 2005. Subsequent rationing of 'gap funding' undoubtedly slowed the process.

Split transfers

In the vast majority of cases, stock transfers have been of the 'whole stock' variety and have involved the setting up of new housing associations as receiving landlords. In most cases such transactions have involved a 'one for one' relationship – i.e. a single new association being created to take on all the stock from the transferring local authority. Occasionally, however, whole stock transfers have been split across two or more newly-created associations. In some instances (e.g. Bexley, Coventry, Tameside) this resulted from the need to comply with contemporary official guidelines on the maximum size of successor landlords (see Chapter 3). However, it is notable that over time these size restrictions were relaxed, undermining the putative disaggregation policy rationale for transfer.

The Scottish Homes stock transfer programme can be seen as a form of split transfer, though in this case the process was drawn out over more than a decade from 1991–2004 rather than being accomplished at a stroke as in the case of most ex-LA split transfers in England. Scottish Homes was established in 1989, inheriting some 75,000 dwellings developed all across the country by the former Scottish Special Housing Association (SSHA). The onward transfer of this stock into local 'community ownership' was one of the new organization's central objectives (Gibb et al. 2005). Whilst local interests were able to influence the nature of Scottish Homes transfers (see Chapter 3), there was no opportunity to consider the policy's appropriateness in local circumstances, nor to 'opt out' of its implementation.

The Scottish New Town transfers of 1995/96 can also be seen as another variant of split transfer. These adopted a 'block' approach whereby tenants were given a choice of potential successor landlords with the outcome for each defined 'block' being determined by majority vote within that block. The process was novel, not only in allowing for the possibility of a ballot choice between future landlords, but also in permitting local authorities to compete with housing associations on equal terms. In the event, the vast majority of the 29,000 homes were acquired by councils rather than by housing associations, an outcome clearly at variance with the general thrust of government housing policy of the time. This was explained by Goodlad and Scott (1996) as resulting from ministers' rhetorical emphasis on tenant choice which placed the government in a position where it 'found itself unable to deny tenants the opportunity to vote for local authorities' (ibid: 327).

Partial transfers

Over 50 councils have carried out partial stock transfers – i.e. where a local authority disposes of a package of tenanted housing whilst, at the same time, retaining stock in its ownership, and therefore a landlord role. A number of authorities have made successive partial transfers, usually involving individual estates or groups of estates. Glasgow City Council, for instance, made over 70 transfers of this kind before handing over its entire remaining stock to Glasgow Housing Association in 2003.

Generally, partial transfers have tended to involve particularly run-down estates with substantial accumulated disrepair. In some instances, packaging decisions have been influenced by the aspiration to create 'balanced portfolios' where better quality housing is included alongside problematic stock to offset negative valuation. In four English partial transfers (all involving London boroughs) stock for disposal was defined by type – sheltered housing – rather than by geographical location. Figure 2.1 illustrates the significance of partial transfers since the late 1990s.

The initial surge in partial transfers visible in Figure 2.1 resulted from the Estates Renewal Challenge Fund (ERCF), a programme initiated in 1996 and aimed at addressing the problems of crumbling and often severely socially deprived estates in inner London and other cities. In three rounds of ERCF transfers in 1998–2000, 23 local authorities shared £488 million in central government grants to underpin transfer business plans to overhaul nearly 45,000 dwellings. As well as forming dowry payments to offset negative valuations, the grants also covered essential pre-transfer repairs and maintenance and the preparatory and set-up costs for the new landlord. The matching funding attracted ERCF transfers in the form of private finance totalled £827 million, a private:public gearing ratio of almost two to one.

Many subsequent partial transfers have also been made possible by a combination of debt write-off for the originating local authority and 'gap funding' for the receiving housing association (see Chapter 3). Although many partial transfers have conveyed property to existing housing associations, 'partials' have also often spawned the establishment of community-based housing associations with a strong local accountability ethic (see Chapter 5).

Two-stage transfers

A transfer variant, pioneered by Sunderland Metropolitan Borough Council in 2001, involved a two-stage transfer, with council stock being passed initially to a city-wide housing association and then subsequently to a constellation of locally based associations across the authority (without the need for a subsequent set of ballots). A similar process was originally envisaged for the Glasgow City Council transfer of 2003. However, partly reflecting the distinct features of Scots law, such a process is inherently far more complex north of the border than in England. Beyond this, as explained later (see Box 5.3 in Chapter 5) the Glasgow Second Stage Transfer

(SST) programme has been seriously compromised by inadequate funding provision in the Glasgow Housing Association business plan.

The changing geography of stock transfers

In England, the geography of stock transfers has seen a very clear shift over time. As shown in Figures 2.3 and 2.4, in its first ten years the process was largely dominated by southern shire districts. From 1998 onwards, however, this changed sharply, with predominantly larger, more urban unitary local authorities accounting for an increased share of the transferring stock. The typically larger landlord holdings of upper tier and other urban councils are reflected in the generally greater average size of (whole) stock transfer transactions post-1997 – see Figure 2.2.

As discussed in more detail in Chapters 3 and 4, several factors lie behind this pattern. Key, here, have been financial considerations. On the one hand, transfer was initially more financially attractive for authorities which had already repaid their housing loan debts. This was disproportionately the case among shire districts – reflecting the fact that, for historical reasons, many such authorities had developed most of their council housing relatively early in the twentieth century. For many urban authorities, on the other hand, heavy post-war and 1960s investment in council housing had racked up substantial loan debt, much of which remained unpaid by the 1990s. In combination with typically higher disrepair liabilities affecting urban council stock, this created a scenario where unsubsidized transfer was financially infeasible. Transactions could proceed in such areas only after 1997 when Ministers first approved Treasury-funded debt write-off for transferring local authorities and/or 'gap funding' for receiving housing associations (as discussed in more detail in Chapter 3).

Political considerations have also been important, with transfer generally seen as unpalatable by Labour-controlled local authorities until 1997. Subsequently, with a Labour government in power at Westminster and with Ministers promoting the policy on a pragmatic rather than nakedly ideological basis, the politics of the situation changed.

FIGURE 2.3   Stock transfers in England: breakdown by local
authority type

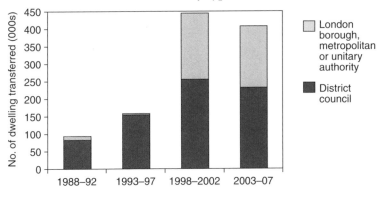

Source: CLG stock transfers dataset.

The geography of stock transfers in Scotland and Wales has
been somewhat different. A strong tradition of urban stock
transfer was established right at the start in Scotland, with the
CBHA handovers of the 1980s (as discussed earlier in this
chapter). Given the national scope of the former Scottish
Special Housing Association, the Scottish Homes transfers of
the 1990s took place in a diverse range of local settings

FIGURE 2.4   The changing regional geography of stock
transfers in England

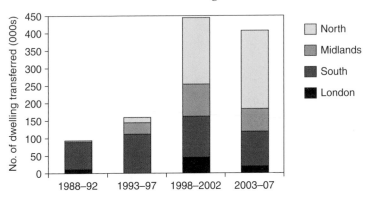

Note: 'South' includes 'East of England' Government Office Region.

Source: CLG stock transfers dataset.

TABLE 2.3 *English housing authorities by landlord/non-landlord status, 2008*

(a) Breakdown by region

Region	LA – retained		ALMO		Post-transfer		All	
	No	%	No	%	No	%	No	%
East	21	44	4	8	23	48	48	100
East Midlands	20	50	8	20	12	30	40	100
London	10	30	20	61	3	9	33	100
North East	6	26	7	30	10	43	23	100
North West	4	9	10	23	29	67	43	100
South East	30	45	2	3	29	52	67	100
South West	13	29	5	11	35	60	45	100
West Midlands	12	34	3	9	27	57	35	100
Yorks & Humberside	6	30	6	30	20	40	20	100
England	122	34	65	18	8	47	354	100

(b) Breakdown by local authority type

Local authority type	LA – retained		ALMO		Post-transfer		All	
	No	%	No	%	No	%	No	%
District	88	37	18	8	132	55	238	100
London borough	10	30	20	61	3	9	33	100
Metropolitan authority	3	8	19	53	14	39	36	100
(Other) unitary authority	21	45	8	17	18	38	47	100
Total	122	34	65	18	167	47	354	100

Note: 'LA – retained' refers to authorities which have retained both the ownership and direct management of council housing.

Source: Data from Local Authority Housing Strategy Statistical Annex returns and National Federation of ALMOs.

including remote rural, suburban and inner urban areas. Nevertheless, much of the SSHA/Scottish Homes transfer programme focused on Greater Glasgow and other larger cities, an emphasis even more evident for local authority partial transfers. Glasgow City Council's whole stock transfer in 2003 only compounds the City's status as the housing association capital of the world. Most of the other post-2003 whole stock transfers have involved rural areas in the South (e.g. Scottish Borders) and West (e.g. Argyll & Bute) of the country.

In Wales, the geography of transfers has been influenced by the fact that virtually none took place prior to 2003, and by the subsequent government funding, which has made transfer a financially attractive proposition to authorities struggling to resource compliance with the Welsh Housing Quality Standard (see Chapter 3). The consequence has been that 'early' transfers have tended to involve Valleys authorities encumbered with poor quality council stock.

As noted earlier in this chapter, by 2008 almost half of all English local authorities, having transferred all their housing, had ceased to operate as landlords – a fact emphasized by Table 2.3a). Post-transfer authorities were in a majority in four of the nine official regions – the North West, South East, South West and West Midlands. Nationally, almost a fifth of authorities had delegated the management of council housing to ALMOs. Only in the East Midlands did at least half of authorities retain the ownership and direct management of council housing.

Tables 2.3(a) and (b) confirm the extent to which whole stock transfer has been much less common in London than elsewhere, while the ALMO option has become dominant. It should, however, be emphasized that partial transfers have been much more numerous in the capital – almost half London's 32 boroughs had undertaken one or more partial transfers by 2008. Outside of London there is something of a contrast between metropolitan authorities – which have tended to opt for ALMOs – and district councils – where stock transfer has been the most popular choice. Nevertheless, with the surge in urban transfers post-1997 a considerable number of metropolitan councils were, by 2008, no longer stock-owning authorities.

Gilmour (2009c) has pointed to the differential impacts of the transfer process on city regions. Box 2.1 takes the example of

Box 2.1   Greater Manchester social housing mix, 1997–2010

In 2007, traditionally owned and managed council housing (or public housing) accounted for nine per cent of England's total housing stock, down from a peak of 28 per cent in 1971 (CLG, 2008). By 2009, in Greater Manchester this proportion was estimated to have fallen to less than one per cent. This has been a recent, sudden and largely un-noticed transformation. As recently as 1997 council housing continued to account for over 250,000 dwellings in Greater Manchester (CLG, 2008). By 2009 the figure was only 3,710. The City of Manchester, where the remaining properties are located, has proposed the transfer of this stock within the next three years to new PFI (Public Finance Initiative) vehicles and local housing associations.

The changes in the structure of social housing in Greater Manchester are shown below. During the first six years of the New Labour government significant changes were limited to the transfer of small overspill estates from the City of Manchester and a large-scale voluntary transfer in Tameside. In 2003 the pattern shifted dramatically as a wave of ALMO formation swept the county, splitting social housing nearly equally between traditional council housing, housing associations and ALMOs. From 2005 to 2008 both ALMOs and housing associations continued to expand at the expense of public housing. Then, from 2008 onwards, housing association tenure looks set to expand at the expense of ALMOs (see Chapter 8).

Notes: Historic tenure data up to March 2007 from CLG (2008; 2009d). Figures as at 31st March. CLG data has been re-modelled by the author to include ALMOs as a separate category, with their housing stock adjusted to date of establishment. March 2008 figures are based on known stock transfers and ALMO formation to that date. Projected figures for March 2009 and 2010 based on proposed further stock changes in Salford and Manchester, and transfer of 12,000 units in Oldham in 2010.

Source: Gilmour (2009c).

the social housing provider mix in Greater Manchester showing how rapidly the pattern has changed in this city region and how this has diverged from the patterns found at national level. This indicates the extent to which the transfer process has produced fragmented geographies of social housing.

Britain's new social landlords

In this section we take a look at the types of landlords involved in each stage of the transfer story. We will return to the question of who are Britain's new social landlords in a summative discussion in Chapter 10.

Throughout Britain, the vast majority of *whole stock* transfers have involved housing associations created specifically to take ownership of the former local authority portfolio. By 2008 such organizations brought into being via the transfer process numbered around 220 in England (of which some 40 had been established in the course of partial transfers). In Scotland, around 40 stock transfer housing associations were set up in the 20 years from 1988 (mostly via the SSHA/Scottish Homes transfer programme rather than through local authority transfers). The handful of post-2003 stock transfers in Wales (see Table 2.1) have also involved newly created landlord bodies. In all, therefore, well over 250 new 'purpose-designed' landlords have come into being as a consequence of the process. Arguably, in combination with the 69 ALMOs created in England since 2002, these have formed 'Britain's new social landlords' – the organizations at the heart of this book. The reasons that newly formed rather than existing associations have dominated the transfer process are explored in Chapters 3 and 4.

As shown in Table 2.4, most stock transfer housing associations have been set up as independent, freestanding entities. In only two instances, prior to 2008, did English authorities transfer to existing associations. In 14 cases, however, the transfer landlord was a new entity set up as a subsidiary of an existing association. Table 2.4 suggests that this has been becoming a more popular option in recent years, with almost a third of the transfers completed in 2006 and 2007 taking this form. The 'group subsidiary' model has accounted for a larger proportion of the new associations set up to take on English partial stock transfers.

The dominance of new organizations as the vehicle for transfers has created the scenario in which it has made sense to refer to 'stock transfer housing associations' and the 'stock transfer sector'. It has facilitated the use of regulatory and statistical data to monitor the management and upgrading of former

TABLE 2.4 *English stock transfers 1988–2007: breakdown by association type at transfer*

Year	New – independent	New – independent group	New – subsidiary	Existing	Total
1988	1				1
1989	2				2
1990	8				8
1991	5				5
1992	2				2
1993	5				5
1994	12			1	13
1995	10				10
1996	6				6
1997	5				5
1998	7				7
1999	10		1		11
2000	13	2			15
2001	12	1			13
2002	11		2		13
2003	6	1	2		9
2004	10		1	1	12
2005	6				6
2006	11		2		13
2007	8		6		14
Total	150	4	14	2	170

Note: Table covers 'whole stock' transfers only (including those undertaken as 'split transfers').

Source: CLG transfers dataset as enhanced by authors.

council homes. However, it cannot be assumed that this reality will necessarily endure. Although they must obtain regulatory consent to do so, housing associations have considerable freedom to restructure themselves and to enter alliances and mergers with other landlords within the sector (Mullins 1999, 2000, Pawson and Sosenko 2008). As discussed in more detail in Chapter 5, many transfer housing associations have in fact made such moves since their original establishment. Nevertheless, the vast majority of transfer associations set up as such since 1988 (89 per cent) remained extant as identifiable entities in 2007. While a few have merged with traditional housing associations or have become subsidiaries of groups led by (or including) traditional associations, the traditional vs. stock transfer dichotomy remained largely intact at this time. Although this seems likely to erode over time, such a process remains at a relatively early stage.

Chapter conclusions

Stock transfer, as currently understood, originally emerged in the very specific policy context of the late 1980s, partly prompted by a 'protective' impulse on the part of local authorities in the face of what were perceived as serious threats to council housing. Despite the shifting policy concerns of the past 20 years, transfers have played a continuing and important role in restructuring social housing in England and Scotland, if not in Wales.

The start of tenanted stock transfer by English local authorities in the late 1980s was pre-figured by earlier initiatives, including estate transfers in Scotland, the handover of ex-New Town Development Corporation dwellings and vacant possession estate disposals aimed at facilitating investment and/or generating capital receipts. The introduction of mixed funding for housing associations in 1989, however, marked a fundamental policy shift helping to prompt the creation of transfer landlords on a new and distinct basis.

Post-1988 stock transfers have come in a variety of guises with an important distinction between the 'whole stock' and 'partial' variants. The latter have tended to involve particularly run-down estates and have been substantially pump-primed by public subsidy.

As the volume of ex-LA transfers in England rose towards the end of the 1990s the emphasis shifted somewhat from rural areas towards cities and from the South to the North. The transfer process and the increased variety of vehicles (including ALMO and PFI) have resulted in geographical differentiation of social housing at several spatial levels including the city region. As transfers have become more urban in character, the policy has increasingly engaged with social inclusion and community regeneration objectives.

Emerging from the stock transfer process, more than 250 newly created registered social landlords have formed a distinct component of the housing association sector in England, Wales and Scotland. These are Britain's new social landlords.

Chapter 3

Stock Transfer Motivations and Processes

Promoting and delivering stock transfers is neither easy nor painless. For elected councillors, it involves exposure to significant political and financial risk, as transfer proposals are inevitably controversial and ballot endorsement can never be taken for granted. For senior management, the process is highly time-consuming and often necessitates extended working weeks and endless evening meetings. For middle managers and staff, transfer preparations bring uncertainty about job security generated by the prospect of major upheaval. For tenants, a transfer means a switch from a familiar landlord to an unknown and usually untested successor body. For central government, the post-1997 promotion of the transfer policy has required Ministers to face down vociferous critics (including party colleagues) and, again, has involved a degree of political hazard given the danger that – as in the Birmingham 2002 bid – a flagship project may be voted down locally. And, with transfer 'transaction costs' averaging £430 per home transferred (NAO 2003: 34), ministerial support for the policy surely implies a conviction that it generates substantial benefits. Given these considerations, how is it that the transfer policy has attracted the necessary support to remain afloat? What have been the policy drivers underlying the policy's continuing prominence?

In describing the emerging pattern of transfers, Chapter 2 hinted at some of the motivations underlying the phenomenon and at the processes involved. This chapter develops the discussion of these issues. Motivations are categorized under three headings: firstly, those related to transfer's potential in facilitating housing investment, secondly, those involving other financial considerations and, thirdly, those linked with other aspirations such as protecting social housing stock, improving housing governance through enhanced tenant and community involvement and delivering higher quality housing management services. In examining financial stimuli, the chapter necessarily explores the economics of stock transfer and the public costs involved. Whilst 'political' motivations have also certainly been important, detailed discussion of these is held over to Chapter 4.

Having analysed what drives transfers, we then discuss the mechanics of the transfer process as it has evolved since the late 1980s. Here we focus, in particular, on the key question of stock valuation – determining the price paid by the new landlord to the former owner. Given the official advice that this should incorporate an early 'stock options appraisal' to identify whether transfer is, in fact, the most appropriate way forward, this section also looks briefly at the main alternative means for boosting housing investment available to local authorities. Both in terms of motivations and processes, it is important to identify the main 'stakeholders' with a potential interest in transfers and to understand their concerns. Before moving to the main body of the chapter, therefore, we first discuss these actors and their interests.

Stakeholder interests

Under British legal and institutional frameworks, ownership transfers of tenanted council housing can proceed only with the support of the local authorities and tenants concerned (see Chapter 2). Both interest groups must be motivated in favour of transfer. In formulating a view here, authorities (meaning their politically elected leaderships) are likely to be influenced by their responsibilities as landlords (e.g. in terms of their ability to maintain and modernize their housing stock, as well as to ensure an adequate supply of affordable housing). At the same time, they may be mindful of their role in delivering a wide variety of other services and their desire to make the best use of limited resources on behalf of local taxpayers. If, for example, a proposed transfer is seen as likely to generate a substantial net capital receipt as well as securing otherwise unavailable investment in the housing stock the authority might be expected to be strongly in favour. If, as has become increasingly common, there is no prospect of spendable proceeds, the attraction will clearly be weaker.

Similarly, local authority tenants, as a stakeholder group, will be primarily motivated by a concern over the stewardship of housing stock in relation to the rents charged (though under the existing Housing Benefit system many tenants are wholly insulated from value for money considerations because any rent increase is fully reimbursed to housing benefit recipients). Other primary considerations for tenants will include the prospects of investment in improving their homes and neighbourhoods, the quality of services and preserved rights such as the Right to Buy.

The framework within which the whole transfer mechanism operates is set by central government, with the rules of the game reflecting government's own stance towards transfers at any one time. This, again, is a product of central government's own interest in the policy as a key stakeholder with particular concerns around promoting housing policies which further Departmental social and political objectives whilst minimizing the impact on the public finances. Considerations such as the impact of transfers on contributions to housing benefit expenditure, on subsidy requirements to facilitate negative value transfers and 'double subsidy' investment of transfer receipts by local authorities have at various times played a key part in shaping and constraining the transfer programme.

Beyond these three main stakeholder groups – local authorities, tenants and government – a number of other parties with a significant interest in the stock transfer policy have been identified (Gardiner et al. 1991). These include new tenants (i.e. households taking up tenancies after the transfer), housing managers and staff (as distinct from local authority councillors), lenders (who finance stock acquisition and upgrading) and consultants who advise on the technical aspects of transfers.

For reasons elaborated in Chapter 7, new tenants' interests are in some respects distinct from those of existing tenants. Particularly in areas where affordable homes are in short supply, prospective tenants have a direct interest in the extent to which transfer might facilitate the development of additional social housing (though concerns about this issue may also be voiced by existing tenants). Local authority housing (and other) staff are likely to be concerned about the potential impact of transfer on their security and terms of employment, as well as on the quality and scale of their workload. For managers, the degree of autonomy is likely to be a particular consideration. For both financial institutions and consultants transfers will be seen as a potentially welcome source of business, albeit one which carries certain risks.

Table 3.1 summarizes the drivers for transfer which have, at one time or another, underpinned the support of the identified stakeholder groups. The nature of each of these drivers – and their changing significance over time – is further discussed below.

Housing investment drivers and financing stock transfers

Most successful transfers are driven by a combination of the factors identified in Table 3.1. However, particularly since 1997, the predominant main trigger has been the need to access housing investment. The backdrop here is the longstanding and widespread under-funding of council housing upkeep since the 1970s, generating the need for a catalogue of remedial works costed at £19 billion by 1996 (NAO, 2003). The potential for transfer to 'unlock extra investment' can be appreciated only in the context of a broader understanding of transfer financing. Hence, this section explains the funding of transfers, and discusses the extent to which the transfer option can be seen as representing 'value for money'.

Funding transfers – the basic model

Under the standard stock transfer model, the seller (local authority) agrees a price with the buyer (housing association) which is based on the tenanted market value valuation (TMV) method – see Box 3.3. Taking into account projected rental (and other income during the term of its business plan – usually 30 years) the housing association then seeks loan (or occasionally bond) finance from a bank or building society to cover (a) the agreed purchase price, and (b) the cost of repairs and modernization. Since works programmes are generally 'front-loaded', most of the repairs funding is also needed 'upfront'. Rental and other income is then used to repay the loans and

TABLE 3.1 *Stakeholder groups: motivations for supporting transfer*

Stakeholders	Financial drivers			Non-financial drivers			
	Repair/ modernization of existing LA stock	Development of new social housing	Development of (non-housing) community facilities	Protective/ defensive motivations	Better governance, management efficiency/ responsiveness	Furthering of vested interests	Political ideology
Central government	x				x		x
Local authorities	x	x (some)	x (some)	x (some)			x (some)
LA senior housing managers	x	x (some)		x (some)	x (some)	x	
LA staff	x	x (some)		x (some)			
Existing LA tenants	x	x (some)			x (some)		
Prospective LA tenants		x (some)					
Lenders						x	
Consultants						x	

interest. At acquisition, the transfer housing association usually 'draws down' a part of the agreed lending facility to cover the purchase price, with this being paid to the local authority. The authority then uses this receipt to repay the outstanding debt attributable to the transferred stock, as well as any other eligible costs arising from the transfer. The latter include 'breakage penalties' – sums payable to the Public Works Loan Board as local authority lender in compensation for breaching the terms of existing housing loans (by repaying them 'early').

Under the framework applicable in England and Wales, local authorities generating a net receipt after repayment of housing debt were, for a time, liable to central government's capital receipts levy. This is a 20 per cent surcharge to 'compensate' the Treasury for the impact of transfer on central government expenditure. The levy was established to offset housing benefit costs no longer covered by contributions from council rents. These arose from the fact that, under the Local Government and Housing Act 1989, local authorities whose housing revenue accounts are assessed as notionally 'in surplus' (potentially generating rental income in excess of landlord expenditure) must contribute to the cost of Housing Benefit payments to local authority tenants eligible for this support. In effect, Housing Benefit expenditure in these authorities was funded through cross-subsidy within the local tenant population rather than by general taxation. Consequently, when an 'HRA surplus' authority transferred its stock the Treasury lost the opportunity to offset its liabilities in funding Housing Benefit payments to the authority's tenants.

However, following changes to the council housing subsidy system from April 2004, notional rental surpluses were no longer applied towards the costs of housing benefit. Instead, they were transferred to central government to help fund the Major Repairs Allowance (MRA), for which some authorities are eligible, as well as other subsidy costs of other 'non-surplus' councils. Before that, the extent of notional surpluses had, in any event, been significantly reduced when, in 2001, MRAs were included as an element of the housing subsidy regime. By the end of 2008, more than £475 million had been 'creamed off' from transfer receipts via the levy. More recently, however, relatively few transfers have attracted levy charges because of the diminishing number involving HRA surplus local authorities. Among the 39 transfers proceeding in 2007 and 2008, for example, only 12 involved levy payments (CLG stock transfers dataset).

Funding 'negative value' and 'overhanging debt' transfers

From a central and local government perspective, one of the main attractions of the stock transfer mechanism has been its potential to facilitate the 're-financing' of social housing without incurring explicit public expenditure. However, the scope for such an outcome depends on (a) the value of the transfer receipt exceeding the local authority's housing debt, and (b) the transfer landlord's projected long term income exceeding its projected expenditure. During the first 10 years of the transfer process (1988–97) all transactions were of this type, hence requiring no government subsidy.

From the mid-1990s, however, Ministers increasingly acknowledged historic under-funding of council housing and saw transfer as central in remedying this situation. Nevertheless, for many of the local authorities with large disrepair backlogs, the scale of investment need and/or outstanding local authority housing debt meant that transfer could be made viable only if underpinned by public funding. Two problematic scenarios are possible. Firstly, the 'overhanging debt' situation. This occurs where the prospective transfer receipt (see Box 3.3 on transfer valuation) is insufficient to repay a local authority's remaining historic housing debt. Consequently, such a transfer cannot proceed without public funding to avoid leaving the local authority with a residual debt but no means of servicing that debt. Secondly, there is the 'negative value' scenario. This is where the estimated cost of acquiring, renovating, managing and maintaining the transferred stock over the business plan period (usually 30 years) exceeds the projected (rental and other) income of the new landlord over the same period (see Box 3.3).

A central funding mechanism to extinguish 'overhanging debt' was introduced in England in 1999. Under this arrangement, qualifying local authorities receive a one-off payment covering the difference between the transfer receipt and the authority's housing debt. The first transfers benefiting from

this treatment were those in Burnley and Coventry. In justifying explicit public funding for stock transfer, central government has pointed to the perceived benefit to the public purse
of transferring risk to the private sector. Also, in common with
ALMO funding (see Chapter 8), such subsidies have been
argued as justifiable in principle because of what are considered to be the benefits of separating the local authority
strategic role from that of housing delivery (paragraph 4.59,
CLG, 2009a).

From 2004, the overhanging debt payment regime was
extended to cover partial transfers. For these purposes, local
authorities have been required to calculate attributable housing
debt on a simple pro-rata basis. If the transfer accounts for 10
per cent of a council's housing stock, therefore, the attributable
debt is 10 per cent of the total. Hence, if the projected value of
the transfer receipt is less than this, an 'overhanging debt' situation applies. By 2008, overhanging debt payments totalled £3.6
billion in England alone. Particularly large sums had been
approved in relation to the whole stock transfers in Liverpool
(£721 million), Bradford (£183 million) and Wakefield (£149
million). Exceeding all these, however, the 2003 Glasgow
transfer involved Treasury financing for £909 million in outstanding debt, plus £196 million in breakage costs – see above
(Social Housing, 2003).

Overhanging debt transfers have not necessarily involved a
'negative value' scenario – it is possible that the valuation pro-
duces a positive receipt but one that remains insufficient to
repay the local authority's debt. Theoretically, it is also possible
that a negative value transfer valuation might not involve overhanging debt – this would be the case for a landlord local
authority which had already repaid all of its housing debt but
which wished to transfer housing with heavy investment
requirements.

In practice, however, overhanging debt and negative valuation issues have usually tended to occur side by side. To
address the latter, central government has made available 'gap
funding' payable to eligible transfer housing associations. In
England, gap funding provision originally made available under
the ERCF (see Chapters 2 and 7) was reintroduced by central
government in 2004 and was available for transfers approved
2004–06. By 2008, the scheme had generated payments

totalling over £600 million. By 2006, most transfers progressing in both England (and all in Scotland) were being
enabled to proceed thanks to overhanging debt funding.
Eighteen of the 27 English transfers proceeding in that year
required such assistance, with two more benefiting from gap
funding (as well as nine where both forms of assistance were
provided).

English transfers in receipt of gap funding have included
Preston (2005, £48 million) and Liverpool (2008, £130
million). However, such sums are dwarfed by the Scottish
Executive's £787 million gap funding approved for the 2003
Glasgow Housing Association transaction – see Table 3.2
(Social Housing 2003). This was on top of £27 million paid out
of the Executive's New Housing Partnerships fund to underpin
the Council's transfer preparation costs (Scottish Parliament
2003).

In Wales, all of the local authority transfers completed by
2008 had involved municipal housing debt write-off. Inclusive
of breakage costs, such funding had amounted to £323 million.
Beyond that, a number of the transfers had also been facilitated
through gap funding. Under the Welsh Assembly Government's
approach, this has been financed by converting the annual
Major Repairs Allowance originally earmarked for the transferring local authority to 'dowry' funding payable annually to the
receiving housing association. The term of such funding is
determined by the calculated 'gap' in the transfer association's
business plan. Total annual gap funding projected in respect of
the seven Welsh transfers completed by early 2009 was some
£28 million. Forward projections assumed a total payment of
gap funding of £821 million although such payments have been
legally committed only for a five-year time horizon (unpublished data provided by the Welsh Assembly Government).

It was suggested in 2003 that gap funding should take the
form of repayable interest-free loans. In this way, the public
purse could share in any post-transfer windfalls arising from
future development gain, advantageous refinancing or out-per-
formance of business plan targets (Webb 2003). Such an
approach addresses concerns (see discussion later in this
chapter) that 'undervaluation' of transferred stock can result in
the subsequent generation of surpluses which equate to 'unjus-
tified subsidies'.

Partly prompted by such thinking, as in Wales (see above), the 2004–06 English gap funding regime has involved designated allocations being paid in instalments over a number of years, with the transfer association's performance being assessed periodically to determine whether the scale of funding needs remains as originally anticipated. This approach has, however, been criticized as amounting to a 'disincentive for housing associations to out-perform their initial business plans' (Social Housing 2009a: 1).

Since 2006, government funding to facilitate transfers has been progressively cut back. First, from 2006, no new applications for gap funding were approved. Second, and potentially much more significant for the longer term, 2009 saw the announcement of an end to local authority debt write-off. This was an element incorporated within proposals for fundamental reform of the local authority housing revenue account (HRA) system to enable remaining landlord local authorities to float free of central control (CLG, 2009a). Critically, the proposals envisaged that 'For the future . . . the financial support available for a transfer would be no different from that on offer for self-financing' (ibid: paragraph 4.55). This clause sets the stock transfer implications of the policy switch within the broader context of the central proposal to re-structure rather than write-off the outstanding housing debt of remaining local authority landlords. The possible consequences of this policy switch for the future of stock transfer are further discussed in Chapter 10.

Transfer housing association business plans, debt profiles and refinancing

Any stock transfer requires a business plan where projected income and expenditure balance over a specified period. Exemplifying the scenario where public funding is required for this purpose, Table 3.2 provides an outline of Glasgow Housing Association's business plan at the point of setup.

Having taken on ownership of the transferred stock and incurred a corresponding initial debt, transfer housing association business plans are typically configured to incur increasing levels of debt during the association's first few years as the association 'draws down' successive tranches of funds under its

TABLE 3.2   *Glasgow housing association business plan projections to peak debt year*

	£ million	% of total
Expenditure to peak debt, 2014		
Purchase price	25	0.7
Responsive repairs	532	14.0
Management and administration	813	21.3
Investment programme	2,256	59.2
Re-provisioning (2,800 dwellings)	183	4.8
Total	3,809	100.0
Financed by		
Net rental income	2,057	54.0
Scottish Executive repayable grant	339	8.9
Scottish Executive other grants	448	11.8
VAT savings	240	6.3
Private finance	725	19.0
Total	3,809	100.0

Source: Adapted from Social Housing (2003) .

agreed lending facility. This debt profile (see Figure 3.1) reflects the typically 'front-loaded' investment schedule as the new landlord carries out an intensive post-transfer programme of 'catch-up repairs' and improvements to comply with the usual five-year 'promises period' as pledged to tenants. Later on, gradually rising rental income should see the association passing 'peak debt' and beginning to generate revenue surpluses, assuming that it does not decide to embark on further investment in new or existing stock or other business activities. The realization of this outcome depends crucially on the validity of key assumptions underpinning the transfer housing association business plan. Some of these factors, such as economic and market conditions (affecting e.g. works and construction costs) and public policy (e.g. rent restructuring, HB reform and RPI based rent increases) are outside of the direct control of the association but are risks which must be managed.

Historically, transfer housing associations have tended to refinance their loan facilities within the first 2–3 years following

FIGURE 3.1 Typical transfer housing association debt profile for 'positive value' transfers

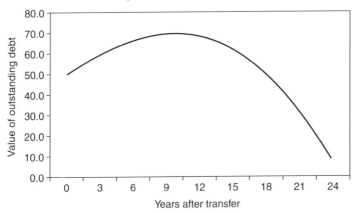

Source: Housing Corporation 1998(b).

transfer (Ernst & Young 2002). Typically, this has involved renegotiating loan facilities to obtain more favourable terms and/or interest rates potentially available as soon as the organization is in a position to demonstrate a post-transfer track record of satisfactory management performance and/or efficiency savings contributing to a strengthened business plan. Aside from securing better terms and rates, post-transfer re-financing may be motivated by the aim of expanding loan facilities on the back of rising asset value of the transfer housing association's housing and other property (see discussion of valuation issues – Box 3.3). This might be inspired by, for example, aspirations to undertake new projects not envisaged at the time of transfer. A more problematic scenario is where post-transfer stock condition surveys have revealed the original loan package as insufficient to meet the promised modernization and improvement programme making it necessary to raise additional finance (e.g. spreading the debt over a longer repayment period). Where re-financing benefits the transfer housing association's business plan and thereby enhances its longer-term potential to generate revenue surpluses, however, an issue arises as to the lack of mechanisms to enable the public purse to share in such benefits. This issue, raised by Malpass and Mullins (2002) is further discussed later in this chapter.

The impact of public expenditure accounting conventions

As noted in Chapter 2, the investment benefits of stock transfer are founded on public accounts conventions and on the 'mixed funding' regime for housing associations established by the Housing Act 1988. With associations being empowered to set their own rents from this point onwards, they were officially defined as being outside the public sector and therefore able to borrow and invest as private bodies (but see footnote). Thus, whilst public capital funding of housing associations (Housing Association Grant and later Social Housing Grant) counts as 'public expenditure' in accounting terms, 'matching funding' and subsequent new loans from financial institutions do not. Unlike local authorities, therefore, associations are free to borrow for investment using the book value of their stock as security. Rather than being restricted by official controls, an association's private borrowing is limited only by its 'encumbered assets' (land and property held as security against existing loans) and by its capacity for loan repayment – i.e. the size of a loan which can be supported by its projected future rental income stream.

By transferring its housing stock into housing association ownership, a local authority may be able to facilitate investment in otherwise unaffordable essential repairs and modernization. That it has been possible for a housing association – but not a local authority – to fund such investment, and that this can be achieved without – necessarily – raising rents, is also a direct consequence of the accounting conventions used by the UK Treasury. Unlike most other European countries, Britain remains wedded to the PSNB – Public Sector Net Borrowing – accounting framework (formerly the Public Sector Borrowing Requirement – PSBR). Crucially, the PSNB definition of 'public spending' encompasses local authority housing capital investment; hence central government's interest in limiting such expenditure, despite the fact that this is integral to a 'trading activity' with the associated borrowing being repaid from rental income. For these purposes, therefore, housing associations are defined as non-state bodies. At the same time, however, associations receive considerable state funding and play an important role as agents of official housing policy. It has also recently been determined that associations are within the remit of European Union procurement rules applicable to public organizations and that in their housing management role they perform a 'public function' (see Mullins and Pawson 2010, forthcoming). All of this emphasizes the tenuous nature of associations' characterization as non-state agencies in PSNB terms.*

Along with a number of other member states, the European Union uses a different definition of public borrowing – the General Government Financial Deficit (or GGFD) measure. Importantly, GGFD (unlike PSBR) excludes expenditure by 'public corporations' (i.e. trading bodies set up and owned by state institutions) and also excludes privatization receipts from its concept of 'public sector income' (Hawksworth and Wilcox 1995a).

During the mid-1990s, the government was seen as moving towards possible replacement of PSBR by GGFD. Hawksworth and Wilcox, for example, noted that even by 1995 central government had begun to submit GGFD returns to the EU and (along with other commentators) they foresaw a possible full-scale switch to a GGFD regime for the UK. This would have opened up the possibility of local authorities creating wholly-owned, but organizationally distinct, social landlord bodies whose investment borrowing would be beyond the definition of 'public sector debt'. In some respects, such organizations are now a reality in the form of local authority ALMOs created since 2002 (see Chapter 8). However, these bodies are not defined as outside the public sector, and are hence denied the full range of financial freedoms available to housing

---

* Partly stemming from these decisions there have been concerns at housing associations being edged towards formal re-incorporation within the public sector. As noted by Wilcox (2004) the EU judgement followed mainly from associations' heavily regulated status. Further worries on this score were generated by proposals for more intrusive regulation in the Housing and Regeneration Bill 2008 (NHF 2008a). Ultimately, the anxiety is that the Office for National Statistics could re-classify housing associations as public bodies in relation to the UK national accounts. Far from being merely a technical matter 'this would challenge not only the financial rationale for stock transfers, but also the financial rationale for housing associations to be the predominant vehicle for the delivery of new affordable housing' (Wilcox, 2004: 60).

associations. In creating the scope for fully liberated ALMOs at an earlier stage, a mid-1990s move to GGFD might have substantially undermined the dynamic towards full-blown stock transfer. In practice, of course, Treasury resistance to the replacement of PSBR/PSNB remained dominant, post-1997 – probably reflecting concern that the financial markets would interpret such as move as indicating a lack of resolve in controlling public spending.

As part of its move to a 'resource accounting' approach to controlling public expenditure since 2000 central government has allowed local authorities to engage in 'prudential borrowing' to the extent that their projected revenue resources can support consequential debt repayments. Since this has entailed the removal of direct capital controls the new regime can be presented as providing authorities with 'additional freedoms' in terms of capital investment. Such a move might, therefore, be expected to have reduced the investment incentives favouring stock transfer. However, since the scope for prudential borrowing is limited by local authority revenue income, and with council rents in England being closely controlled by central government post-2001, the system did not lead to more council housing investment here without additional revenue subsidy. 'High debt authorities . . . will [continue to] achieve more financial freedom through transfer because their old housing debt will be paid off. Low debt authorities will also get more financial freedom through transfer because they "escape" the pooling arrangements whereby they pay into the national pot' (CIH 2002c: 2). Crucially, in contrast with the housing association financial regime, prudential borrowing is limited by rules prohibiting local authorities from using the asset value of their housing stock as loan security. Some of these factors could be altered by the Westminster government's local authority housing revenue account (HRA) reform proposals (CLG, 2009a) – see Chapter 10, potentially reducing or removing key financial incentives for transfer, previously inbuilt.

Being outside the kind of redistributive HRA regime operating in England, Scottish local authorities have enjoyed a slightly more favourable position in relation to their scope for prudential borrowing. Those with low debt have significant potential to finance housing investment in this way. Also, their borrowing is deemed to be entirely prudential, and is accounted for as 'Annually Managed Expenditure' – and is therefore not counted against the Departmental Expenditure Limited (DEL) budget of the Scottish Government.

Overhauling local authority housing through transfer: value for money considerations

Stock transfer critics have long contended that the policy is an expensive and disruptive process made necessary only to evade PSBR/PSNB restrictions rather than a cost-effective way of upgrading council housing. These arguments seemed to be given new force by the National Audit Office's revelation in 2003 of a previously unpublished official assessment of stock overhaul procurement costs calculated in 2001. This had estimated that a hypothetical 5-year stock transfer programme involving 1 million local authority homes would cost the taxpayer an average of £4,200 per property spread over a 30-year period as compared with an average unit cost of only £2,900 for the same investment if carried out directly by local authorities themselves (NAO 2003: paragraph 3.37).

In part, this finding reflected the NAO's estimate that the transaction costs associated with transfer averaged some £430 per dwelling. Such costs include the consultants fees, stamp duty, opportunity costs of staff time integral to achieving ownership handover (NAO 2003: 34). In the main, however, the 'lower taxpayer cost' of direct LA investment – as calculated by the NAO – was also a function of a council (as a state institution) being able to borrow at a lower rate of interest than could a housing association.

As the NAO acknowledged, the 2001 official comparison took no account of the risk transfer from the public to the private sector implied by stock transfer. To the extent that this is inherent in the policy, it is arguably a relevant consideration, since the apparent differential between the two cost estimates results largely from the fact that local authorities – as public bodies – can borrow at lower rates of interest than private organizations, and this in turn reflects the fact that, under the 'direct council investment' option, financial risks (e.g. due to cost over-runs, misplaced investment), continue to be borne by the state rather than being passed to a private body. Klein (1997) contends that 'the low cost of borrowing by governments does not reflect superior capabilities to choose or manage projects . . . [rather] it reflects the fact that governments have recourse to taxpayers who de facto provide a fairly open-ended credit insurance to the government. [Hence] if taxpayers were remunerated for the risk they assume in the case of tax-financed projects, then ex ante there would be no capital cost advantage to government finance' (ibid: 29). In other words, to the extent that the apparent cost differential shown by the NAO's comparative figures is attributable to 'cheaper government borrowing', the comparison is, as argued by Jeff Zitron, a leading consultant in this area, 'a red herring'.

Other debateable aspects of the 2001 'cost comparison' were identified by Wilcox (2003) who pointed out that the assessment 'did not compare like for like in terms of the time profile of major repairs and improvements programmes under the different options' (ibid: 54). This refers to the fact that, whilst transfer housing associations typically 'front-load' their works expenditure within a 30-year business plan framework (see Figure 3.1), local authorities are more likely to plan for a smoother rate of spending across the period. Hence, the debt profiles were not comparable. All other things being equal, the same volume of investment would be 'more costly' under the transfer option because – with tenants benefiting sooner from investment – the cumulative interest costs would be higher.

Taking all this on board, therefore, the belief that 'official figures' self-evidently prove stock transfer to be an 'expensive' means of upgrading local authority housing (e.g. as re-cited by the ODPM House of Commons Select Committee – House of Commons 2004) could be seen as questionable. Equally, there is certainly no conclusive evidence to show that the transfer policy is fully justified in purely 'value for money' terms.

An important issue closely related to the value for money debate concerns the longer-term financial impact of transfer. As shown in Figure 3.1 the typical transfer housing association business plan projects a scenario where, having passed its 'peak debt' year, it has the potential to generate growing revenue surpluses. The potentially very considerable scale of these surpluses reflects the valuation methodology used to determine the transfer price – see Box 3.3. The existence of such a scenario raises two public policy concerns. Firstly, the potentially rather 'comfortable' position of post-peak debt transfer housing associations may be seen as providing relatively few incentives for such organizations to maximize their management performance to the benefit of their tenants as well as the taxpayer. Secondly, as argued by Malpass and Mullins (2002), housing associations generating such surpluses are unlikely to be operating 'in the areas of greatest need for housing investment' (ibid: 678). Since housing associations are, as Malpass and Mullins observed, formally independent of the state, such surpluses cannot be re-directed consistent with the geographical pattern of housing need (a traditional function of central government subsidy frameworks relating to local authority landlords).

The problem here can be seen as one reflecting what Zitron (2004) describes as the 'undiscriminating' public funding regime applicable to housing associations. The 'comfort margin' built into transfer valuation assumptions in practice could be depicted as a capital subsidy similar to that of up-front Social Housing Grant funding for new housing association development. Valuations on this basis can be justified on the grounds that there is a need to allow for unforeseen risks faced by a transfer housing association and to protect the organization's viability. More practically, with transfer funders naturally sharing such concerns it is possible that any attempt to reduce such comfort margins below their familiar level could render proposals un-fundable. The National Audit Office cited the case of one (1995) transfer where a valuation reflecting the actual cost of funding as subsequently experienced would have been over 50 per cent higher (less generous to the association) than the valuation fixed in practice. (The debate here concerns the appropriate 'discount rate' used to value transferring stock – see Box 3.3.) It could, therefore, be argued that in this instance the public purse 'lost out' to the extent of £19.5 million in implicit 'subsidy'. As the NAO points out, however, the higher valuation 'could have been achieved in practice only if lenders were still prepared to fund the transfer [on these terms], and (ODPM) believes that there is no evidence that a higher price would have been achievable had one been sought' (NAO 2003: paragraph 3.12).

One solution to the 'indiscriminate' system of funding housing associations through up-front capital grant would be to re-instate revenue funding similar to the pre-1974 framework. However, as Zitron argued, such an approach 'means instability, funding by political fiat and inability to plan' (Zitron 2004: 4). Instead, Zitron advocated a PFI approach to upgrading council housing on the grounds that contractual terms agreed by the local authority and its private sector (or housing association) partner can specify target performance standards and create linkage between achievement of these standards and contract payments. Under such an approach, the public sector 'retains significant risk but both rations and targets its subsidy' (Zitron 2004: 4). This strategy could be seen as consistent with the Labour Government's conviction that PFI should play a central role in public sector reform, and its efforts to extend PFI's remit to social housing and regeneration (HM Treasury 2003) (see also Box 3.2).

However, questions have also been raised about the PFI model of funding public service investment. For example, in the context of its application to finance NHS hospitals Pollock et al. (2002) argued that the alleged superiority of PFI on value for money grounds rested on dubious accounting assumptions with respect to discount rates and risk transfer. On a slightly different tack, Lonsdale (2005) drew attention to the typically lengthy contract periods (often 30 years for hospital and school projects), arguing that this implies a strong likelihood of the 'statement of work' needing to be renegotiated during the contract term. Lonsdale contended that such negotiations would be likely to take place under conditions of 'supplier dominance' such that the public bodies concerned will be under pressure to make financial concessions eradicating any economic advantage enjoyed by such schemes as calculated at the outset. While such arguments may be less relevant in the housing context, the small number of PFI housing projects approved in recent years have involved highly complex contractual agreements which have made such projects expensive to arrange and challenging to implement (Weaver 2005).

As ever, it seems that the question of value for money to the taxpayer is dependent upon the range of considerations included, the assumptions that are made and the extent to which such assumptions are delivered in practice.

Box 3.1   The Decent Homes Standard

As originally formulated, the Decent Homes Standard required that dwellings satisfy four broad criteria:

- Fitness for human habitation (as defined by the Housing Act 1985)
- Disrepair (a dwelling fails this test if either (a) it has one or more key building components which are old and, because of their condition, needing replacement or major repair, or (b) two or more other building components which are old and, because of their condition, needing replacement or major repair)
- Having 'reasonably modern facilities and services' (e.g. kitchen 20 years old or less; bathroom 30 years old or less)
- Providing a 'reasonable degree of thermal comfort' (including both 'effective heating' and 'effective insulation').

(ODPM, 2002: 6–9)

It was estimated in 2001 that around 1.7 million social rented sector dwellings in England (41 per cent of the total) were 'non-decent' on this measure (ODPM, 2002). Most of these will have been local authority-owned homes. Subsequently, however, this figure rose as a result of a revision to the Standard involving replacement of the 'unfitness' criterion with an assessment of a home's health and safety rating. A dwelling fails the Standard on this criterion if it contains one or more hazards assessed as serious under the Housing Health and Safety Rating System (HHSRS) framework. Such hazards could include, for example, dampness and mould growth, excess cold, or pollutants such as asbestos or carbon monoxide.

Impact of Decent Homes and quality housing standards

The significance of 'unlocking investment' as a motivation for stock transfer became far stronger after 1997 and particularly after 2000 when government adopted time-specific targets to eliminate unsatisfactory housing. In England, ministers defined an official Decent Homes Standard in 2001 (see Box 3.1), whilst committing to upgrading all social housing to this benchmark by 2010. Similarly, in Scotland and Wales, social housing standards and time-specific targets to achieve these were set by the devolved administrations in 2002/03 (Welsh Assembly Government, 2002; Scottish Executive, 2003). Importantly, the Scottish and Welsh standards have been interpreted as significantly more demanding than the DHS – e.g. in the Welsh case, in relation to requirements about the condition of the immediate surroundings of the dwelling.

Introducing this new approach, the English Housing Green Paper (DETR 2000c) also advanced a number of other arguments in favour of transfer (see below). However, an increased flow of transferring stock – with an annual target of 200,000 homes – was seen as essential in achieving the Decent Homes objective.

Development of new social housing

The great majority of new housing associations spawned by early transfers in England subsequently became active in developing new social housing (Pawson and Fancy 2003). Some early transfers were largely based on an aspiration to generate funds for the development of new social housing. This was particularly the case in the earlier 'shire district' transfers in the South of England, where the short and dwindling supply of affordable housing (rather than the condition of the existing stock) was often the most pressing housing policy concern. Many of these local authorities were in a position where their housing debt had been substantially repaid or even extinguished (see Chapter 2). Hence, the transfer receipt was likely to be sufficient to generate a considerable net capital receipt after the repayment of any remaining debt.

Nearly half of all pre-1999 transfer housing associations created in England were contractually required to develop new housing under the terms of agreements with founding local authorities. Under the East Lindsey District Council transfer contract, for example, the transfer housing association partner, Linx Homes, was required to develop 400 homes during the first five years after set-up in 1999 (Pawson and Fancy 2003).

Aspirations to boost social house-building tended to become less important in motivating transfers in England after 2000. This is partly because of the demise of the Local Authority Social Housing Grant (meaning that transfer receipts could no longer be 'recycled' more than once) and partly because the main focus of the transfer programme moved from high demand Southern shire districts to predominantly urban authorities with more seriously dilapidated housing stock and often operating in more mixed housing markets. In Scotland, however, a number of proposed transfers (e.g. Edinburgh, Highland) were promoted substantially on the basis that these would unlock major funding for new housing development, as well as for renovation of existing council stock. Thus, authorities falling into line with the Scottish Executive's strongly pro-transfer agenda stood to earn 'rewards' in the form of assurances as to the future scale of that funding.

In rather a different way, generating capital receipts to fund new house-building was also a crucial driver underlying the Scottish Homes stock transfer programme of the 1990s. While Scottish Homes was tasked with the disposal of the 75,000 dwellings inherited from the Scottish Special Housing Association in 1989, the agency was also responsible for funding new housing association development in Scotland. The ministerial requirement that Housing Association Grant payments to (non-transfer) housing associations be underpinned by transfer receipts placed considerable pressure on Scottish Homes, not just to push through transfers at the fastest possible pace, but also to maximize valuations (Taylor 2004: 128).

Other financial drivers

Much of the impetus behind early stock transfers in England derived from a financial driver unrelated to accessing investment. Here, the Local Government and Housing Act 1989 had strengthened ministers' ability to force up local authority rents seen as needing to be raised to more 'economic' levels, in the process helping to cut public spending by cross-subsidizing local Housing Benefit expenditure (see above). Particularly for many district councils, this New Financial Regime brought with it a prospect of very substantial rent increases, quite possibly accompanied by unavoidable service economies. Transfer was, in a number of instances, seen largely as an opportune device for avoiding this outcome – many early transfers gave tenants estimates of their future rents under a non-transfer scenario and where the projected charges greatly exceeded those specified in transfer promises. With the advent of resource accounting in 2000/01, however, the advantage for HRA-surplus local authorities in avoiding cross-subsidization of local Housing Benefit spending became less clear-cut (Perry 2002). As noted above, the restructuring of the 'redistributive' council housing finance regime in 2004 meant that such transactions involved national pooling rather than local cross-subsidy.

The introduction of the national rent restructuring framework in England from 2001 had an important impact on the stock transfer debate. Particularly following on from the adoption of a single rent target formula for both local authorities and housing associations in 2004, the possibility that choice of staying with the council or transferring could have implications for future rent levels was effectively removed.

Another aspect of the 1989 legislation pushing English authorities towards transfer involved the new rules on Right to Buy receipts. Rather than being able to substantially 'recycle' these funds into housing capital works, the new regime required that 75 per cent of receipts were used to repay housing debt. Again, the less regulated financial regime enjoyed by transfer housing associations appeared attractive in this context.

The aspiration to generate capital receipts, for uses other than social housing investment, also loomed large in a number of early transfers where stock in reasonable condition allied to low levels of council housing debt held out the prospect of substantial net proceeds for transferring local authorities. The proportion of transfer receipts which 'leaked' into investment in leisure centres, village halls and the like is believed to have been substantial, though precise figures are unavailable.

Non-financial drivers

Protective and defensive motivations

As noted in Chapter 2, the origins of the local authority stock transfer process in England have been traced to concerns stemming from the 'radical' housing policy agenda of the incoming

Conservative government in 1987. The fear of Tenants' Choice as a mechanism facilitating 'hostile takeovers' was, for a time, a potent force inspiring transfer proposals, though its impact had long declined by the time that Tenants' Choice was repealed in England under the Housing Act 1996. In Scotland, however, Tenants' Choice remains on the statute book and has until recently continued to have a significant impact in isolated local circumstances. Its corrosive effects were seen as having had a significant role in motivating the 2003 Scottish Borders Council stock transfer (Taylor 2004). Here, the local ex-Scottish Homes transfer landlord, Waverley Housing, had – even by 1998 – acquired over 400 dwellings from Scottish Borders Council through Tenants' Choice (Tulloch 2000).

Aside from the Tenants' Choice scenario, the same kind of 'protective' or 'defensive' impulse has remained important as an argument for transfer throughout the policy's history. Because housing association tenants have been generally ineligible for the Right to Buy, for example, transfer has sometimes been portrayed as a means of insulating social housing from its erosive impact (since whilst transferring tenants enjoy a contractually preserved Right to Buy, new tenants re-housed under the new regime do not). Pollitt et al. (1998) saw it as highly significant that most (pre-1997) transfers had taken place in rural and suburban areas and medium-sized towns where the council stock tended to be attractive houses set within generally buoyant housing markets. Indeed, the continued impact of the retained Right to Buy in these areas meant that some or all of the stock increases achieved through recycling the transfer receipt were wiped out by continued stock losses.

The broadening of the Compulsory Competitive Tendering regime to cover housing management in 1992 likewise stimulated a degree of interest in stock transfer. For a period, authorities actively exploring transfer were exempted from preparing Compulsory Tendering plans, thereby avoiding what many local authority staff and councillors saw as unnecessary disruption and dislocation in prospect as housing departments were forced to split into client and contractor interests. However, with abolition of Compulsory Competitive Tendering (formally repealed in 2000), such concerns were rendered obsolete.

'Better governance' motivations

In this section we consider some of the assumptions and less explicitly stated motivations that have inspired central government to construct a policy regime favouring transfer over stock retention by local authorities.

A first assumption, underpinning support for stock transfer at ministerial level and among civil servants (particularly in the Treasury), is the view that social housing is a capital asset and that its husbandry should be run as a business with decision-making motivated by hard-headed commercial considerations. In this sense, transfer is part of the (New Labour) 'modernization project' which seeks to bring to bear commercial disciplines on the running of public services (see Chapter 1). An important aspect of this argument is that shifting social housing into the ownership of housing associations working within (it is hoped) robust 30-year business plans creates a stable investment framework free from the uncertainties of stop-go public funding which have dogged local authorities' attempts at long-term investment planning. In a sense, therefore, such 'better governance' motivations have an important financial component.

A second Whitehall assumption is a belief that harks back to a long-held view that associations – perhaps because they are not distracted by party political concerns – are generally more effective housing managers than local authorities. A key change highlighted by this view is that the influence of elected local councillors is reduced in housing associations and that decisions are therefore less prone to being made on 'political grounds' (see Chapters 4–6). A common feature of the discourse of stock transfer organizations is that 'we are non-political', usually meaning that local councillors have less say in the decision-making process than before transfer and that all board members are bound to make decisions in the 'best interests of the organization' rather than in pursuit of other goals. There have been local conflicts over issues, such as lettings and 'Members' enquiries', where the role of councillors has been diminished following stock transfer.

Based on these assumptions, some have argued the case for transfer primarily as a means of improving the effectiveness of housing management services. For example, Clapham and

Kintrea (1994) contended that Glasgow's community-based housing organization transfer programme of the 1980s had demonstrated the potential of (this form of) transfer for radically improving customer service standards by comparison with Council provision. As noted in Chapter 7, however, this was seen as resulting largely from the creation of smaller, more accountable organizations in place of hierarchical control or bureaucracy – a consequence of transfer not always replicated.

This brings us to another oft-cited governance-related transfer motivation – the contention that transfer provides a means of breaking up 'remote and monopolistic landlords'. Arguably, this is predicated on the public choice economics view that large landlords are less efficient and that the disaggregation of such organizations would facilitate consumer choice. Such a view informed Westminster government thinking on size limits for transfer packages (in force in England until 2004) as well as the plan to fragment Glasgow Housing Association into over 60 landlord entities (see Chapters 4 and 5; also Pawson et al. 2009, McKee 2009). The 2000 DETR Green Paper, for example, contended that 'transfer presents an opportunity to move away from large monopoly providers of social housing to a greater number of smaller bodies . . . based in or closer to the communities where the homes are transferred' (DETR 2000c, paragraph 7.14). However, as the NAO (2003) acknowledged 'transfers have not significantly reduced the monopoly supply of social housing at the local level'. Moreover, the potential advantages of local accountability and responsiveness associated with landlord breakup must be set against the potential of larger organizations to deliver scale economies and bulk procurement savings and to avoid the duplication of functions and governance which are part and parcel of the 'fragmentation' option. Organizational scale considerations and impacts on transfer landlord corporate structure and governance are further discussed in Chapter 5.

Another important 'improving governance' motivation for transfer is the assertion that the policy is crucial in facilitating greater tenant involvement in organizational management. Styling it as 'community ownership', for example, the 1999 Scottish Office Housing Green Paper argued that stock transfer 'provides an opportunity for tenants to have a real say in the ownership and management of their houses' (Scottish Office

1999: paragraph 3.11). As well as involving tenant representation at board level, it was stressed that 'The structure of the (transfer landlord) organisation should provide opportunities for widespread community participation at all levels' (paragraph 3.12). This approach has subsequently become important in England, thanks in part to the stimulus given by the Community Housing Task Force in requiring residents to be at the heart of option appraisal processes (Mullins et al. 2004). Also, through the development of tenant-led transfer organizations, often building on pre-existing tenant management organizations, e.g. WATMOS in Walsall, and the promotion of the 'community mutual' and 'community gateway' models (CIH 2002a). In the same vein, it has recently been suggested that ALMOs might be subject to stock transfer involving a new landlord body registered as a housing association but structured as a Tenant Management Organization (TMO) (NFA, 2009). Some of the governance and accountability issues involved here are further discussed in Chapters 5 and 8).

'Vested interest' motivations?

The prospect of greater freedoms, including, in some cases, the opportunity to engage in new housing development, has understandably stimulated enthusiasm for stock transfer among senior managers in local authority housing departments. Pollitt et al. (1998) found that transfer was seen by senior staff as 'protecting . . . the sphere of influence of housing managers' (ibid: 157). Case study research also brought to light 'behind the scenes discussions by managers, anticipation of higher salaries and better-quality company cars' (ibid: 157). The authors, nevertheless, argued that the 'self-seeking' nature of managers' behaviour should not be over-stated since the managers were clearly interested in transfer as a means of improving the quality of their work and providing them with enhanced means of solving previously intractable problems such as homelessness and housing disrepair.

It is also important to emphasize that transfer brings a degree of uncertainty about the employment security of senior managers as well as staff more generally. Whilst transfers have in practice often involved the setting up of a new housing association headed by the former local authority director of housing, this is not an inevitable outcome. Indeed, the former Housing Corporation's approach (in considering registration of a newly-created landlord) was 'based on external competition when recruiting senior executives, particularly the Chief Executive's post' (ODPM 2003e: 90).

As Gardiner et al. (1991) argued, stock transfer consultants and advisers may also be seen as transfer stakeholders with some form of 'vested interest' in the policy. Consultants have undoubtedly played a significant role in driving the policy forward. Not only has transfer represented an important income stream for firms who advise all the parties to such transactions, but also consultants 'have a vested interest in ensuring that . . . transfer models [have] extended the process to a widening range of circumstances' (Malpass and Mullins 2002: 680). While consultants have been influential in working with trade bodies and with central government to develop new approaches and to lobby for more favourable rules and funding arrangements, they have also had a vested interest in restricting innovation so that the same recipes can be 'stretched' to provide an ongoing income stream.

Linked with 'vested interest' explanations for transfer motivations, Nygaard et al. (2007) analysed the transfer phenomenon within a 'property rights' framework. This refers to the contention within new institutional economics that 'commodities have multiple attributes and that rights to these attributes are, in principle, separable' (ibid: 92) and a distinction between *de jure* and *de facto* property rights. The analysis also differentiates between tenants, local authorities and central government as distinct interest groups with respect to stock transfer. It sees social housing as constituting an 'attribute bundle'. As well as a physical asset, a social landlord's housing stock is also a source of employment (management of the asset), a source of patronage and a vehicle for discharging statutory responsibilities. From this perspective, transfer is a mechanism for rearranging property rights. However, while it involves *de jure* rights being acquired by a new entity (transfer housing association), *de facto* rights 'remain un-transferred or have been redistributed within the public sector' (ibid: 90). This underpins an argument implying that transfer can be attractive to local authorities and/or central government as a 'value extraction strategy'.

Political ideology

At root, many critics see official enthusiasm for stock transfer as being 'ideological' in nature. The political aspects of the debate are discussed in detail in Chapter 4.

Developing and delivering stock transfer proposals: the process

Under the post-Decent Homes framework, the usual stages through which (successful) English local authority transfer proposals passed can be summarized as:

1. The local authority commissions (or carries out) an options appraisal to weigh up the potential benefits of transfer by comparison with the main alternatives (see Box 3.2)
2. Officers in the council's housing department decide to pursue the idea of transfer and councillors agree to develop the idea in principle
3. Consultants are appointed to work up a proposal and there is consideration of the potential successor landlord to take on the transferred stock – usually leading to the establishment of a new housing association requiring registration
4. The council seeks a place on the national transfer programme (this might entail a bid for financial support in relation to local authority debt write-off and/or transfer business plan gap funding – see above)
5. Having selected (or created) a successor landlord, the local authority begins to negotiate a valuation. Potential private funders are sounded out
6. Formal consultations are held with tenants leading to the drafting of an official transfer proposal and draft business plan
7. Tenants are balloted
8. Further negotiation takes place involving the council, the new landlord and its financial backer(s) to produce a finalized valuation, a transfer contract and an implementation plan encompassing practical issues such as recruitment (including staff transfer) to the successor landlord

9. The Secretary of State approves the transfer and the stock passes into its new ownership.

The following sections discuss some of the issues which arise at various stages in the process sketched out above.

Stock options appraisal

Particularly since the late 1990s, local authorities have been expected to carry out a formal 'options appraisal' in advance of starting through the stages set out above. In establishing its 1998 New Housing Partnerships fund, for example, the Scottish Office encouraged authorities to undertake such assessments. However, although almost every Scottish local authority took up the resources offered for this purpose, the credibility of some of the outcomes was somewhat prejudiced by defects such as failure to involve key stakeholders – for example local authority tenants – and by the significant proportion of those which concluded in favour of stock retention on 'non-financial' grounds (Pawson 2002).

In 2003, ODPM introduced a requirement that all remaining landlord local authorities in England should, by 2005, carry out an option appraisal on the future management of their stock (ODPM 2003d). This was to involve a formal assessment of the funding needed to eliminate non-decent housing by 2010 and (for those unable to finance Decent Homes Standard compliance from mainstream resources) an assessment of the relative merits of the three management options available to achieve this (see Box 3.2). Under a similar process, Scottish local authorities (and housing associations) were required by the Scottish Executive to draw up (Housing Quality) Standard Delivery Plans by 2005 (though the options available to Scottish local authorities were limited to transfer or retention). By 2007, most Standard Delivery Plans had been officially 'signed off' as credible assessments of investment need and the means to finance such need (Communities Scotland 2007b). An obligation to undertake stock options appraisal was also imposed on Welsh local authorities by the Welsh Assembly Government.

In a review of English practice in this area, the Westminster government criticized what were seen as inadequacies in prac-

Box 3.2   English landlord local authorities Decent Homes Standard funding options

Factor	Stock option			
	Private Finance Initiative (PFI)	Arms Length Management Organization (ALMO)	Stock transfer	
Stock ownership	Remains with LA for HRA and remains with housing association for non-HRA	Remains with LA	Passes to new landlord	
Tenant rights	Tenants of an HRA PFI retain their secure tenancies	Unchanged	Change to assured tenancies (preserved Right to Buy for transferring tenants)	
Stock management	Split between LA and PFI contractor depends on terms of the contract	ALMO manages stock but strategic functions (including homelessness) retained by LA	New housing association landlord; LA retains some strategic and enabling functions	
Consultation requirements for approval	Must demonstrate that consultation has taken place and residents' views considered	Must consult and demonstrate evidence of active support	Formal consultation requirement and evidence that majority of tenants not opposed	

Ballot	Not anticipated		
Independent tenant adviser	Not mentioned but increasingly common	Some LAs employ one	Good practice requirement
Specific guidance re: tenant consultation/involvement	Housing Act 1985 S105	Referred to but no detail	Yes
Future governance arrangements	Depends on terms of the contract. No board required but resident steering groups may be involved in contract monitoring	Company board of directors with third= tenants expected	Housing association board. Newly established board to include tenants

Source: based on Mullins et al. (2004).

tice. There was concern that '(some) councils either fail to address the underlying problems or they give option appraisal a very narrow financial/technical focus that effectively disenfranchises tenants' (ODPM 2003a: 23). On this basis, local authorities were subsequently obliged to have their appraisals 'signed off' by the relevant regional Government Office. The assessments were to check that tenants and leaseholders had been properly involved in the process and supported the conclusions, that the underlying assumptions were reasonable and the analysis was sound (ODPM 2003a).

In addition, specific official guidance was produced to facilitate the involvement of black and minority ethnic communities in stock options appraisal exercises (Mullins et al. 2004).

As the ODPM guidance emphasized, councils were required to involve tenants and leaseholders, not just in the consideration of defined 'options' but in the formulation of these options. Only just over a third of the Scottish local authority stock option appraisals carried out between 1999 and 2002 passed this test (Pawson 2002).

Successor landlord selection

As noted in Chapters 1 and 2, the great majority of stock transfers have involved landlords newly-created by local authorities. From the early 1990s, central government sought to engineer a greater role in stock transfer for existing housing associations, mainly on the grounds that established housing associations could bring to bear (a) financial expertise, and (b) strong existing relationships with potential transfer funders (ODPM 2003c). Through the stock options appraisal process, English councils looking at transfer have been encouraged (though not required) to organize a formal competition between putative successor landlords. At a minimum, authorities have had to 'demonstrate clearly . . . that tenants have been made fully aware of all the new landlord options, and provide evidence that they have been fully involved in deciding the eventual landlord choice' (ODPM 2003e: 40). However, while possibly beneficial in terms of maximizing the transfer purchase price (see below) the National Audit Office saw increased competition between potential successor landlords as liable to complicate tenant choice (NAO 2003).

The stage at which a local authority selects its putative successor landlord has important implications in terms of the
extent to which the latter takes 'ownership' of the transfer business plan. There is a view that transfer housing associations
have typically had little commitment to initial business plans,
seeing these as having been inherited from – and previously
owned by – the local authority and requiring immediate post-
transfer review (ODPM 2003c). The corollary that the transfer
association should be chosen at the earliest possible point in the
development of a transfer proposal, however, sits uneasily with
any contention that the process should be 'more competitive' in
terms successor landlord selection.

Box 3.3 makes clear that the discount rate used in Tenanted
Market Value calculations crucially affects the valuation attributed to transferring stock. The higher the rate, the lower the
estimated value of the stock. Generally speaking, a lower valuation benefits transferring tenants because it implies lower rents.
The public purse, however, benefits from lower discount rates
which generate higher valuations. These result in larger capital
receipts which maximize local authority debt repayment,
provide 'surplus' resources from which the LSVT levy is paid,
or minimize the amount of public subsidy required to enable
the transfer to proceed at all. Given these considerations, it is
perhaps unsurprising that local authorities tend to argue for
reduced discount rates, a tendency said to have hardened since
the early phase of the process (Williams and Wilcox 2001). All
of this connects with the 'value for money' debate discussed
earlier in this chapter. The National Audit Office noted that
central government reduced the standard discount rate applied
in English transfers to 7 per cent in 1999 and, from 2000, recommended that authorities adopt an 'appropriate' rate in the
6–8 per cent band. Application of a 6 per cent rate might, for
example, be relevant 'where the stock is in relatively good condition and/or demand for the homes is buoyant' (NAO 2003:
27) – see also Box 3.3.

A related issue here concerns the valuation timescale.
Conventionally, the Tenanted Market Value calculation projects income and expenditure flows over 30 years, implying
that the transferred stock would have no value in Year 30. This
could be justifiable in instances where there are doubts over
long-term housing demand. For most stock transfers, however,

Box 3.3 Valuing stock transfers

Somewhat akin to the sale of a business, 'The basic idea behind the LSVT valuation model is to value a bundle of social housing as a going concern in its existing use' (Bramley et al. 2004: 123–4). The valuation has to take account of the current and intended future use of the stock as social housing. Hence its notional open market sale value is irrelevant (except insofar as a housing association's 'book value' is treated as security against loans). Instead, the transfer price is based on the Net Present Value of expected future income less future expected expenditure, conventionally estimated for a 30-year timescale. Hence, the Tenanted Market Value (TMV) calculation involves figures for income and expenditure after Year 1 being 'discounted' in a way which 'allows for the lower cost value of a certain amount in the future than the same amount today' (Gardiner et al. 1991: 9–10). Consequently, applying a real discount rate of 8 per cent means that £108 in real terms (i.e. already adjusted for inflation) would, in one year's time be valued as equivalent to £100 today.

The discount rate is related to the cost of capital but also, as used in this context, reflects the financial risk to which transfer housing associations are exposed and 'the additional margins that (they) . . . have to pay in their private finance deals with lenders' (NAO 2003: 26). As well as reflecting the cost of capital (interest rates), it is recognized that discount rates as used in this context need to build in a 'degree of comfort' to produce a demonstrably 'robust' transfer business plan acceptable to funders.

The critical importance of discount rates has been highlighted – albeit obscurely – by the case of Glasgow Housing Association where the original valuation for the 2003 transfer involved an effective 'discount rate' of only 4–5 per cent rather than the 6–8 per cent standard for other stock transfers (e.g. 7 per cent in the case of former Scottish Homes transfers). Because of the exceptional size of the Glasgow Housing Association transfer (80,000 homes), a risk allowance was not seen by funders as essential. The organization's scale was viewed as creating a 'portfolio effect'; that is, spreading risks in such a way that no specific risk allowance needed to be built into the valuation. Another factor may have been a judgement on the part of funders that the scale and political significance of the Glasgow transfer meant that central government could not allow it to fail.

The effect of the low discount rate was to increase the price of the acquisition (raising it just above zero), hence minimizing the albeit large amount of public subsidy required to enable the transfer to proceed at all (see Table 3.2). In the process, however, a critical financial barrier to second stage transfers (SSTs) was established. This reflects the fact that, because the usual considerations about the

→

need for 'risk allowance' were applicable to SSTs, valuations for such potential acquisitions needed to be based on a 'standard' discount rate rather than the 'low' rate used for the initial Glasgow transfer. From Glasgow Housing Association's viewpoint, however, this would require the organization to effectively 'subsidize' such transactions because the use of a higher discount rate would lead to a putative successor landlord bidding a smaller unit value for each dwelling than the amount paid by Glasgow Housing Association in its original acquisition. Therefore, because any transactions agreed on this basis would leave the association 'in deficit' they could not satisfy the 'financial neutrality' test specified in the transfer prospectus.

The UK Treasury's 'Green Book' discount rules were changed in 2003. The previously applied 8 per cent figure was based on a Treasury 6 per cent standard rate plus 2 per cent for risk. From 2003 onwards the Treasury moved to a basic 3.5 per cent discount rate, but with elements related to risk and optimism bias that were contained within the earlier 6 per cent standard rate to be assessed separately and added as appropriate to the 3.5 per cent rate. In practice, however, there has been little reduction in discount rates incorporated within subsequent transfer finances; not least because of lender concerns about loan security.

The single most important item in transfer valuations is usually projected rental income. Exactly how much rental income will be generated over the valuation period will depend on many assumptions – e.g. in relation to the numbers of tenanted homes (which will, in turn, be affected by void rates and stock losses through sales and demolitions), and in relation to rent levels and bad debts. Other significant components in most valuations include estimated costs of remedying disrepair, carrying out programmed maintenance, and paying management staff over the valuation period. Scheduling of major repairs and improvement programmes is also a key factor in valuations and often a focus for negotiations between parties to the transaction.

In practice, the task of valuing stock for transfer purposes is 'more of an art than a science' (Gardiner et al. 1991: 31) and the figure eventually found acceptable to the local authority, the new landlord and central government will be the outcome of often protracted negotiation. While an initial valuation is necessary in advance of the tenant ballot (as a foundation for rent projections and 'promises') the actual agreed figure may be finally determined only at a very late stage before the transfer actually takes place. In cases where there is a competition to select the successor landlord this opens up the possibility that an organization may be chosen largely on the basis of an initial 'bid' which is subsequently reduced below that of other initial bids, but where the process is too far advanced for the selection of the recipient landlord to be re-opened.

this could be seen as unrealistically pessimistic. The National Audit Office estimated that the potential transfer value of eight pre-1998 transfers would have been 14 per cent higher, had the life expectancy of the transferred properties been assumed as 40 years rather than 30 years (NAO 2003). Responding on this point, the Westminster government accepted that future transfer valuations should factor in post-transfer life expectancy of between 30 and 50 years (ODPM 2003c).

Securing a place on the national transfer programme

Since 1993, English local authorities have been required by central government to secure a place on a national annual transfer programme. This provides ministers with a means of making an initial judgement on whether a local authority's outline plans are consistent with official requirements (e.g. in relation to tenant involvement, nature of successor landlord, selection of successor landlord, etc.). With the advent of over-hanging debt and negative value transfers this device also became important in rationing the scarce resources of public subsidy. A similar 'annual programme' framework was established by the Scottish Executive in 2004 (Scottish Executive 2004).

Balloting tenants

To secure ministerial consent for stock transfer a local authority must demonstrate majority support for the proposal among the tenants concerned. This is achieved through a formal ballot (a legal requirement in Scotland (Housing (Scotland) Act 2001, Sch. 9), though simple custom and practice south of the border). The franchise is limited to existing tenants on a given date. Whilst transfers often have significant implications for people living in former council flats previously purchased under the Right to Buy, this group generally has no voting right. The ballot outcome relates to the votes cast, irrespective of turnout. In practice, however, this is generally substantial and far in excess of local election turnouts. Across the 345 ballots held in England between 1988 and 2007 recorded turnout averaged 73 per cent (unpublished CLG data). It has, nevertheless, been argued that since a majority vote under the LSVT model involves all tenants transferring (irrespective of their personal preference) it would be logical for Ministerial consent to be given only where Yes voters represent a majority of *all tenants* rather than a majority of those voting (Gardiner et al. 1991).

In preparation for the ballot there is typically a great deal of activity aimed at influencing tenant opinion in favour of or against the transfer proposal. While local authorities often commission marketing or communications consultants to assist at this stage, a local authority and its agents are restricted in the way that their case is presented. Under the terms of the Local Government Act 1986 publicity material produced by local authorities must be 'informative' rather than 'persuasive'. However, an early evaluation of transfers (Mullins et al. 1992) highlighted the issue of fairness in the ways in which information was presented and new guidance was produced with the expectation that tenants would have access to independent advice, usually through engagement of consultants working for the tenants. Subsequently, this became a standard part of the process. Nevertheless, the issue of bias in presentation has remained and concerns have re-surfaced from time to time – e.g. the case of a local authority being reprimanded for having breached these rules (Audit Commission, 2004a). No such restrictions apply to the content of anti-transfer literature however, and local authorities have criticized the 'scaremongering' bias allegedly sometimes present in this material, particularly where it is felt to have contributed to ballot defeats.

In the ballot, tenants are presented with the opportunity to vote for or against the package of 'transfer promises' (see Chapter 7) as put forward by the local authority and the new landlord. Superficially, transfer can be portrayed as a customer choice-driven policy because it involves a tenant vote. This creates an important discipline because the proposal needs to be made sufficiently attractive to secure majority backing. The extent to which transfer can be fairly portrayed as choice-driven is further discussed in Chapters 4 and 10.

Chapter conclusions

The multiple motivations underpinning stock transfers reflect the diversity of stakeholders involved in the process. However, while financial incentives have been crucially important throughout the policy's history, the extent to which transfers are always justified in purely financial terms remains somewhat uncertain. The economics of transfer are crucially wrapped up in the technical details of the valuation exercise. Through its control over the valuation rules, over access to the stock transfer programme, and over the disposal itself, central government is able to exercise huge influence over the process. At the same time, however, transfers can happen only where there is support from both local authorities and tenants and where, in the case of negative value stock and/or overhanging debt, some form of public subsidy is available. And the limits on the influence of central government are also evident from the fact that Ministers' oft-repeated advocacy of a greater role for existing housing associations has, after more than 15 years, had relatively little impact.

Transfer is often presented as consistent with the government's 'consumer choice' agenda – an assertion justified by the observation that a local authority must secure majority tenant support for its proposal. However, it is hard to present transfer as genuinely part of the consumerist agenda because proposals to date have seldom if ever been bottom-up in the sense of being motivated by tenant preferences and because majority 'yes' votes are generally achieved only where the local authority is fully behind the proposal and presents its case forcefully. The increased emphasis on tenants being at the heart of option appraisal processes, post-2001, and the more recent promotion of community gateway/community mutual models of transfer, may indicate recognition of this discrepancy as weakening the legitimacy of the transfer programme.

Chapter 4

The Politics of Stock Transfer

Some early proponents argued that transfer would 'take the politics out' of social housing. By this they were generally referring to the internal politics of local government in which the housing service was sometimes seen as a pawn in games between political parties and between service departments. There were also concerns about clientelism and the way in which some ward councillors sought to influence lettings and management issues in their patches. Stock transfer was presented as a combination of managerialist common sense with the involvement of people of goodwill (without a 'political axe to grind') in governance. This 'de-politicization thesis' is common in both the discourse of stock transfer organizations and public policies concerning transfer and is found amongst some opponents of transfer who see transfer as part of a long-term trajectory in which housing questions are removed from political debates (see, for example, Kaufman in DCH 2006) as well as by advocates of transfer who favour a pragmatic approach to housing.

Yet our review of the literature on stock transfer and case study research over two decades presented in this book suggests that politics has never been far beneath the surface in stock transfer policy and practice. That contests with a political flavour have usually accompanied debates around the prospect of transfer has been plain for all to see. Often in quite fundamental ways, political considerations have also influenced the operations of post-transfer landlords and the shape of post-transfer local housing systems (for a classic analysis of such debates within a specific local context see Kearns and Lawson (2009)).

Thus, every chapter in this book is informed by consideration of the politics of transfer: Chapters 1 and 10 provide the links between transfer and the big political themes of housing and the welfare state, privatization and public policy; Chapter 2 shows the chronology and the emergence of transfer as an alternative to more politically inspired forms of de-municipalization including 'Tenants' Choice' and Housing Action Trusts (HATs); Chapter 3 considers the variety of drivers and motivations for transfer of which political ideology is one commonly cited; Chapter 5 highlights the big and small 'p' political questions associated with the governance of stock transfer landlords; Chapter 6 includes some of the political implications of organizational change for transfer landlords particularly around trade union membership and influence and the consequence of ministerial decisions on organizational form and function. Chapter 7 pays particular attention to tenants' perspectives in assessing impacts of transfer and critiques the (limited) evidence for political views of transfer as 'privatization' leading to rent rises, tenants' rights and 'hard nosed' management approaches to evictions, etc. Chapter 8 includes a full discussion of the politics of ALMOs highlighting the political origins of the ALMO option and the sharpness of opposition encountered to this 'stepping stone to privatization' from defenders of council housing. Chapter 9 highlights the consequences of transfer for the role of elected local authorities in local housing systems, in securing affordable housing, meeting homelessness and wider community needs and in allocating housing, all of which are relevant to the de-politicization thesis.

This chapter brings together consideration of these political dimensions of transfer by highlighting the national and local politics of transfer and by exploring a number of inter-connected dimensions. In this chapter, we draw particularly on detailed case study research in Glasgow which has been the most continuously political, as well as the largest, transfer completed in the UK. Other examples of successful and failed transfers have been subject to research which has highlighted the ways in which housing transfer has been shaped and negotiated through both national and local political structures.

The politics of transfer have been contested at both national and local levels. The next section of this chapter reviews developments in the national political arena, considering in turn the links between transfer and politically driven policies of 'de-municipalization' and 'modernization', political ideologies favouring and opposing transfer, national political organization against transfer and the politics of choice. The chapter then focuses on the local resolution of these contests. Here, we consider, in turn, the option appraisal and ballot stages in which transfer has been politically contested in authorities across the country, and the longer-term political issues that have surfaced as transfer organizations have bedded down and evolved. The final section of the chapter returns to bigger picture questions concerning the association of transfer with privatization and the impacts of transfer for the role of housing in the welfare state.

National politics

At national policy level it is impossible to understand the rise of transfer policy in isolation from political developments. First, the active 'de-muncipalization' agenda pursued by successive Conservative governments in the 1980s sowed the seeds for local authorities to 'invent' the transfer model. Following the focus on the Right to Buy in the first two Conservative administrations after the election of Margaret Thatcher in 1979, the third-term government turned its attention in 1987 to alternatives to municipal renting. As discussed in Chapter 2, measures to boost the 'independent rented sector' included schemes to enable council tenants to vote to move to new landlords (Tenants' Choice) and to transfer blocks of council housing to Housing Action Trusts (HATs). Both these cases were interesting in that their implementation involved considerable political bargaining between local and central government actors with outcomes considerably at variance to the original demuncipalizing policy intentions.

The largest, and by far the most well-known, Tenants' Choice transfer achieved in England was the Walterton and Elgin Community Homes transfer from Westminster City Council. Here, the local tenants' organization used the Tenants' Choice scheme to develop an alternative to a proposed sell-off of their estates by Westminster council following the discovery of a major asbestos problem (Rosenberg 1998). A key factor in the generally low take-up of Tenants' Choice was political miscalculation by the Conservative government who had anticipated a greater interest in the scheme from both tenants' groups and private sector landlords; while the former were not attracted by the image of private landlordism, the latter were put off by the regulatory regime (Mullins 1990). Meanwhile, as discussed in Chapter 2, the HATs policy was subject to political negotiation to make it workable and was considerably modified during the implementation process.

While neither of these mechanisms had a direct long-term impact on the social housing sector they were part of the climate that encouraged the first authorities to develop transfer as a voluntary initiative from 1988 using enabling legislation passed in 1986.

Ginsburg argues that de-muncipalization was 'not so much a question of pragmatism as of ideology reflecting the Government's lack of belief in local authorities as direct providers of public services and its commitment to restraining public borrowing' (Ginsburg 2005: 117–18). However, as illustrated in Chapter 3, a key underlying attraction of stock transfer to UK governments of both colours has been in taking borrowing to finance stock re-investment off the public accounts balance sheet, in the same way that transfer of the new build role for social housing to housing associations had already done.

Then came the 'modernization' agenda pursued by 'New Labour' from 1997 which made it clear that there would be no return to support for stock retention. As the Centre for Public Services put it in 2004 'the ALMO and LSVT options fit snugly with the growth of quangos, trusts, joint ventures, partnerships and other company models that are part of Labour's so called "reform and modernisation" agenda' (Centre for Public Services 2004: 13). Modernization was described by its proponents as a pragmatic rather than an ideological agenda. As reported in Chapter 1, Labour's first Environment Minister Hilary Armstrong embodied this approach by adopting an argument resonant of local 'taking politics out' arguments.

As well as influencing the incentive structures which led to local stock transfer initiatives, increasingly from 1993 stock transfer policy was nationally steered (Malpass and Mullins 2002) and Ministerial objectives loomed increasingly large in defining and configuring what had started out as independent local initiatives. These objectives were not uncontested, and national opposition to transfer was mobilized through essentially political campaigns, notably Defend Council Housing (DCH), supported by critiques equating transfer with privatization, neo-liberalism and the retreat from welfare (Ginsburg, 2005), by periodic bouts of questioning the rationale for transfer policy and the performance of transfer landlords from well known national politicians including Austin Mitchell, George Galloway, Gerald Kauffman and Jon Cruddas, and by local organization and campaigns by tenants groups and trade unions.

Over the years, political obstacles to transfer were addressed, for example by modifications to transfer governance and management models. First, in 1996, the Local Housing Company model – see Chapter 5 – enabled greater local authority and tenant representation on the board of transfer housing associations to maintain local accountability while at the same time facilitating access to investment off the public balance sheet (Wilcox and Bramley 1993, Zitron 1995).

Later, in 2000, the creation of the ALMO model (DETR 2000a) in which the local authority remains property owner, legal landlord and normally sole shareholder while contracting, housing management functions to a new 'arms length' body was widely seen as reflecting a Ministerial recognition of the politics of stock transfer. The ALMO concept would be more acceptable to councils sympathetic to the portrayal of transfer as 'unacceptable privatization'. The politics of ALMOs are more fully discussed in Chapter 8. Meanwhile, in post-devolution Scotland, the wide-ranging Housing (Scotland) Act has been seen as centrally concerned with addressing political as well as administrative barriers to transfer (Kintrea 2006), with the creation of a single form of social housing tenancy a crucial aspect.

A core issue for opponents of transfer has been the absence of an alternative route to substantial investment for local authorities wishing to retain ownership of housing. This issue achieved considerable prominence under the Brown government from 2007 and is discussed below in our coverage of the politics of choice and the role of the House of Commons Council Housing Group.

Political ideology

Chapter 3 provides an overview of some of the main drivers and motivations that have been seen as explaining the process of stock transfer. One of the most commonly argued positions by transfer critics is that the policy reflects an 'ideological' stance rather than a rational assessment of policy options. Such an explanation would appear to fit quite well with the genesis of transfer in a period associated with an anti-muncipalist stance by Conservative governments of the 1980s and the early take-up of transfer by Conservative or independent administrations who predominated in the rural and suburban areas where transfer was born (see Chapter 2). However, this fit could be seen to be looser as transfer spread to the urban heartlands where the ideology of de-muncipalization had seen least support and came under the more pragmatic (and less ideological) rubric of 'moderniszation'.

Examples of political ideologies hostile to council housing are indeed easiest to find on the political right during the high tide of the Thatcher era. For example, Wandsworth's right wing Conservative administration of the early 1990s was one of the earliest urban administrations to consider transfer. The flavour of some of the political debate associated with Wandsworth's decision process was decidedly ideological in nature. A council report on the question dismissed transfer as insufficiently radical to match its market-based ideology and as:

> only in effect moving one block of insulated and subsidised housing stock from the direct public sector to the quasi-public domain of the housing association. (Wandsworth Borough Council 1993: 8).

A similar ideological disposition was encountered by the Walterton and Elgin Action Group (WEAL) formed in 1986 to campaign to prevent Westminster Council's proposed sale of their homes to a private developer who would demolish and replace at higher density following the discovery of asbestos. Here, it was claimed that the council had a hidden agenda to reduce the number of social housing tenants in order to influence local election results. In a six-year saga this case enjoyed extensive national publicity, featured in a Panorama exposé of 'gerrymandering' and attracted comment from leading political figures. While not involving transfer on the LSVT model, this celebrated case highlights some of the political issues associated with asset disposals by local authorities and landlord choice by residents.

As noted earlier, Walterton and Elgin residents used the Tenants' Choice scheme to develop an acceptable escape route from Westminster Council after a prolonged campaign against the sale, demolition and replacement of their former Greater London Council homes, inherited by Westminster in the demise of that bastion of muncipalism. The properties were finally transferred to Walterton and Elgin Community Homes (WECH) in 1992 following a protracted dispute with the council over valuation and the size of a dowry to cover historic disrepair. Box 4.1 highlights some of the political disputation from the perspective of WECH drawing directly from their website.

Critics of later transfers under New Labour's modernization agenda have continued to claim that official support for transfer is primarily a matter of ideology. For example, a parliamentary report concluded 'We believe that the target of achieving Decent Homes in the social housing sector is being used as a Trojan Horse by the Government in a dogmatic quest to minimise the proportion of housing stock managed by Local Authorities' (House of Commons 2004: 3). The report also described as 'dogmatic' the government's belief in the intrinsic benefits of separating 'strategic' and 'operational' roles in housing and, therefore, the attractiveness of stock transfer (House of Commons 2004). Ministerial advocacy of a strategic:operational split dates back at least to the early 1990s, having been initially applied through the creation of a client:contractor division, integral to housing management Compulsory Competitive Tendering imposed by the Major government in 1992.

Notwithstanding the post-1997 repeal of CCT, Ministers have continued to assert that 'we strongly favour the separation of authorities' strategic and landlord responsibilities for housing. This will strengthen both roles' (DETR 2000c: paragraph 3.2). This view, while informed by principal:agent perspectives from economics and given some legitimacy by rational planning models, is at variance with much modern management thinking which stresses the emergent nature of strategy and the need for learning from operations to inform strategy development (see also Chapter 9). In the ODPM Select Committee's view, such arguments were unconvincing bearing in mind the Housing Inspectorate's assertion that:

Box 4.1   Political Ideology and the Walterton and Elgin Tenants' Choice Transfer

In 1986, with the GLC set for abolition, responsibility for major works as well as daily maintenance passed to Westminster Council. In great secrecy, without any warning to the residents, the Council drew up a scheme to sell the estates to private developers. The developers planned to demolish the Walterton Estate and rebuild at twice the density. About 350 houses, let as about 900 units, would become 1,800, while one of the Elgin towers would become a hotel.

The Council accused the Action Group of being politically motivated and yet at the same time the Council itself had a second, hidden agenda – *to win the 1990 Borough Council elections by manipulating the electorate.* The City would sell the estates to a private developer. He would build for sale and so change the local voting patterns. The new properties would bring in people with enough money to buy, instead of rent, and who would be more likely to vote Conservative. This policy was carried out particularly in marginal wards. The ruling group on the Council never admitted to this policy, talking instead of 'Building Stable Communities'.

Unexpectedly the tenants found what they were looking for in a piece of legislation introduced by the Thatcher government. The 'Tenants' Choice' provision in the 1988 Housing Act was intended to encourage the sale of council housing to private landlords. However, there was a clause which said that prospective buyers had to seek approval from the Housing Corporation and, through a ballot from the tenants.

WECH signed up three quarters of the residents as members and in March 1989 became the first landlord to be approved by the

$\longrightarrow$

> there is no indication that the 90 authorities who had sold their stock were better at strategic work than the ones who had not . . . I do not think there is any evidence to support the fact that splitting the roles guarantees better performance. (Witness statement by Head of Housing Inspectorate – House of Commons, House of Commons 2004: 3).

Also relevant here is Murie and Nevin's contention that politicians at both local and national level have tended to see

Housing Corporation under 'Tenants' Choice' and the first to lodge an application to take over Council property.

> 'When WECH went for Tenants' Choice there was gossip that the then Secretary of State, Nicholas Ridley, said, "This was not supposed to happen!". It was very much a triumph over adversity by ordinary people who wanted to live in decent homes.' Malcolm Levi, (CEO) PCHA (Paddington Churches Housing Association). Ben Wilson, Director of Operations. PCHA, said: 'PCHA brought experience in running housing, and resources to match WECH's commitment and determination. Our involvement reinforced PCHA's founding ideal of responsibility to local communities. Personally I found it very exciting. It was what I came into housing for.'

At first the Council argued that WECH should pay them almost £1 million for the properties. WECH maintained that, because of the poor condition of the estates, the price should be negative and the Council should pay it £63 million to rehabilitate the estate. A protracted dispute began which was referred to the District Valuer for resolution.

In September 1991 WECH published a manifesto for residents. Residents could finally vote on whether to transfer to WECH or stay with the Council. Some 82 per cent of the residents voted, of which 72 per cent were in favour of the transfer to WECH. The properties were finally transferred in April 1992. The Council exercised its right to pay the dowry in five annual instalments, adding interest of about £4.5 million to the total.

Source: www.locallocalhistory.co.uk/municipal-housing/walterton/index.htm, consulted 15 June 2009, Reproduced with permission.

council housing as a 'public relations liability' and have hence favoured the idea of divesting managerial responsibility to another agency. 'Although tenants were not enthusiastic about other landlords, the criticism of local authorities' performance in relation to housing was a consistent source of difficulty for Labour councils ... For those ... concerned with the modernisation agenda the legacy of municipal housing was an embarrassment. Offloading embarrassments is a long-established part of central government's traditions' (Murie and Nevin 2001: 35).

Political organization against transfer

National opposition to transfer has embraced a range of ideological positions including involvement of groups such as the Socialist Workers Party, public sector trade unions, tenants' organizations, and some prominent politicians from mainstream political parties.

Set up in 1998 to fight the privatization of social housing and to campaign for direct investment, Defend Council Housing (DCH) has been by far the most influential organization involved in opposing stock transfer and other forms of demuncipalization. The group's founder was Alan Walter who sadly died suddenly in March 2009 while working on the campaign. According to his obituary in *The Independent*, Walter was 'a political, community and trade union activist, he understood that the cause of ordinary people was manifold and therefore had to be fought at every corner'. In 1982 Walter had joined the Socialist Workers Party, remaining a committed member until his death in March 2009. The obituary went on to note that Walter had 'worked tirelessly against the notion that council housing was outdated and for the principle of making it a tenure of choice for all those who sought it. Transferring council housing stock became the mantra of councils around the country, and local tenants were persuaded that privatization was the only hope for winning extra resources to have improvements made to their homes. Yet through consistent campaigning, Walter and the DCH began winning the argument that council housing was a viable option' (Simon, 2009).

Walter's *Guardian* obituary by DCH supporter Austin Mitchell MP argued that 'Almost singlehandedly he brought an issue which both political parties were anxious to bury back to centre stage; that the campaign is now on the brink of success, with both the prime minister and the housing minister having given their backing to more council housing, is in no small part due to his efforts'. Walter persuaded trade unions to finance the campaign and organized tenants all around the country. DCH was not a one-man band, but, despite a sometimes crippling bad back, Walter did most of the research and propaganda work. He dragged the issue on to the national stage, working with the council housing group of MPs and organized public consultations in parliament (Mitchell 2009).

DCH has taken an uncompromising stand against stock transfer nationally through its website, conferences, newspaper and briefings and locally through support for campaigns during option appraisals and ballots. DCH helps local activists, tenants and trade unions to produce hard-hitting local campaign newsletters and to organize meetings, arguing that 'It is crucial that tenants hear both sides of the debate. The council will give tenants the hard sell promoting privatisation' (DCH 2009).

DCH has sometimes disparaged the role of independent tenants' adviser consultants who were introduced to address the criticism of hard-selling campaigns in an early evaluation of transfer ballot campaigns for government. This was a response to the research-based observation that 'analysis of fairness in the transfer process [suggests] that there should be stronger regulation of the consultation process, groups organised to oppose transfer should be given access to space to air their views within rather than in parallel to the official campaign . . . A transfer proposal insufficiently robust to stand independent and critical scrutiny would not be in the interests of anyone concerned' (Mullins et al. 1992: 83). In its local campaigns, DCH has argued that Independent Tenant Advisers have promoted the council's transfer plans rather than offering genuinely balanced advice.

National level trade union support for DCH is evident from the DCH website, sponsorship of publications by a broad coalition of unions (Amicus, GMB, Unison, UCATT, T&G, PCS, and the Communication Workers Union), and by contributions to DCH publications by leading trade union figures such as Dave Prentis (Unison Leader), Mark Serrwotka (CPS Leader) and Derek Simpson (Amicus). However, as case studies reported in Chapter 6 indicate, local representatives of the same unions have sometimes taken a more pragmatic stance towards specific local proposals for transfer to reflect the views of their local memberships (Box 6.1). While transfer has generally been detrimental for trade union membership figures, the relationship between union representatives and stock transfer organisations has often been generally constructive as the Glasgow case study referred to in Box 6.1 suggests.

Tenants' groups have sometimes been involved in opposition to stock transfer at both national and local levels. However, TAROE (Tenants and Residents of England), a group formed from the National Tenants Organization and the National

Tenants and Residents Federation) has developed a neutral stance and is not directly represented in DCH. However, some local tenants' federations, notably Camden and Newcastle, are active members of DCH and have been involved in active local campaigns. In Camden, for example, this involved the establishment of a joint campaign with local trades unions to oppose the Council's plan to establish an ALMO in 2003 (Jones 2009). However, Grayson (2006) argues that the Labour Party's abandonment of the Council housing project has led to 'a process of weakening and destroying tenants organisations. Many of the powerful "feds" have been forced to disband' (Grayson 2006: 66). Nevertheless, the failure of some local authorities to win over established tenants groups to support transfer proposals has been a key factor in failed ballots. Meanwhile, there has often been a disruptive effect on existing structures of tenants' representation as a result of option appraisal and ballot processes and subsequent changes to the landlord body.

Turning to transfer opposition on the part of national politicians, a key focus has been the House of Commons Council Housing Group, which according to its website 'works closely with Defend Council Housing'. The group's 2005 report on the 'fourth option', and the case for direct investment was eventually taken up when in 2007 Ministers launched a 'Review of Council Housing Finance' with the promise to 'ensure that we have a sustainable, long term system for financing council housing' and 'consider evidence about the need to spend on management, maintenance and repairs'. This review signalled a new approach with the then Housing Minister consulting on rules to enable local authorities to start building new council housing again (HCCHG 2009). (See Chapter 10.)

Politics of choice

In the new millennium, much of the political debate about transfer has been organized around competing ideas of choice. The modernization agenda pursued by Labour governments from 1997 brought with it a rather different set of debates about politics. Now the concern was with the politics of choice, and the extent to which the government's clear commitment to community engagement would lead to enhancement of real choice, and the extent to which certain choices were out of scope.

However, description of stock transfer as a 'consumer choice' policy is, at the very least, questionable. Firstly, it has to be recognized that the drivers for transfer have tended to lie with national and local government; in very few instances has the impetus come from tenants themselves. Hence, the 'choice' of whether to endorse a stock transfer proposal has been offered to those council tenants whose local authority landlords have seen this option as appropriate to their financial circumstances. Secondly, while there might be an official desire to see tenants being offered the opportunity to select from a range of (transfer) options, the 'choice' has in fact generally amounted to a take-it-or-leave-it proposal. Given the highly unequal access to financial resources conferred by the two 'choices' on offer, transfer critics have often dubbed the policy as tantamount to 'blackmail'. Undoubtedly, given the public finance environment in which they have taken place, stock transfers have brought many benefits but as a device to 'enhance tenant choice' the policy has significant shortcomings.

Ginsburg (2005) highlights the absence of choice to remain with the council and the government's 'punitive approach' to the councils and tenants who have not followed the privatization route. In a Parliamentary debate on 30 June 2004, Austin Mitchell MP referred to this as a 'crime against council housing'. The same debate saw considerable opposition to government policy emanating from the Labour and Liberal Democrat backbenches and an endorsement from former Labour deputy leader Roy Hattersley (cited by Ginsburg 2005: 132–3).

When the Westminster government introduced requirements for authorities to undertake stock options appraisals and presented authorities with a set of policy alternatives to meet the required Decent Homes standard in all of their stock by 2010 (initially) this led to political debates about the meaning of choice. In particular, opponents of transfer mounted a prolonged campaign for a 'fourth option' of stock retention and investment by municipal authorities to add to the long-term option of stock transfer and recently introduced options of ALMOs and PFI. As the campaign organization DCH has put it:

Box 4.2   DCH arguments on the politics of choice

✔ No 'Level Playing Field' Between The Different Options Available
  - regime of 'negative subsidy' on local council housing revenue accounts
  - stock transfers would not be financially viable unless the government wrote off all overhanging debt prior to the transfer
  - Arms Length Management Organizations and PFI receive extra public subsidy: money that is not available directly to council housing

✔ In Housing, 'Choice' is Only One-way
  - existing RSL tenants or private tenants cannot choose to become council tenants
  - cannot choose to go back to the council if they find the promises are not kept
  - no cases where council tenants have campaigned for stock transfer, PFI or ALMO

✔ Conflicts of Interest
  - senior managers who are recommending the 'change' and conducting the options appraisal usually stand to personally gain financially from that change

→

Government pays lip-service to 'choice' in public services, and claims that it places tenants at the heart of the decision-making process on stock options. The reality is very different. The government's present dogmatic commitment to privatisation and refusal to grant the 'fourth option' is designed to bully and blackmail tenants. It does not offer tenants the main choice they want – to stay with the council and get direct investment. Real choice for council tenants must involve allowing them to choose direct investment in council housing. (DCH 2004c)

As detailed in Box 4.2, DCH has identified numerous ways that the post-2000 regime has offered little real choice to council tenants and local authorities While several of the more procedural aspects of these arguments are subject to debate, the

> - a small number of highly profitable companies specialize in assisting councils and RSLs with promoting transfer
> - consultancies in high demand get their reputation for successfully promoting the council's option
>
> ✔ Denial of Access To Information
> - 'commercial confidentiality' limits the information available to tenant representatives
> - one-sided glossy PR campaigns
> - local authorities blatantly disregard principles of accurate and balanced publicity material set out in government's Transfer Guidance Manual
>
> ✔ Undemocratic Ballots
> - no legal right to a ballot for either PFI or ALMOs
> - councils control timing of transfer ballots (DCH cites examples where this power has been used to hold 'snap ballots' before opposition campaign material was published)
> - discourage the local press from giving equal space/airtime to opponents
> - refuse to provide opponents with the addresses of residents being consulted
> - threaten and bully tenants, union representatives and councillors
>
> *Source*: Based on DCH (2004c)

underlying critique of the absence of real choice between options has proved hard for government to refute, leading eventually to some shift of stance in relation to the 'fourth option' of investment in retained local authority stock.

Another campaign publication produced by the Centre for Public Services (2004) set out 'the case for the fourth option for council housing', stating that there was a 'growing momentum of support from local authorities, tenants, local authority associations, trade unions and MPs for a 4th option which allows increased housing investment for stock retention' (ibid: 5). In critiquing other options, the authors argued that there was opposition in principle to stock transfer and PFI and that the ALMO option was simply a 'stepping-stone to further privatisation' (ibid: 5) because separation of ownership and management would have made future ownership decisions less politically sensitive. Further arguments cited for the fourth option, and against ALMOs, included avoiding loss of democratic accountability, staff disruption, set-up costs and other risks. Vindication of this position was claimed when Camden tenants voted down the Council's proposed ALMO in 2004. The extent to which stock transfer can fairly be portrayed as part of the New Labour 'choice agenda' is further discussed in Chapter 10.

Contestation around local transfer proposals

As Malpass and Mullins note the idea of transfer 'had to overcome resistance from tenants fearing loss of hard won social rights, from staff fearing the loss of reasonable terms and conditions and from local councillors whose power base is threatened' (Malpass and Mullins 2002: 678). Political arguments developed by opponents of transfer locally have been varied reflecting the different interests potentially threatened by the process. One set of arguments relates to a general lack of political trust in housing associations. Despite the fact that most stock transfer associations were initially formed as new standalone local organizations, it is the image of large monolithic associations into which these local bodies may later be absorbed that tends to dominate the critiques. For example, housing associations are described by Alan Walter as 'increasingly remote and unaccountable multi million pound national businesses generating huge surpluses' (DCH 2006: 88). Gerald Kaufman MP, in the same publication, reflected on the consequences of his ministerial decisions to finance housing associations in 1974, leading eventually to them becoming sole providers of new build housing as 'not their job, not meant to be their job and they are far from marvellous at carrying it out' (ibid: 31).

The political nature of transfer is even more apparent at local level, where some celebrated contests have been associated with option appraisals, stock transfer offers and ballots and subsequent implementation processes, often over several years. It is also at the local level that the lobby and campaign organizations described above have had greatest impact – although, in practice, the scale of 'no vote' campaigns has varied enormously.

Ballot results analysis

As noted in Chapter 3, securing ministerial consent for stock transfer requires a local authority to demonstrate majority support for the proposal among the tenants concerned and eligible to vote. Despite the seemingly unstoppable advance of the process across the country, it is important to recognize that in each historical phase a significant minority of transfer ballots have been lost. Over the history of LSVTs up until 2007, just under a quarter (24 per cent) of the 344 transfer proposals put to tenants in England had been voted down. As shown in Figure 4.1, rejection rates were relatively high in the first few years of the process although they were again creeping up after 2003.

One factor lying behind the pattern shown in Figure 4.1 is that partial transfer ballots tend to have been somewhat more liable to result in 'yes' votes than those for whole stock handovers. Only 13 per cent of the former have been voted down by tenants, as against 26 per cent of the latter. Even if attention is focused on the period since 1997 we find partial transfers being somewhat more likely to attract majority support (87 per cent) than whole stock transfers (81 per cent). This may well be because partial transfers are generally configured to encompass concentrations of poor quality housing where most, if not all, tenants stand to gain directly from the extra investment

FIGURE 4.1   Outcome of transfer ballots in England, 1988–2007

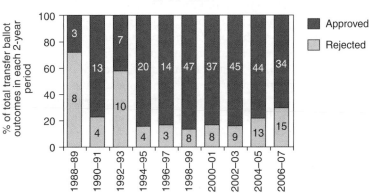

Note: Figures within graphic show no. of ballots concerned.

Source: CLG – unpublished data.

transfer it is intended to facilitate. In any whole stock transfer – even in cities with considerable stock condition problems such as Birmingham or Glasgow – there will be substantial numbers of tenants living in good quality housing in satisfactory repair. Arguments about the essential need for transfer as a means of facilitating refurbishment may cut little ice with this constituency. Similarly, arguments for transfer to access better housing management may be of more direct relevance to tenants living in what are perceived to be the least popular and/or most stigmatized neighbourhoods.

While Figure 4.1 indicates that rejection rates have remained at relatively low levels since 1993, it is perhaps worth bearing in mind the DCH assertion that its campaigns (particularly visible since 2000) have prevented many embryonic transfer proposals from even reaching the ballot stage 'because it could be shown that they were just a quick fix option being forced on the tenants by the council' (Wheal 2002).

Other than the partial transfer/whole stock transfer dichotomy, what else influences tenants' choices when faced with a transfer ballot? Focusing on the period around 1990 when transfer rejections were relatively common, we have identified a number of factors which apparently contributed to this outcome (Mullins et al. 1992). The presence of 'active opposition' seemed to have a noticeable effect. Vocal opponents 'raised awkward questions and doubts about the [transfer] offers being made . . . in the absence of opposition, consultation material was largely unchallenged and the press supportive because there was nothing else to report' (ibid: 70). Another relevant issue was the extent to which the local authority and the transfer landlord were perceived to be acting in harmony. In one instance, where the two were seen as 'clearly demarcated', there was an impression that the parties were to an extent opposed and in competition. Resentment of this state of affairs was believed to have influenced the ballot rejection of the proposed transfer.

The evaluation of the 'first generation' of stock transfers (Mullins et al. 1992, 1995) included case studies where local politics had loomed large during the development and consideration of transfer options. One hypothesis explored in this research was the importance of trust between elected politicians and housing department staff promoting the idea of transfer and tenants whose ballot endorsement was needed if transfers were to proceed. Where such trust was strong, the strategy of selling transfer as a 'least change' option – 'keeping the service and staff that you know' – seemed to be the best one to achieve ballot success. Where such trust did not exist, it seemed that rather than seeing transfer as an opportunity to escape, distrust meant that tenants lacked the confidence to support transfer proposals. Ironically, therefore, arguments for change of ownership were most positively received where existing rates of satisfaction were high and existing relationships between tenants and councils were strong.

Analysis of these early ballot outcomes suggested that, from a council perspective, prospects of success were dependent on:

- the extent to which the transfer was successfully 'sold' through simple publicity
- how effectively rent and other personal advantages to tenants were spelled out
- communicating the message that there was no risk-free 'no change' option – remaining with the council would bring its own hazards
- staging a campaign of an appropriate length – long enough to convey the message; short enough to maintain momentum
- strength and organization of opposition campaign
- reassuring tenants about the status of the transfer association (dispelling any linkage with 'exploitative' private landlords) – including through having tenants on the shadow HA board.

This last point connects with the fact that, despite government wishes to the contrary (Mullins et al. 1995: 22, DETR 2000c: 63), newly created – rather than existing – HAs have continued to dominate the stock transfer scene (see Chapter 2). This has been attributed in part to predecessor landlords' preference for creating successor bodies with a degree of 'local accountability' in terms of the representation of elected councillors (see Chapter 5). This motivation may, in turn, be explained by 'the local political judgement . . . that only a new local organisation will bring the support needed for transfer both in the community generally, and in the ballot' (NHF 2002b).

Political factors seemed even more significant in the 'second generation' of large urban transfers. This was partly because in

many of these authorities housing services were more politi-
cized, and key interest groups such as tenants' associations and
trade unions were more used to participating in political decision processes. A pivotal moment for the second generation of
transfer policy occurred in 2002 when the two largest transfer
ballots in Britain occurred, covering 175,000 tenants in two
major cities with contrary results and implications for future
transfer policy. Daly et al. (2005) compared these ballot outcomes in Glasgow and Birmingham. Both ballots involved high
turnouts (67 per cent in Birmingham and 64 per cent in
Glasgow) from very large constituencies (90,000 homes in
Birmingham and 85,000 in Glasgow). Outcomes were strik-
ingly different, with just 33 per cent in favour of transfer in
Birmingham compared with 58 per cent in Glasgow. The three
factors identified by Daly et al. to explain the different outcomes were the commitment of political leadership, the unity of
the opposition campaign and the different ways in which
tenant mistrust of councils played out (for more details on the
transfer debate in Glasgow see Box 4.4).

In Birmingham, there were clear divisions within the majority
Labour group and opposition from local members of parliament,
as well as a well-organized anti-transfer campaign run by trades
unions and tenants. Here, strong mistrust of the council was
mobilized to undermine confidence in its proposals: 'people did
not trust them or believe anything they said' (evidence of residents to the Independent Commission of Enquiry 2002) with
tenants 'punishing' the council by voting to remain its tenants. In
contrast, the Glasgow transfer proposal was solidly backed by
both local and national politicians as the only way to solve the
city's problems. A persuasive image of community ownership
and enhanced tenant management was also presented as a credible alternative to the widely mistrusted Housing Department
(see Box 4.1). Another factor was the different national political
context in Scotland, with the critical importance attached to the
plan by national politicians reflected in substantial Treasury
funding made available (see Chapter 3). This provides a further
link between the local politics of transfer and central–local relations and supports the view that while stock transfer has not
been nationally directed it has been strongly steered by central
government and that the local decision-making context is partly
constructed by this national steering.

While the Glasgow ballot produced a 'yes vote' the controversy which has subsequently dogged the transfer (see Box 4.4) compromised subsequent transfer proposals in other parts of Scotland. Most critically, negative publicity about complications affecting Glasgow Housing Association's Second Stage Transfer programme were identified as a material factor leading to the 53–47 per cent defeat of Edinburgh Council's transfer proposal in 2005. Here, a post-ballot survey of 1,067 tenants undertaken by MORI found that 'Glasgow' was the factor most commonly cited by 'no voters' as a reason for opposing the plan. Some 20 per cent of those who had cast their ballot against transfer reported that this issue had swayed their decision (City of Edinburgh Council 2006).

Consequences of negative ballots

Particularly pointed issues are raised where tenants have rejected proposed transfers, revealing a stark difference between 'official' judgement of tenants' best interest and tenants' own evaluations. Given the limited menu of options available to secure the investment needed to bring the housing stock up to standard, there have been cases of tenants in certain authorities being balloted repeatedly on the same decision – albeit on slightly different terms.

Following the 'no vote' in Birmingham, an Independent Commission of Enquiry (2002) into the future of council housing in Birmingham was convened, chaired by Professor Anne Power of LSE. Drawing on consultation with tenants and councillors, their report included an assessment of why the proposed transfer had been rejected at ballot, a review of the consequences of the ballot defeat and a proposal for future options for 'flourishing neighbourhoods'. Box 4.3 summarizes some of the Commission's conclusions.

The Commission's analysis of the ballot outcome mirrors some of those from the first generation research particularly in relation to trust, presentation and planning on the council's side and vigour and quality of opposition campaign. A new factor that had emerged since the first generation transfers was the influence of the national campaign Defend Council Housing. Another specific factor (shared with Glasgow) was the unprecedented scale and complexity of the proposed

Box 4.3   Implications of Birmingham's 'no' vote

Factors affecting Ballot Defeat

- Proposals unconvincing
- Presentation off-putting
- Process rushed and tenants did not feel properly consulted
- Older and BME tenants feared the consequences
- 'Privatization' was not popular
- Rumours and misinformation, e.g. existing tenants feared they might lose right to buy
- Only one option and the proposed housing associations did not reflect local boundaries
- Failure to modify proposals in response to concerns; staff fed back a higher level of support than proved to be the case
- Changes in senior staff during the process
- Other housing associations in the city were not involved
- Scale of repair problems made whole stock transfer 'virtually unmanageable'
- Union campaign against transfer consistent and well organized
- Some union members were directly involved in Defend Council Housing and were involved in jobs related to the transfer
- The service deteriorated during the push for transfer as management took their eye off the ball
- Government rules made it hard to offer solid prospects for improvement

→

transfer (to ten new housing associations), the extent of the repairs backlog and the difficulty of offering solid prospects of improvement. Other contextual factors apparently overlooked by the Commission were the troubled outsourcing of housing repairs 18 months prior to the ballot which had further soured staff and tenants' perceptions of 'privatization' options and the ill-judged decision to employ the former manager of one of the city's two rival football teams in the promotional video!

The Birmingham case highlights the impact of the limited choices available to local authorities to invest to meet the Decent Homes Standard, with the Commission of Enquiry seeing the most important consequence of the ballot defeat as being that there are 'no easy ways to close the funding gap'.

Consequences of Ballot Defeat

- Accept that 'one size does not fit all'
- Areas of the city that have already pursued new options seem to work better
- A patchwork of solutions is desirable
- Some tenants want options with greater local control
- Strong case for involving existing housing associations
- Costs are too high and performance too low
- Address problems of housing management value for money
- Improve repairs spend and quality
- Deal with unpopular and hard to let housing
- Staff are demoralized and need new sense of direction
- No easy ways to close the funding gap

Future Options

- Community based housing organizations in many shapes and sizes
- Many tenant-driven experiments
- Staff and residents training to develop capacity
- Devolution to constituency level
- Harnessing the council's significant resources
- Reduced inter-ethnic competition
- Community engagement
- Re-establish 'pioneering city' reputation created by Joseph Chamberlain

Source: based on Independent Commission of Enquiry (2002)

Subsequently, however, following a change in political control, the City's Conservative-controlled administration insisted that the transfer proposal had been, all along, unnecessary and that compliance with the Decent Homes Standard could be funded from within the Council's own resources. Specifically, it was envisaged that this would involve land disposals, supplemented by prudential borrowing. 'It was estimated that the disposal of around 315 acres of land and the clearance of 5,500 non-decent properties would generate a receipt of £203.1 million (gross), £113.5 million net between 2005 and 2010' (Rollo 2008: 5). Prudential borrowing capacity was anticipated as amounting to £12.5 million, annually, in the same period.

Whether Birmingham's post-2002 Decent Homes strategy remains tenable given the post-2008 property market downturn, remains in some doubt. It is also uncertain whether the extent of the works to be funded from the additional investment will be equivalent to those which would have followed from the transfer. In the case of another 'failed transfer' council – Edinburgh – it has become clear since the 2005 ballot that while the Council may achieve Scottish Quality Housing Standard compliance by 2015, the works involved in the associated investment programme will be considerably less extensive than would have resulted from transfer. Specifically, £100 million of investment in environmental improvements has needed to be removed from the plan. Paying for this reduced programme will be achieved mainly through substantial real-terms rent increases. While the transfer would have led to rents pegged to inflation for five years, the 'rescue plan' will see annual real terms increases of 2.7 per cent, compounding to a real-terms rise of over 20 per cent by 2015. Consequently, housing benefit dependence is forecast as increasing to 84 per cent (Rollo 2008).

A third example of an authority seeking alternative funding for stock improvement following tenant rejection of a 'new management option' is Camden. Camden's initial strategy following its ALMO ballot defeat in 2003/04 was to lobby Ministers for special treatment. As an authority with a housing service highly rated by the Audit Commission, the Council argued that it was illogical for it to be denied the public funding offered to similarly rated authorities simply because it was unable to adopt the ALMO organizational format. Having been rebuffed by government, the Council proposed to fill the resource gap mainly through selling 500 valuable central London flats on the open market. As in Birmingham, however, the viability of this strategy has been placed in doubt by the housing market crash and this led, in early 2009, to the floating of an alternative proposal to raise funds through letting the 500 homes at market rents.

The politics of post-transfer local housing

Turning to consider the longer-term political impacts of the transfer process the case of successful ballot outcomes provides a more telling test for the de-politicization thesis that transfer takes the politics out of housing. This thesis might suggest that following on from the overt politics of the transfer decision itself, ballots etc., the new landlords would settle down to a quieter post-transfer life in which they could focus on the housing business. Case study evidence from stock transfer organizations suggests that this is rarely the case.

Politics of localism

An important political impact of stock transfer has been the changed relationship between housing organizations and local political structures. As outlined in Chapter 5, the early period of stock transfer coincided with the removal of a range of public services from local democratic control associated with local government and was subject to a 'democratic deficit' critique (Davis and Spencer 1995).

Perhaps as a result of the fear of loss of local control, almost all early transfers involved the creation of new special purpose organizations, quite different to the 'remote and unaccountable multi million pound national businesses generating huge surpluses' depicted by opponents of transfer (DCH 2006: 88). Early transfer landlords often adopted names that were associated with their founding areas, frequently simply adding 'housing association' after the former district council name (and many of that generation of transfers were in the shire districts).

One of the growing pains experienced by the more entrepreneurial and expansionist of these early transfers was associated with the move away from their parent authorities. This was often signalled by a change of name to one without such localized geographical associations; jokes about the strange new names chosen by these associations abound in the industry. Sometimes such growth was organic, associated with a competitive approach to new development opportunities, with associations such as Sovereign taking the opportunity of a competitive procurement policy by the South West region of the Housing Corporation to expand rapidly out of West Berkshire into nearly 50 local authorities by the mid-1990s. In some cases expansion was through amalgamation with other housing associations, often through group structures (and

occasionally through mergers). Within group structures political tensions sometimes arose from conversion of the original
stock transfer organization into a subsidiary organization in a
larger group. Sometimes particular concerns arose from the
parent local authority being offered representation on the local
subsidiary board only, rather than on the new group parent
board.

Exemplifying related tensions is the case of Bedfordshire
Pilgrims HA which expanded rapidly between transfer in 1990
and 1994, by which time it had a management presence in ten
local authorities. A proposal by the association's then Chief
Executive to establish a group structure in 1994 was interpreted
by the parent local authority as seeking to create a formal distancing of the two bodies. The appointment of a new Chief
Executive in 1995 brought a consolidating, collegiate regime
which restored and strengthened some relationships strained in
the association's early years. While emphasizing a primary link
with the founding authority, the new post-holder was able to
provide firmer foundations for continued expansion.

Even greater tensions have sometimes been encountered where
the original transfer landlord has been 'taken over' by an 'alien'
housing association group. In addition to potential political tensions with the founding authority, this also raises political issues
for tenants who, while holding the veto over the original
transfer through the ballot, have no power of veto over any subsequent merger proposal (see Chapter 10). This happened in
Leominster (at the time a district council within Herefordshire).
When the stand-alone 'Leominster Marches' association ran
into financial difficulties it was 'rescued' by a traditional
regional association, Jephson, which was able to amalgamate its
own smaller stock within the Marches region, as well as offering
the association a substantial interest-free loan in return for a
'golden share' in its governance. While Leominster Marches has
to this day retained its name and identity, this is as a subsidiary
of Jephson. Ironically, the association has retained its operational base and public offices in the heart of the market town at
the centre of the old district council area, meanwhile democratic
accountability has upscaled away from Leominster to the new
Herefordshire unitary council. Albeit as a subsidiary of a
regional landlord, the association can now be seen as having a
stronger local presence than the local authority itself!

Second Generation transfers were, if anything, even more strongly influenced by localist politics than were the first generation. Like the ALMO alternative developed after 2000, the local housing company model placed a strong emphasis on locally accountable boards (within the general limits associated with company law or industrial and provident society status requiring the first duty of all board members to the best interests of the company rather than any external constituencies). They were also sometimes locked in by the transfer agreement to operate only within the parent authority area for the first five years of operation. Again, however, there were potential tensions as a result of the competing logics of scale and efficiency that were leading to substantial restructuring in the housing association sector at that time (Mullins 2006). This, combined with greater absorption of transfer associations into the wider housing association sector, led to new tensions.

Two rather unusual cases illustrate some of the political tensions arising from conflicts between localism and scale and efficiency in the 2000s. The first case study involved a former stock transfer association that had become a subsidiary in a federal style group structure led by a large traditional association. This was seen by local stakeholders as a positive arrangement, increasing the management scope and capacity of the subsidiary. Later, the group parent decided to explore possible merger with another large association. The merged organization would operate across several regions and would adopt a centralized structure with a strong emphasis on balance sheet performance to improve credit ratings. While the merger as a whole proceeded, the case study association decided to withdraw from the arrangement after failing to agree terms. Its board and residents felt that they had less say over this merger than over their original partnership. They anticipated that the deal would increase costs of support services and group membership and reduce autonomy. This would leave them as a branch plant with a disempowered board and higher costs. However, withdrawal from the group meant the loss of a contract to manage stock for their previous partner and a consequent reduction in viability. Standing alone does not appear to be an option and the case study association was required by the regulator to find a new partner. It joined a regionally based group with a headquarters much closer than the initial group parent. Within this context it was hoped that the association would be able to maintain regional focus and maximize autonomy.

The second case study relevant here involved a stock transfer direct into a traditional national housing association group. It was argued that it was possible to construct this unusual deal because of the long-established presence of the national association within the local authority area and a positive trust-based relationship with councillors. While a local committee was established to cover all of the association's operations in the district (and surrounding areas), the acquiring association was unwilling to offer the local authority the usual comfort of a local subsidiary. It was clearly the intention to absorb the local committee, over time, into the wider regional structure of the association. While highly unusual, this case illustrated the impact of the increased emphasis on scale and efficiency over local accountability within the sector, which was, at the time, threatening the continued independence of local subsidiaries in other group structures.

Against the trend illustrated by these cases is a resurgent drive of localism, evident in early pronouncements from the Tenant Services Authority in England and also reflected in the tenant-focused Community Housing Mutual and Community Gateway models developed in recent years and implemented in Wales and England (see Chapter 5). But the aspiration to achieve a better balance between local accountability and scale economies and efficiency was perhaps exemplified by the aspirations of the Glasgow transfer to proceed in two stages to devolve power to community based associations through a programme of second stage transfers. (See Box 4.4.)

Politics of the welfare state

It is appropriate to end this chapter on the politics of transfer by considering the broader political considerations associated with the position of housing within the welfare state. After all, it is partly differing views about the role of the state that have led stock transfer to be the subject of political controversy both nationally and locally. One aspect of this debate concerns the

Box 4.4   The Glasgow stock transfer: a case study in local political contestation

Glasgow Housing Association was established to take ownership of Glasgow City Council's 80,000 homes under the stock transfer of 2003. The story which has subsequently unfolded has richly illustrated the politics of stock transfer. And, while this case study is unique in certain important respects, it is useful in exemplifying political tensions experienced (albeit usually much less acutely) in some other transfers.

A long history of under-investment meant that, by the late 1990s, Glasgow City Council faced a huge backlog need for repairs and modernization. A particular problem was the burden of historic debt which resulted in around half of rental income being pre-committed to loan interest and repayments. As early as 1986 it had been recognized that, as a social landlord, GCC was akin to 'a business that has gone bust'. The possibility of 'floating off' the Council's housing stock under some form of trust vehicle was investigated at around this time. From 1997 onwards, a tenanted transfer into housing association ownership was seen as the only possible means of accessing essential investment on the required scale. Following Scottish devolution, Ministers investigated the feasibility of multiple small scale transfers. And although subsequently conceding that a single unit transaction was the only practicable way forward, this was now presented as simply an initial step in a two-stage process, involving a later round of 'second stage transfers' (SSTs).

As explained in Box 3.3, there were major financial hurdles to the achievement of this plan. However, although these were fully recognized by central government, the Council and its advisers in 2003, they were not immediately made plain to the wider public. Instead, a key clause was included in the transfer prospectus stating that SSTs could proceed only where such moves were 'financially neutral' for GHA. Nevertheless, included within its 2003 business plan the organization committed that: 'At the end of our first 10 years of operation, we will survey all of our tenants to seek their views on secondary transfer' (GHA 2003: 64). With hindsight, and bearing in mind the funding settlement finally agreed by the Scottish Executive, the package was flawed by the inclusion of incompatible objectives (Kearns and Lawson 2008); fitting with the analysis of competing institutional logics existing simultaneously in individual organizations and across the sector (Friedman and Alford 1991, Mullins 2006).

→

The transfer proposal evoked vigorous debate and trenchant opposition as reflected in the 58 per cent 'yes' vote – a less than overwhelming tenant endorsement. However, transfer critics were members of somewhat disparate groups lacking a common agenda. Divisive issues included the court challenge mounted by some political opponents of the transfer which cast as 'unlawful' the Council's uncompetitive award of the GHA housing repairs contract to the GCC Direct Labour Organization. Trades Union critics saw the challenge as inimical to workforce interests, since assurances about continued work for the DLO was the one significant 'concession' won by union campaigners in their negotiations with the City Council and Ministers. Similarly, while bitterly criticized by some advocates of existing community based housing associations in the city (see, for example: Robertson 2003), the GHA single transfer model was preferred by the unions because of the continued relationship between the new landlord and the DLO and because defending staff rights was seen to be simpler as a result of the retention of a unitary transfer body.

As well as creating GHA as an entity, the transfer agreement also provided for delegation of management of the transferred homes to a network of 62 Local Housing Organizations (LHOs), each with its own semi-autonomous management committee. LHOs were a mix of 'management only' housing associations, newly created and registered for the purpose, and units linked with existing community-based housing associations.

As further explained in Box 5.3, managing the tensions built into the relationship between GHA headquarters and the LHOs has proved highly challenging for all concerned. The expectation was that, over time, each LHO would have the opportunity to bid for stock ownership through the SST process (McKee 2009). Only in 2005, however, did it became clear to GHA's senior management and board that, within the existing financial envelope, it would be impossible to fulfil what many had believed were unqualified SST undertakings. And although this analysis was reluctantly accepted by the Holyrood Government in 2006 and confirmed by the regulator in 2007 (Communities Scotland 2007a), it triggered accusations of betrayal and failure which have continued to this day. Managing the resulting controversy has absorbed huge amounts of GHA senior management time and sapped the organization's morale. Nevertheless, in a close analysis of the many and varied critiques of GHA, Kearns and Lawson (2009) dismiss the depiction of the transfer as a simple case of 'policy failure'. Critical

→

allegations were, instead 'a mixture of the ideologically-informed, premature and simplistic; from some quarters the arguments could also be seen as self-serving'.

Renewed political tensions surfaced in 2009 in connection with the re-tendering of GHA's housing repairs contract with the City Council's direct labour organization. Here, with the prospect of losing one of the three contracts at issue, the Council stepped in to scupper the deal with a rival bidder by raising last minute doubts about the transfer of pension liabilities. Ironic here is the fact that while the Council itself had favoured the transfer of the DLO to GHA back in 2003, this had been prevented by Ministers.

The first SSTs (six packages totalling just 2,000 homes) took place in 2009, and up to another 20,000 homes were tagged for possible LHO handovers by 2011. However, a declaration by GHA that this would be the limit of the SST programme (GHA 2008) was rebuked by the Council on the grounds that the association must make good on its 2003 Business Plan pledge to consult all remaining tenants on the issue – see above (Glasgow City Council 2009).

At the time of writing, the City Council has recently floated the idea that Ministers should split GHA into five 'federal' units, as a step towards SSTs involving all the association's remaining 70,000 homes. This suggestion drew a sharp riposte from a number of tenant chairs of Local Housing Organizations (Inside Housing, 15 May 2009). Declaring 'We do not want to return to the days of no investment, no repairs, no choice and big rent rises', the authors criticized the Council for failure to consult on its proposal and asserted that breakup could not proceed without tenant backing.

At the same time, the Council has rejected GHA aspirations to assert itself as a regeneration agency as an unacceptable challenge to its own primacy in this field (Braiden 2009). In a similar vein, the Council was reportedly lobbying for GHA to be stripped of its new build powers, with earmarked funding for 2,100 homes instead being divided between established associations. Meanwhile, other critics (for example Robertson 2009) continued to label GHA a 'policy failure' notwithstanding its substantial record of success in meeting the objectives with which it was originally tasked and for which it was funded (Pawson 2009b). Short of dramatic and decisive Ministerial intervention, it seems highly likely that this controversy will run on for some considerable time.

For a more detailed account of GHA's first five years see Pawson et al. (2009)

extent to which stock transfer can truly be regarded as privatization. Beyond this, there are broader questions about the direction of travel in the organization of the housing welfare state indicated by stock transfer and the significance of this for the rights and responsibilities associated with the welfare state.

Stock transfer and privatization

As our analysis of the national and local politics of transfer has illustrated, the label 'privatization' has often proved a telling factor in galvinizing opposition. The sources reviewed so far in this chapter have tended to use the term privatization in a fairly general way. For example, the Centre for Public Services (2004: 23) states simply that 'LSVT is privatisation of local authority housing as the council retains no control of the stock'. Similarly, Walter (2007) categorizes transfer as one of 'the government's three privatisation options'.

Other politically committed writers have also emphasized the perceived dominance of financial interests in decision-making by housing associations. Glynn (2007: 128), for example, argues that associations must place the interests of financiers ahead of those of tenants because they are 'in hock to private finance'. In a similar vein Mooney and Poole (2005) contrasted the position of Glasgow Housing Association (GHA) to the former City Council Housing Department which had also raised private loans to fund its housing investment: 'What is [however] new is that [banks] will have [a key role] in policy-making and in shaping the future management of transferred housing' (ibid: 35). In Mooney and Poole's analysis this meant that GHA 'would be required to operate like a profit-making company to ensure that lenders saw a healthy return on their investment and on their loans' (ibid: 35). As a result they argued that 'the welfare role of social housing will be severely curtailed if not completely eroded as a result of stock transfer' (ibid: 34).

We would not seek to deny the role of loan covenants and financial ratios in housing associations' business planning; nor the limited 'headroom' enjoyed by new stock transfer organizations in view of their high debt to assets ratios (Mullins et al. 1995). During the 2008–09 credit crisis, the unwillingness of funders to extend or amend loan agreements without substantial increases in margins has made life difficult for many housing associations who have been further hit by the slump in the value of land and unsold housing for sale and shared ownership, all of these potentially impacting on financial ratios and covenants. However, the model of debt finance adopted for transfers in the UK can be contrasted to more direct equity investment by profit takers in the structures of housing companies for example in the system of category A and B shares used by some housing companies in Finland.* In short, financiers do not have a direct seat on the boards of UK housing associations, nor do they benefit directly from the relative levels of profitability of stock transfer landlords, merely from the ability of the landlord to repay debt in line with loan agreements.

Moreover, there is little evidence for the assertion that stock transfer landlords (and/or all housing associations) tend to be 'hard nosed' operators, treating tenants in a manner more similar to private landlords than to local authorities. Analysis summarized in Chapter 7 demonstrates that, to the contrary, transfer HAs record significantly lower eviction rates for rent arrears than local authorities and for traditional associations (Pawson et al. 2004).

Components of privatization

The wider academic literature on privatization of public services/assets suggests that it may involve several distinct processes. For example Heald (1984) identifies four forms of privatization:

- Commercialization which involves shifting the way in which services are paid for from the taxpayer to the service user
- Contracting out the management of public services to the private sector
- Sell-offs of public assets to the private sector
- De-regulation; enabling private companies to compete in public service provision and reducing the burden of regulation to make market entry easier.

---

* Category B shares being held by pension funds and other investors with the expectation of a profit, while category A shares are held by municipalities in lieu of a transfer receipt.

Murie's (1993) analysis of housing restructuring in the UK added further processes to Heald's list:

- De-muncipalization, or the removal of assets and services from local authority control was a clear ideologically-driven change as the earlier part of this chapter establishes.
- Preparing services for privatization is a less clear cut process that could include policies to move council rents closer to private rents and to introduce HRA business planning and resource accounting for housing.

Some changes of direction were apparent under New Labour's post-1997 'modernization' policies (see Mullins and Murie 2006). Best Value provided a broader framework for choices about contracting out services. The focus on 'contracting-out' which had shaped the Conservatives' 1995 Consultation Paper *More Choice in the Social Rented Sector* was still evident in Labour's 2000 Green Paper *Quality and Choice: The new way forward for housing and elaborated in the PSA Plus review* (ODPM 2003d) which sought a level playing field between a number of contracting-out models.

As explained in Chapter 3, the main driver for transfer as a form of 'housing privatization' has been to secure investment 'off balance sheet' so that the backlog of repair in existing stock could be tackled without increasing public debt within the Public Sector Net Borrowing framework (Hawksworth and Wilcox 1995b). This is perhaps a technical view of privatization but has been a key policy driver. Finally, there is the popular image of privatization, reflected in some anti-transfer campaigns, that views the process as asset-stripping in which historic state subsidized public goods are exploited for commercial gain. This raises questions about the valuation of assets at transfer and the controls needed to prevent unacceptable profit-taking.

As it has evolved in England, stock transfer is essentially an administrative transaction involving application for a place on a government programme, formal consultation with tenants, registration with the regulator, agreement between the two parties, approval by the Secretary of State and securing private finance. A distinctive feature of this process is the very significant 'voice' given to existing tenants whose vote in a ballot has significantly shaped most transfer proposals and seen around quarter of such proposals defeated (Munro et al. 2005). Subsequent transactions involving transferred assets (e.g. sales of vacant properties, or mergers with other social landlords) remain administrative rather than market-based, requiring the approval of the regulator, and usually of private funders and consultation with tenants (although not a further ballot).

Hence, most aspects of initial transfer transactions are administratively determined, following rules specified by legislation or regulation. A transfer landlord's ability to enter into subsequent transactions (involving the former council stock) is severely constrained and there are few early opportunities to exploit the transferred asset in a purely commercial fashion. While sales of tenanted properties require regulatory consent, scope sometimes exists for disposal of commercial development of land around housing sites. Over time, as initial debt is repaid and asset values have appreciated, the 'headroom' to engage in more commercial activities increases. It is often said that one of the main changes introduced by stock transfer is the discipline of private borrowing and the associated need to keep within the 30-year business plan. Usually, this results in a more commercial approach than operated under the local authority.

Table 4.1 summarizes the main forms of privatization identified in the above discussion and applies these to the case of stock transfer drawing on a more detailed analysis in which Mullins and Pawson compared right to buy and stock transfer as forms of privatization (Mullins and Pawson 2009). This table indicates that stock transfer can only be regarded as an unequivocal example of privatization in relation to de-municipalization and funding off-balance sheet through private finance. In all other respects it is either debateable whether transfer is privatization or it is clear that it is not. Even in relation to transfer of risk and commercialization, there are important qualifications which distinguish transfer organizations from purely commercial companies. In relation to contracting out, deregulation, free consumer choice and full exploitation of assets for private profit there are significant differences between stock transfer landlords and market based profit distributing companies.

TABLE 4.1   *Stock transfer as a form of 'privatization'*

Form of privatization (and definition)	Evidence in relation to stock transfer
De-municipalization – Reducing municipal ownership and development	YES – reduced LA stock by 1.3 million dwellings between 1988 and 2008.
Transfer of risk – Risk of maintaining the assets and protecting future income no longer borne by the state ('off-balance sheet')	Technically YES – HA borrowing is outside PSBR and responsibility for assets is with HAs. BUT borrowing is effectively underwritten by regulation and lenders have first call on assets in event of landlord bankruptcies.
Commercialization – Increasing user charges and reducing subsidy and tax finance of state activity	Partly YES – transfer landlords must ensure rental and other income enables loans to be repaid; higher rents for new tenants one outcome of this. BUT HA rents increasingly regulated from mid 1990s and state policies on rent restructuring have underpinned post-2000 transfer HA business plans.
Contracting out – Outsourcing the management of services where responsibilities and assets remain state owned	Technically NO – ownership of assets transfers to HAs. BUT after 2000 government has viewed transfer landlords as one delivery agent to achieve Decent Homes Standard. Other agents (ALMOS, PFI) closer to contracting-out model (no asset transfer).

→

Beyond 'privatization' – housing and modernization of the welfare state

Ginsburg (2005) associates stock transfer with 'neo-liberalism and the retreat from welfare'. However, he argues that 'true privatisation' is just one of three possible interpretations of stock transfer. For Ginsburg, the term, in this context, denotes

TABLE 4.1 *(continued)*

Deregulation – Reducing or removing state regulation of private activity	NO – stock transfer a highly regulated process and all (other than very small) HAs routinely subject to heavy regulation. Funding policies have attempted to harness HA assets to subsidize new social housing. BUT difficult to see how any regulatory intervention to influence use of surpluses accrued by transfer landlords could be implemented without threatening landlords' 'independent' status.
Promotion of consumer choice – Enabling consumers to choose between alternative providers and options to meet their needs	Largely NO – despite rhetoric of tenant choice, choices have largely been made by LAs. Even when these were enforced, size limits had little impact on tenants' ability to choose between landlords. BUT considerable evidence of increased 'voice'; greater tenant involvement after transfer and post-2000 option appraisals emphasize early involvement of tenants.
State investment exploited for private profit – Assets undersold, historic state investment fuels current private profits	Largely NO - Low asset valuations reflect requirement to continue as social tenancies. Valuation process intended to be cost neutral. Status of transfer landlords as non-profit distributing protects tax-payer. BUT under-valuation through cautious assumptions and changes in economy led to strong surpluses in some cases. Concerns about 'fat cat remuneration' of senior staff and, post-2003 board member payments. High consultancy costs and 'leakage' of public funds to private sector.

Sources: Developed from Mullins and Pawson (2009). Framework adapted from Murie (1993); stock transfer evidence drawn from case studies

a scenario where 'transfer marks a decisive shift towards monopolistic private landlordism, with public control and accountability fading away over time' (ibid: 132), and where change in the character of 'social housing' will be 'driven by the increasingly commercial interests of the landlords, albeit regulated by inspectorates and partnerships with local authorities' (ibid: 133). While acknowledging that 'the evidence in support of this interpretation is limited, so far' (ibid: 132) Ginsburg's analysis is that a staged process leading to the ultimate destination of full privatization is the most likely long-term impact of stock transfers.

This leads us to question whether transfer is principally about a change in the mix of actors involved in delivering social housing, with a shift from state to non-profit with few implications for the overall balance of rights and responsibilities between citizens and the state on the one hand. If the latter is the case, will this lead to a more fundamental shift in the direction of a market based system with non-profit actors themselves likely to be replaced by fully private actors and rights? Malpass and Victory (2010, forthcoming) follow Ginsburg's broad line of argument in considering the potential impact of proposed regulatory changes for housing associations. They argue that there has been a 'consistent direction of travel away from the overwhelming municipalist and collectivist dominance of the period from 1919 to 1979 . . . The Cave review can be seen as setting up the next phase, with greater emphasis and reliance on private finance and profit-seeking companies . . . this could be the end of social housing and housing associations as we have known them. Parallels with those other paragons of 19th century mutuality, the building societies, spring to mind. Despite assurances given by Labour ministers about issues such as PLC status, it is not hard to imagine a future Conservative Government pressing forward with the privatisation of social housing' (Malpass and Victory 2010, forthcoming: 117–18).

Malpass and Victory are clearly referring to a further move away from the privileged position enjoyed by housing associations in the 1980s and 90s when they became the monopoly providers of new social housing and helped to define the socially based regulatory norms in partnership with the industry regulator. Mullins (1997) referred to the move from this form of 'regulatory capture' towards a form of regulated competition in which the role of the regulator is increasingly separated from the sector and is seen as stimulating competition between a range of provider types (Mullins and Sacranie 2008). Initial pronouncements by the newly established Tenant Services Authority (TSA) indicated a further distancing from housing associations and an intention to promote competition including with private sector bodies. Discussion papers issued by the TSA in June 2009 indicated a willingness to 'think the unthinkable' in relation to aspects of social rights traditionally associated with social housing. (e.g. for secure tenancies to become conditional on the supply/demand balance in particular areas' (TSA 2009a).

Chapter conclusions

We started this chapter by referring to the common sense notion that transfer has taken the politics out of housing by removing social housing from direct democratic control. The examples discussed in this chapter would suggest, to the contrary, that transfer is an intensely political process involving the potential for political contests of various types during each life cycle phase from options appraisal and ballot through to post-transfer governance and accountability structures, the impacts of geographical expansionism and diversification and modes of engagement with locally based governance networks. The 'de-politicization thesis' has not been supported by the material presented here which suggests that not only has the process of transfer been associated with high profile political contests at national and local levels, but the outcomes and consequences of transfer have often been politically potent.

Our discussion of the transfer process hinged on the politics of choice, central–local relations and the ability of local authorities to continue to provide social housing. The politics of localism were also found to be an important part of the transfer story.

The early years of transfer became part of a narrative of 'democratic deficit' as a range of local services moved away from direct local political control (see also Chapter 5). Subsequently, and despite the inauguration of a new generation of transfer vehicles as 'Local Housing Companies' and the later introduction of the ALMO option with greater local authority linkage (see Chapter 8), localism continued to be a potent source of political debate.

Notably, as a result of trends to geographical expansionism and restructuring of the housing association sector through group structures and ensuing 'streamlining' (see Chapter 5), the connection between individual local authorities and social land-lords has been weakened. Concerns about the dominance of efficiency over local accountability within such enlarged struc-tures, led Glasgow to propose a two-stage transfer process with the aim of devolving management functions to a network of community based housing associations (CBHAs) in line with the Scottish CBHA tradition (see Chapters 2, 3 and 5). More generally, micro-political issues were apparent in stories of the governance of the new transfer bodies (explored more fully in Chapter 5) and the roles played by different stakeholders, par-ticularly local authorities.

The consequences of transfer for the position of housing in the welfare state are still being worked through. The key ques-tion here is whether the shift in the mix of institutions involved in delivery of social objectives will eventually lead to a weak-ening of the social rights and obligations formerly embodied in those institutions. Simplistic privatization critiques are under-mined by the careful unpacking of component elements of pri-vatization, most of which are not evident in transfer. However, a wider perspective on the implications of the shift from munic-ipal to third sector provision followed by regulated competition between a mix of for-profit and non-profit providers of housing suggests that a gradual elision towards more marke-tized forms of provision with the potential for lower degrees of social protection is potentially the case. We return to the ques-tion of the wider impacts of transfer on welfare in Chapter 10.

Chapter 5

Governance and Accountability Consequences

The spectacular implosion of the UK's top banks in 2008 cast a renewed spotlight on corporate governance failings in large private enterprises. How, it was asked, could the boards of HBOS and Royal Bank of Scotland have provided such weak oversight of senior manager activities? Were the banks' directors in fact properly qualified for their role and were they properly accountable to shareholders? What was the balance of power between non-executive and executive directors and was there a risk that 'the very experience which is the reason for their appointment may itself have become out of date . . . past experience was no help in responding to the . . . huge technological and psychological shift in banking between 1990 and 2008 – it was the young executives who had the real experience of the new world' (Rees-Mogg 2009). Such questions are neither entirely new, nor of exclusive relevance to the world of private business. The corporate casualties of the recent banking crisis have only served to re-invigorate debates about reforms of organizational governance originally stimulated by highly publicized 'governance failures' of the 1980s and 1990s such as those involving BCCI, Enron and Equitable Life.

What parallels can be drawn with large housing associations, players in a sector that has also changed enormously since 1990, where there is often a mismatch of ages, experience and assumptions between non-execs and execs and where 'the nuclear button' may appear to be the only option to reconcile genuine differences of judgement? While housing associations are social enterprises rather than profit-orientated businesses, influential critiques of corporate management (e.g. Cadbury 1992, Higgs 2003) have also focused attention on governance in *this* sector. Equally important in stimulating such interest have been the concerns around the quality and probity of elected representatives and board members in public bodies and QUANGOs (or Quasi-Autonomous Non-Government Organizations). Indeed, a number of the recommendations of the second Nolan Report were specific to housing associations (Committee on Standards in Public Life 1996), with some of these stimulated directly by local authority housing stock transfers with the transfer process having become established in the early 1990s (Davis and Spencer 1995).

As highlighted in Chapter 4, the apparent 'loss of accountability' inherent in transfer transactions has formed a central element in the political critique of the policy. Instead of being answerable to elected councillors, housing managers in transfer organizations are overseen by a board of management whose primary responsibility is to the organization itself, rather than being directly accountable to any broader constituency. At its starkest, the transfer process is thus portrayed as replacing publicly accountable bodies with quasi-private landlords, remote from the communities in which they operate and insulated from local opinion as well as being 'in hock' to private lenders (Glynn 2007). A contrary view is that the loss of democratic accountability resulting from transfer is at least largely compensated by enhanced tenant involvement in the governance of the new landlords (Gibb 2003).

Exploring such arguments and picking up on some of the issues raised in Chapter 4, the main body of this chapter is structured as follows. First we revisit the era in which the early transfers took place and review the debates around the accountability of quasi-public bodies taking place at this time. This is followed by an analysis of the organizational frameworks used to facilitate stock transfers and the development of new models as the process has unfolded over the past 20 years. We then look at empirical evidence on the 'governance practice' of transfer landlords and the light this sheds on some of the tensions inherent in the structures established for this purpose. The fact that transfer landlords have been stripped away from predecessor local authorities adds an edge to much of this. However, many of the issues are relevant to debates around the governance of all housing associations. In the penultimate section we look at the evolution of transfer landlords' organizational governance frameworks and the competing institutional logics that have influenced such change.

Then, ahead of our conclusions, we focus more squarely on the accountability consequences of transfer.

Ahead of the main discussion, let us step back to review exactly what is meant by the terms 'governance' and 'accountability' in this context. As the former term is most commonly used in the social housing world, the focus is mainly on 'corporate governance' or the oversight and policymaking processes within landlord organizations. In the housing association context, 'corporate governance' is about the framework and operation of the formally constituted board of management to which senior staff are accountable. Corporate governance, as characterized by Malpass (1997a), concerns 'the overall management of organisations, the accountability of staff to board members and the arrangements for the organisation to be accountable to the outside world' (ibid: 3). However, as we argue below, while the board is a key element of this framework, the corporate governance of transfer housing association typically encompasses other mechanisms – especially in relation to channels for tenant influence on organizational decision-making.

More broadly, the concept of governance also encompasses 'the systems or principles within which decisions are located' (Malpass 1997a: 2). Reid (1995) captured the way that local housing services are increasingly co-ordinated by local networks of actors who have replaced the formal hierarchy once provided by local government in a shift described by Rhodes (1997) amongst others as the move from government to governance. As well as looking at the corporate governance of transfer landlords, therefore, this chapter also reflects on the wider impacts of the transfer process on the distribution of power within the social housing system and on local network relationships with other actors.

Accountability is about the mechanisms which facilitate oversight and the people or institutions by whom an agency is 'held to account'. As defined by Gregory and Hicks (1999), organizational accountability is the controllability or answerability of public service organizations to bodies that hold them to account. As noted in Chapter 4, contestation around these issues has formed a central element within political debates on stock transfer. In this chapter we explore in more detail the new accountability landscape for social landlords after council housing.

Early transfers and the local public spending bodies debate

The gradual shift of social housing away from local democratic control seen over the past 20 years has been seen as paralleling similar changes in other services such as education, health and urban regeneration (Greer and Hoggett 2000). Even in its early stages this process produced an array of 'local public spending bodies' (LPSBs): organizations which – while not directly accountable to the taxpayer or local electorate – were characterized as largely publicly funded and integral to public policy (Committee on Standards in Public Life 1996). Bracketed alongside housing associations as LPSBs were bodies such as Training and Enterprise Councils, Local Enterprise Companies and Further Education colleges.

Common to LPSBs was their adoption of a governance framework involving salaried managers accountable to boards of largely lay members. This was seen as amounting to the incorporation of a 'board of directors' model into the public sector (Ferlie et al. 1995).

Reflecting concerns raised by Davis and Stewart (1994), among others, the Committee acknowledged that the rise of LPSBs raised issues in relation to governance and accountability. As seen by the Committee, these called for mechanisms:

- to enable such organizations 'to respond to local needs, and to have arrangements in place which enable local concerns to be raised'
- to facilitate 'appointments procedures, openness, codes of conduct, training, and whistle-blowing' incorporating similar principles as those set out in the Committee's first report in relation to national public organizations.

(Ibid: summary 1)

Recommendations relevant to housing associations included the call for organisations to strengthen accountability through membership recruitment (see below), and through increased tenant involvement in housing management. Although these suggestions were directed at all associations, the Committee expressed particular concerns in relation to stock transfer landlords. This reflected a perception of transfer associations as 'near monopoly' providers of social housing in many localities and worries that local authorities might retain insufficient leverage over the new landlords to act as a channel for 'local influence' on the new bodies. In these circumstances, the Committee recommended stronger regulation for transfer landlords (as well as other associations with a quasi-monopolistic position in their district).

Another dimension to this issue, and one which has become more important over time, has been the tendency for some associations' geographical growth strategies to reduce the relative importance of their 'home authority' to their operations, thereby creating pressures for reduced involvement of local authority nominees in their corporate governance structures. Related issues can be a perceived 'leakage' of resources from the home area as over time associations re-invest surpluses generated in the home area in new investment in other areas.

One practical issue Lord Nolan may well have had in mind here is the relationship between councils and housing associations on accommodating homeless people. As discussed in more detail in Chapter 9, a local authority's legal duties to secure housing for certain homeless households remain in place following transfer. For a local authority no longer a landlord, discharging such duties will be possible only with the help of local associations. Concerns that transfer might place stockless councils in an impossible position here have been frequently voiced over the years (see, for example, Bennett 2001, Taylor 2008) and have in some authorities contributed to doubts about proceeding on this course. Related issues are further discussed in Chapter 9. At this point, suffice it to say that although tensions over 'local authority nominations' have been far from unusual post-stock transfer, most informed observers would probably concede that the 'strong regulation' advocated by Lord Nolan has been fairly effective in ensuring that these are kept in check.

Changing governance models

Early transfers

What were the specifics of the stock transfer model which contributed to the critique of housing associations in the LPSB debate? As noted in Chapters 1 and 2, virtually all transfers conveying a local authority's entire housing stock have been to newly created housing associations. Although the recipient of one 1990 transfer (Rochester-on-Medway) was allowed to remain an unregistered private body, the standard model for all others in England (and virtually all in Scotland) was the not-for-profit housing association, registered with the Housing Corporation and – at least until 1996 – legally constituted as an Industrial and Provident Society.

Established under the Industrial & Provident Societies Act 1965, I&P organizations are businesses 'for the benefit of the community'. Other than those which are also co-operatives, housing associations constituted on this model have an 'ordinary shareholder' membership of individuals with an interest in the organization. Such shares can be purchased for a nominal amount (normally £1). Although shareholding members may be tenants of the organization membership is also open to others. Given that they do not make or distribute profits, ordinary shareholding members receive no financial return. Legally, however, shareholding members wield a degree of influence in that they form the body to which the organization's board is accountable.

Formally, board members are subject to shareholder election through the organization's Annual General Meeting. In practice, however, it is widely acknowledged that such 'accountability' lacks substance. Few associations have taken the opportunity to create large shareholding memberships amongst their residents and local communities, perhaps fearing that such recruitment could backfire and reduce the flexibility to introduce key changes such as mergers. Committee member elections are typically staged so that positions are uncontested, with the shareholder membership simply endorsing a candidate or candidates solicited by senior staff and/or existing committee members, inviting the charge that association boards are essentially 'self-perpetuating oligarchies' (Kearns 1997: 49). More generally, the Industrial & Provident Society model can be seen as less appropriate outside the context of relatively small locality-focused landlords.

Distinct from most 'traditional' housing associations, early transfer landlords tended to adopt rules recognizing distinct 'constituencies' in terms of board member backgrounds

Pawson and Fancy 2003: Tables 11–12). Hence, a specified number of seats on the board were designated for tenants and for nominees of the founding local authority – in practice, almost always sitting councillors. Remaining board members were termed 'independents'. In most pre-1996 English associations between a fifth and a third of board member seats were for tenants, while council nominees usually also guaranteed up to 20 per cent of board places (the legal limit to 'local authority persons' at the time to prevent the association being deemed local authority controlled'). Constituting boards in this way was seen as a means of providing reassurance to local authority Elected Members and to tenants that, as stakeholder groups, their interests would be upheld by the new organization. However, for reasons discussed in more detail below, this is problematic and, consequently, the representative model cannot operate fully.

Local housing companies

An important change in the policy context emerged in 1996 with the Westminster Government's acceptance of a new social landlord governance model, the Local Housing Company format. This was bound up with a re-definition of the rules on what constitutes public expenditure. Treasury rules, embodying the PSBR definition of public expenditure, include within 'public borrowing' any loans taken out by organizations 'controlled by local councillors'. Under the Local Government and Housing Act 1989, any organization governed by a board containing more than 20 per cent 'local authority persons' was defined as 'council controlled'. With the Housing Act 1996, however, these rules were relaxed, allowing the Housing Corporation to register as 'housing associations' new landlords with up to two thirds of board member seats designated for council nominees and tenants, provided that seats reserved for each group remained below 50 per cent.

This opened the way for the Local Housing Company (LHC) model first floated by Nick Raynsford, the then parliamentary opposition housing spokesperson (Raynsford 1991). As subsequently fleshed out by others (Wilcox and Bramley 1993, Zitron 1995) LHCs were, from the start, presented as a means of preserving a social landlord's local accountability while at

Box 5.1   Contestation around Local Housing Company operation and the 'golden share'

Example 1

This example concerns a stock transfer housing association established on the Local Housing Company basis in 2003 with constituent interest groups (tenants, local authority nominees, and independents) having assigned places on the committee. Early perceptions on the part of the association's staff were that the local authority nominees (all sitting councillors) tended to act as a block rather than as individual committee members, with the individuals concerned often seeing their role as primarily to represent the interests of the council rather than identifying with the landlord.

Because of the perceived need for sufficient representatives from all three constituencies, the Committee was seen by the chief executive and senior staff as being unmanageably large – at 19 members. At the same time, 'constituency group' members acting in concert had the power to frustrate decision-making through the constitutional provision that at least one member of each group needed to be present to form a quorum. The constitution drawn up at transfer was also found problematic in that disciplinary action against a committee member in breach of undertakings would be binding only with the support of at least 75 per cent of participating members. Similarly, as incorporated within the organization's memorandum and articles of association, the local authority as an entity held 26 per cent voting rights in Association General Meetings. Hence, given the 75 per cent vote required to amend the organization's rules (e.g. those on quorums and disciplinary action against members), held an effective veto over constitutional change.

→

the same time facilitating access to investment off the public balance sheet.

Usually involving equal numbers of tenants, local authority nominees and independents, the LHC constituency framework has become the standard model for transfer landlords set up since 1996. In most cases, these bodies have been legally established as companies limited by guarantee rather than Industrial & Provident Societies. Guarantee limited bodies are constituted

The difficult atmosphere was exacerbated by a lack of adherence to a code of conduct, so that details of 'confidential' board business were being disclosed to the press. This reflected a strongly held view by some board members that the code was too prescriptive and that it allowed the organization to keep too much secret that was of great importance for many (ex-local authority) tenants. Here, an unfavourable comparison was being drawn with the openness of the business conducted by the association as compared to the local authority. This refers to the fact that, whilst the proceedings of official Council committees are normally made available to the public, housing associations are under no such obligation. It is, nevertheless, important to recognize that decisions by such council committees are often little more than an endorsement of conclusions reached in private by local authority controlling political groups.

(Case study example drawn from Pawson et al. 2005b).

Example 2
Senior managers and board of Sunderland Housing Group sought to restructure their organization in 2007. Given the 'golden share' powers of Sunderland City Council under the Group's (LHC) constitution, Council approval for the move was required. Local controversy was stirred by the proposed consolidation of five existing landlord subsidiaries into a single landlord entity, and the creation of a new higher level group board where none of the seats would be explicitly designated for tenant members. Recognizing that Council support for the restructure was legally required, the City's decision to back the plan was challenged through Judicial Review – although this was unsuccessful.

under the Companies Act 1985 and differ from the latter in that they have no shareholding membership. Instead, three distinct 'classes of membership' are created – including the founding local authority as a corporate member – with each class having voting rights over a third of the total member votes.

Unlike their Industrial & Provident counterparts, LHC board members are not (even technically) accountable to such a wider body. LHC board member recruitment processes are specific to the constituency from which members are drawn. Council nominees are simply nominated by the local authority. Independent board members are effectively selected by the existing board – as advised by senior staff. In common with traditional associations, such recruitment is increasingly formalized, nowadays often involving the specification of required 'capabilities' (e.g. defined to reflect perceived 'skills gaps' in relation to existing members) and open advertising.

Another significant aspect of the LHC model, as usually structured in practice, is the constitutional rule stipulating that constitutional reforms require the assent of 75 per cent of the membership. This provision, promoted by the Housing Corporation, gives each 'constituency' effective 'veto' power over any fundamental change which might be proposed by executive staff or members of another board member constituency. Given the formal position of the founding local authority as a 'corporate member' (see above) the power remaining in the hands of the local authority is sometimes referred to as the 'golden share'. The potential significance of such provisions is highlighted by the two examples detailed in Box 5.1.

Among early transfer landlords, tenant board member recruitment was sometimes a fairly ad hoc process, partly reflecting the absence of pre-existing tenant representative structures. Among 'second generation' transfer landlords (those established since 1997). it appears to have been more common for the initial cohort of tenant directors to be selected through open elections with little restriction on candidate eligibility. However, subsequent rounds of Tenant Board Members recruitment have tended to involve more top-down filtering of potential candidates to assess capabilities, motivation and commitment (Pawson et al. 2009).

Particularly where the transfer proposal had been locally contentious, some transfer housing associations found that an initial round of open election generated a tenant director cohort including prominent anti-transfer campaigners. While this could turn out to be a means of 'incorporating' former 'dissidents' some of the new landlord bodies found to their cost that attempting such 'conversion' was a high risk strategy.

In common with other local spending public bodies, transfer housing associations have been seen as adopting a form of stakeholder governance. While this was, to some extent, true from the start, it was strongly emphasized under the LHC format. This terminology refers to the stakeholder principle as advocated by Hutton (1995) as a new organizing principle of corporate governance, and as adapted by Lord Nolan in his initial recommendations for local public spending body boards incorporating 'a balance of skills, interests and backgrounds in order to promote healthy debate and effective decision-making' (Greer and Hoggett, 2000).

Linked to this point is the observation that stock transfer brings significant changes in the map of key stakeholders involved in social housing decision making. While the tripartite LHC structure institutionalizes a 'council voice' on the new board, no one would argue that this is more than a very limited recompense for the overall loss of influence on social housing for local councillors and, by extension, local voters. Councillor frustrations with their 'downgraded' housing policy role post-transfer have often emerged as the successor landlord seeks to exert its independence and pursue evolving corporate objectives – e.g. in relation to area regeneration or out-of-borough housing development activity or functional diversification.

Stakeholders gaining influence under the new framework include senior staff, funders, and regulators. As further discussed later in this chapter, there are good grounds for arguing that tenants constitute another stakeholder group usually substantially empowered through transfers.

Transfer landlord governance models: the Scottish agenda

The preceding discussion mainly concerns policy developments in England. These are relevant to Scotland only to a limited extent. Reflecting the distinct origins of stock transfer north of the border, the policy context for post-transfer social housing governance has always been somewhat different here. As discussed in Chapter 2, early Scottish transfers took the form of estate-level disposals by the then Glasgow District Council in the 1980s. In accordance with the locally strong traditions of working class organization, these transfers were to local tenant-controlled landlords (Clapham et al. 1991 Clapham and

Kintrea 2000). In this, the process reflected the existing establishment of the community-based housing association (CBHA) model in the West of Scotland.

The CBHA model also strongly influenced the transfer programme facilitating the breakup of the former Scottish Special Housing Association portfolio by Scottish Homes during the 1990s (Taylor 2004). Hence, the SSHA stock was parcelled up into over 100 geographical units and hived off sequentially between 1990 and 2004 (Gibb et al. 2005). Generally speaking, the smaller parcels of stock were absorbed by existing housing associations, with the larger ones (more than 500 homes) being acquired by over 30 associations newly created for the purpose on the CBHA format with tenant board members often in the majority.

Reflecting the perceived success and political acceptability of the CBHA model, the post-devolution Ministerial drive to encourage local authority whole stock transfers in Scotland appropriated the slogan 'community ownership' (Kintrea 2006, McKee 2009). In practice, Scottish whole stock transfer landlords have been expected to adopt the tri-partite LHC-type governance structure, though not in all cases within a Company Limited by Guarantee legal form. Also, with the partial exception of Glasgow (see below) all six local authority whole stock transfers carried through since 2003 have involved a single, authority-wide successor landlord. Whether such arrangements can accurately be described as 'community ownership' has been questioned (Kintrea 2006).

This model was influential in structuring the Glasgow transfer of 2003. While this transaction conveyed all 80,000 homes to a single new entity, Glasgow Housing Association, it incorporated an aspiration for an array of second stage transfers to progressively dismember the association into over 60 local entities. However, as discussed in Chapter 3, the realization of this plan has proved highly problematic – mainly due to the inadequate financial provision within the original transfer business plan (see also Pawson et al. 2009, Pawson, 2009b).

Governance models: community empowerment

A somewhat distinct post-transfer governance agenda has also been evident in Wales. This reflects the political priority attached to community empowerment and a perception that existing transfer models have given insufficient attention to this (CCH 1999, Bromiley et al. 2004). As noted earlier, however, the lack of emphasis on recruiting a mass membership for transfer I&P societies was more a product of implementation than the model itself, which assumes board accountability to a (potentially mass) shareholding membership. Following from this critique, Welsh Ministers have advocated a 'community housing mutual' (CHM) model for transfer landlords. This involves ownership of ex-local authority housing passing to the tenants, collectively, via a new landlord entity where tenants are the only shareholders. Indeed, a key feature of the CHM format is that all tenants are members (unless they decline to join). It is on this basis that CHM advocates argue that, under these arrangements, a stock transfer portfolio is 'sold to the tenants and not to a third party company or housing association' (Waite 2008: 3).

However, while the CHM model has been promoted as a 'Welsh solution', it should be recognized that only five of the first nine stock transfer associations established in Wales have in fact been set up on this basis. Also, in parallel, a very similar 'bottom-up' style of stock transfer has been developed in England in the shape of the community gateway model (CIH 2002a). Like its community housing mutual counterpart, the gateway format has a strong participative theme and an emphasis on decentralization of decision-making and control to the neighbourhood level. Also critical within the CG model as originally developed by the Confederation of Co-operative Housing (CCH), was the commitment to heavy investment in community capacity building. Arguably, this has been less prominent within the CHM model.

The first community gateway stock transfer was completed in Preston in 2005. While the aim of mass membership is shared with the community housing mutual model, Preston's Community Gateway Association opted for rules where tenants would need to make a positive choice to join. Nevertheless, by 2009, some 2,500 members had been enrolled – around 40 per cent of tenants. While governed by a tri-partite board, the Preston Gateway Association has established an elected Gateway Tenants Committee charged with representing tenants to the board and electing tenant board members. All board reports are first considered by the GTC. The Association has defined 10 'local community areas' as its managerial and participative framework. By 2009, three other community gateway-style transfer landlords had been established elsewhere in England. Importantly, however, not all of these had involved investment in community capacity building on the scale seen in Preston.

Post-transfer social housing governance in practice: tensions played out

Empowering tenants?

Arguably one of the most novel and striking aspects of stock transfer has been the involvement of tenants in post-transfer organizational governance. While direct evidence is far more limited, much the same could probably be said of ALMOs (see Chapter 8). How far such measures have resulted in genuine – and lasting – tenant empowerment has been an important bone of contention in political debates around stock transfer (see Chapter 4). Most of the research attention here has concentrated on tenants' role as board members and this is the main focus of the following discussion. Importantly, however, many transfer landlords have developed a range of other mechanisms and frameworks to facilitate tenant influence over organizational decision-making. Some of these are discussed at the end of this section.

As regards the formal 'governorship' of social housing, the routine inclusion of tenants as governing body members marks a clear change from the local authority housing model. While some local authorities experimented with the co-option of tenants onto housing committees during the 1980s and 1990s, this was never a widespread phenomenon. Similarly, only in Scotland has it been common practice for tenants to be substantially represented on governing bodies of longer-established, non-LSVT, housing associations. Survey evidence for England implies that as recently as 2003, tenant board members accounted for less than five per cent of all traditional association governing bodies members (Cairncross and Pearl 2003).

Constituting transfer landlord boards with at least a third of seats reserved for tenants has been widely presented as a means of bringing social housing closer to the communities it serves. The model attempts to compensate for what was described by Skelcher (1998) as the glaring 'democratic deficit' resulting from the removal of public services such as social housing from oversight by elected councillors. However, while Skelcher's argument clearly has force, it is fair to question how effectively the traditional framework has provided tenants with a real say on the running of council housing. Equally, given the typically low turnouts at local authority elections (especially in areas with large amounts of social housing) the electoral legitimacy of local authorities is weaker than once was the case.

Putting such arguments to one side, nonetheless, tenant board members are thus seen as bringing consumer values and a sense of legitimacy to the restructuring of social housing (Maltby 2003). Practically, however, as emphasized by Bradley (2008) tenants' role here is 'ambiguous and contested'. The 'ambiguity' of the tenant board member role stems, in part, from the already mentioned regulatory guidance which stresses that board members (whether tenants or local authority nominees) must accept an obligation to prioritize the interests of the organization rather than acting as agents of their constituency (Housing Corporation 1998). Within such a 'neutral allegiance model' (McDermont et al. 2009), tenant (and councillor) board members become 'representatives without the means to represent' (Clapham and Kintrea 2000: 547). Hence, tenant (and councillor) board members are required to avoid not only any form of 'mandating' by their 'constituency' group, but also any organized 'bloc voting' or other factional behaviour.

How do such observations and rules square with empirical evidence on the role of tenant board members? While substantially represented on most transfer landlord boards, tenant members have rarely played a leading (i.e. chairing) role. Significant exceptions have included Glasgow Housing Association where tenant convenorship is a constitutional requirement. Implicitly acknowledging the 'ambiguity' point outlined above, an argument voiced by a managerial interview in our 2003 research was that such a role would place a tenant director incumbent in an 'over-exposed' position.

Our own research has brought to light perceptions that – not simply as a consequence of their typical status as 'backbench' members – tenant directors have sometimes played only a very limited part in transfer association board decision-making. In one case study association from our 2003 study, for example, a senior manager reported tenant directors as having made little contribution, with 'several of them never opening their mouths once in four years'. In another association, there was concern that they remained 'very much the silent partners' in terms of active involvement in decision-making. While many associations profess to have invested considerable sums in training tenant directors, these have not always been found to have a transformative impact.

More positively, another study focusing on stock transfer landlords and ALMOs found that tenant board members were willing to accept the dominance of the commercial discourse and did not appear to see this as negating their own opportunities for influence in 'championing a tenant identity' (Bradley 2008). Moreover, tenant directors 'actively sought out tenants' views in order to inform the board's policy making and, at a neighbourhood level, used their influence to pioneer a participatory approach to decision-making' (ibid: 893). In the midst of a debate where empirical research evidence remains very limited, this could be seen as important backing for the view that tenant directors can, indeed, participate effectively within the stakeholder model of organizational governance.

Nevertheless, our own research findings have been more consistent with those of an official study which found tenant directors often reluctant to conform to the demands of strategic governance in their tendency to focus on 'estate-level issues' at committee meetings, seen by Chief Executives as properly concentrating exclusively on wider issues (Audit Commission, 2004a). Similar evidence was found in a small-scale case study of a Tenant Management Organization (Mullins 2003) which found a tendency for 'reverse delegation' of strategic matters to paid staff while tenant board members focused their attention on more immediate and operational issues. In comparing TMOs with housing association group structures, this small study concluded that governance structures were not necessarily the most important determinant of active involvement of residents in different types of decisions.

Although not exclusively concerned with their role in stock transfer housing associations, proposed solutions to tensions around the role of tenant board members have included:

- Selection by interview rather than election (Audit Commission 2004b)
- Wholesale rejection of tenant board membership as incompatible with efficient business operations (Appleyard 2006)
- Involving tenants as directors only with respect to organizations with a direct service delivery remit rather than those with a strategic role (Elton 2006).

Central government has remained officially supportive of tenant board membership as a key component of the stakeholder governance model. Behind the scenes, however, (perhaps influenced by the Appleyard critique – see above) Bradley reports that English Ministers have been more ambivalent on the issue. Citing evidence from the Tenant Participation Advisory Service (Morgan 2006), Bradley reports that in 2006 the government 'seriously considered removing tenants from the management boards of social housing organisations' (Bradley 2008: 884).

Reviewing relevant evidence from a more theoretical perspective, McKee and Cooper (2008) observed that tenants accepting the opportunity to become board members effectively need to trade off any resulting empowerment for the restrictions and responsibilities that come as part of the package. In this Foucauldian view, such 'tenant involvement' as initiated via stock transfer is properly conceptualized as 'responsibilization'. Seen from a social constructionist standpoint, Bradley argues that critical perspectives wrongly view housing associations as 'fixed and given structures to which individuals must adapt'. Instead, he argues that tenant directors should be recognized as 'contributors to the construction of meaning in housing organisations rather than . . . problematic individuals who have failed to slot into their defined roles' (ibid: 880).

As noted at the start of this section, tenant board membership has constituted only one means by which transfer landlords have attempted to facilitate tenant involvement. Arguably, other techniques and frameworks have actually been more significant. These can be divided into 'consumerist' or 'choice' initiatives on the one hand, and representative or 'voice' mechanisms on the other. As also discussed in Chapter 6, there has been a widespread aspiration to operate in a more 'customer friendly' way than the former local authority housing department. Hence, the stress on developing customer-feedback mechanisms such as surveys, focus groups and panels, as well as techniques such as tenant-led inspection and mystery shopping.

Initiatives to facilitate tenants' 'voice' have typically included convening annual tenants conferences, assistance (including funding) for registered tenants' organizations, and the establishment of representative forums at estate, neighbourhood or borough-wide level. The Preston Gateway Tenants Committee – see above – is a radical interpretation of this.

Our research suggests that, at the very least, many such developments have been stimulated by stock transfer – both through the process of preparing for the transaction and through the typical zeal of the new organization to distinguish itself from its predecessor landlord. Equally, there is a strong sense in some transfer landlords that the novelty of the new regime is not simply the increased range of channels for tenant influence but the higher status accorded to the messages evoked.

Having said this, it is important to acknowledge that not all of these developments are unique to transfer landlords. Indeed, in many respects they have probably been paralleled by trends across social housing – particularly among ALMOs. To some extent, therefore, the moves described above are likely to be a microcosm of governance developments taking place across the sector over the past two decades.

It is also fair to ask how far any such changes are sustainable into the future. While acknowledging stock transfer as a stimulus to tenant empowerment, Ginsburg (2005) rightly warns that such gains as registered in a transfer landlord's early years 'may be much harder to sustain in the longer term' (ibid: 132). Indeed, many landlords would accept that, having eliminated sub-standard property and improved day-to-day services, retaining tenant enthusiasm for participation is a major challenge.

Councillor participation on governing bodies

Like their tenant board member counterparts, councillor board members have usually participated on governing bodies as 'backbenchers', although there have been examples of councillors successfully sustaining the role of Chair and embedding their associations in local governance networks over extended periods. More commonly, however councillors may be nominated to housing association boards for limited terms of office (see below). A housing association's need to demonstrate 'independence' could also mitigate against councillor chairpersonship. An additional issue for some is that this might be seen as inappropriate in instances where a transfer landlord is active outside the boundaries of its original local authority.

Some of the ambiguities characteristic of the role of tenant directors are also true for councillors. In particular, like their tenant counterparts, councillors are liable to face conflicts of loyalty between the constituency they 'represent' and the organization they govern. Particularly in the early phase of a transfer landlord's existence, experience shows that there is a high risk of such conflicts leading to problematic board operation.

Rochester and Hutchison (2002: 17) report observing 'two extreme kinds of [local authority] reaction to the transfer process'. Some saw the transfer as marking the termination of their responsibility for housing in any form, whilst 'others [are] "in denial": their representatives on the transfer association board continued to act as if little has changed'. Echoing this latter sentiment, many English transfer landlords in our 2003 study had experienced an initial period where local authority 'representatives' acted as though association board meetings ought to be conducted just as those of the predecessor local authority: stances on any question would, for example, be determined by reference to party decisions as agreed in advance.

Respecting confidentiality has also been a common flashpoint (see Box 5.1). In one case study association a 'communications protocol' had been established as a guide for councillor board members confused about their respective loyalties. Reportedly, what is seen as inappropriately assertive council board member behaviour in the early life of some transfer landlords tends to generate alliances between tenant 'representatives' and 'independents'.

Seen from the perspective of senior managers and other board members, a common frustration about councillors is their reportedly limited commitment to their board member role. However, statistical evidence does not support claims of inconsistent councillor board attendance (Pawson and Fancy 2003: 28). A more valid complaint may be that local authority representation lacks continuity and that this impedes efforts to train nominees and to inculcate 'housing association values and norms'. Here, survey evidence from our 2003 study did appear to substantiate concerns about 'high turnover'.

Given their typical position as sitting councillors, the term of housing association office of a council nominee board member may be interrupted by a change in party control, by personal electoral defeat or simply the operation of traditional 'rotational' systems for determining local authority representation on outside bodies. In response, some transfer associations have sought Council commitment to three-year councillor board member terms. While regulatory rules allow for the possibility that nominees might be local authority staff or former councillors such practice has been rare.

Despite their typically rather high turnover rates there is evidence that councillors quite often 'go native' to the extent that they progressively transfer their prime loyalty from the local authority to the association (Mullins 1996). This is consistent with the finding that they commonly see their role as 'representing the housing association to the local authority' (Audit Commission 2002: 44).

Evolving organizational forms and governance frameworks

Constitutional restructuring, organisational size and form

As registered housing associations, transfer landlords are part of a sector which has seen substantial restructuring over the past 10–20 years (Mullins 1999 and 2000; Mullins and Craig 2005). Such change has involved both intra-organizational consolidation and the agglomeration of previously unrelated bodies, including the rise of national 'supergroups' with ownership portfolios exceeding those of all but a handful of local authorities. One impact of such changes has been the 50 per cent increase in the average size of associations registered in England in the six years to 2007 (Pawson and Sosenko 2008).

Relevant here is the implication of pre-2004 government rules that transfers should facilitate the breakup of large municipal housing departments. Partly to this end, a ceiling on the size of post-transfer landlords was originally set for transfers in England and Wales in 1993. The threshold – 5,000 dwellings – reflected the government's wish 'to avoid the risk that future transfers will perpetuate a local monopoly by creating a single new predominant landlord in an area' (DoE 1992: 7). Underlying this was 'an assumption that smaller landlords would be more efficient and would provide a greater element of consumer choice' (Malpass and Mullins 2002: 677).

Recognizing that the size limit was acting as a deterrent to some authorities contemplating transfer, the threshold was raised to 12,000 in 1996, a figure which remained current in England until its abolition in 2004. During this period, the limit compelled a number of large urban authorities – notably Bradford, Coventry, Sunderland and Walsall – to structure their transfers such that portfolios were geographically split across two or more individually registered successor landlord entities. Reflecting municipal inclinations to retain a semblance of unity, these 'local companies' were linked together in city-wide group structures. For the authorities, this was seen as a second-best option, in that it entailed 'unnecessary' duplication of functions and the loss of scale economies.

The removal of the size limit in 2004 facilitated a few transfers involving larger successor landlords such as the 2005 transaction conveying all Wakefield's 32,000 homes to a new body, Wakefield & District Housing Trust. More importantly, it allowed the Housing Corporation to consent to the consolidation of successor landlord group structures back into city-wide entities – as in Bradford, Coventry and Sunderland (in each case under new names disconnected from locality). Perhaps of more importance for the future, it removed any bar to the regulator in consenting to group structure or merger proposals agglomerating transfer landlords within larger groups or entities.

As shown in Table 5.1, the 'group consolidations' mentioned above have involved just a small proportion of the multiple 'constitutional change transactions' in which English transfer landlords have engaged in recent years. As a class, transfer landlords have, in fact, been the most active participants in this process (Pawson and Sosenko 2008). As indicated in Table 5.1, most of this activity has involved setting up or joining group structures and there have been few 'full mergers'. For example, of 154 transfer associations set up as independent entities between 1988 and 2007, just over half (84) retained this status in 2007. Forty-nine had come together with other landlords although in only eight cases had this involved a full merger such that the transfer landlord was entirely absorbed within the partner organization. Significantly, however, more than half of the 59 transfer landlords established as 'free-standing' entities in England from 1988–97 had, by 2007, merged with others (6) or joined a group structure as a subsidiary unit (28) (Pawson et al. 2009).

As in the sector more broadly, a number of drivers underlie the appetite for the constitutional changes enumerated in Table 5.1. In a few cases, such moves have reflected weaknesses in original business plans which left associations subsequently in need of 'rescue' by a (financially) more robust partner. Probably more common has been the opposite scenario, where a transfer landlord's long-term financial prospects – its capacity to generate ongoing revenue surpluses – is seen as attractive to potential suitors (see Chapter 3).

A distinct form of constitutional change highlighted in Table 5.1 is the establishment of an 'internal group'. This has often been associated with aspirations for 'business diversification' into activities such as commercial property management, development of low- cost market housing or social enterprise. Another very specific form of 'diversification' relevant in a few cases has been where a transfer landlord seeks to position itself to take on a new landlord subsidiary via a future stock transfer. Moves of this kind have often been seen as timely at the point where a transfer landlord has completed the stock overhaul programme specified in its original commitments (usually after five years). As they approach this point, many associations have recognized the need to seek out 'new business' so as to capitalize on the project management, property development and financial planning skills they have needed to develop in delivering the initial 'promises programme'. Put another way, attraction of 'new business' is essential if the organization is to

TABLE 5.1 *Constitutional changes of English stock transfer housing associations*

Original status when established, 1988 to 2007	Constitutional change type					Total
	None – remained as at set-up	Established internal group	Joined group as subsidiary	Merged		
				Group consolidation*	Other	
Independent housing association	84	21	41		8	154
Subsidiary of existing housing association	34				3	37
Subsidiary of new housing association	7			13		20
Grand total	125	21	41	13	11	211

*With respect to group parent body as at transfer.

Sources: authors' analysis of Regulatory and Statistical Return (RSR) data; kind assistance also provided by Housing Corporation regional office staff.

avoid shrinking its operations and the risk of staff redundancies.

Business efficiency and local accountability: competing institutional logics?

Constitutional change transactions which involve associations coming together with others through mergers or group structure establishment contribute to the sector-wide trend towards organizational agglomeration (Mullins and Craig 2005, Pawson and Sosenko 2008). As we have discussed elsewhere (Mullins 2006), such moves can be attributed largely to the 'institutional logic' of scale and efficiency in a world where associations must operate as commercially astute organizations and where they are under constant regulatory pressure to deliver more for less. In this section we look, in turn, at organizational and governance restructuring guided largely by a 'business efficiency' model, and at an example of 're-constitution' driven mainly by a priority for greater local accountability. This discussion leads to the final main section of the chapter which analyses accountability impacts of the transfer process.

'Efficiencies' potentially realizable through group consolidation may be partly about scale economies. Complementary attractions may include reduced tax exposure (VAT, corporation tax, stamp duty) as well as cutting the regulatory burden (a single set of landlord returns).

Associated with the institutional logic of 'business efficiency' is the adoption of governance structures more akin to those of the commercial (profit-maximizing) world. Some large housing associations have flirted with the idea of pushing to establish themselves on a public limited company basis – a move confidently predicted as inevitable by one informed observer (McIntosh 2007). However, this would have far-reaching ramifications and could be achieved only through fundamental changes to the regulatory and public finance regimes.

More modestly (and in common with their 'traditional associations'), many stock transfer landlords have been seeking to develop more 'professionalized' governance arrangements. Key features of the model include the clearer differentiation of 'strategic' and 'operational' decision-making, sometimes leading to a tiered governance framework with a relatively small 'business board' at its apex. This kind of forum differs from the typical board as established at transfer in that it is likely to be smaller (perhaps 6–10 members rather than 15–18), and not structured on a 'constituency basis'. Following the prescription of Elton (2006) – see above – continuing involvement in governance on the part of tenants and councillors may be mainly via a subordinate 'operational' forum.

Whether or not within the context of the kind of structure described above, board member payment is often seen as another hallmark of moving to 'more businesslike' form of governance. Here we refer to a landmark change in the Housing Corporation regulatory regime introduced in England in 2003 and which allows housing associations to 'opt for' board member payment (Ayton 2004). In Scotland, by contrast, the (then) regulator, Communities Scotland, in 2005 rejected calls for a similar change on the basis of research evidence suggesting the balance of opinion within the sector was strongly opposed (Communities Scotland 2005, Pawson et al. 2005b).

The Corporation's decision marked the conclusion of a long-running and fairly polarized debate. Advocates for change had argued that, given the status of many housing associations as multi-million pound businesses, there was a need for stronger and more professional corporate oversight. Echoing the conclusions of the Cadbury Enquiry (1992), such a change was seen as essential to curb what Greer and Hogget (2000) termed 'the hegemony of the executive' (ibid: 514). Defenders of the status quo pointed out that such a change – even on an 'opting in' basis – would render obsolete the term 'voluntary housing' and damage the housing association brand.

Even by 2006 – only three years into the new regime – Housing Corporation RSR data showed that almost a quarter of English associations (excluding those with less than 1,000 dwellings) had already opted for board member payment. It should, however, be noted that these data do not differentiate between associations paying all board members and those where only board chairs received payment. As a class of association, transfer landlords were only slightly less likely to have adopted board member payment than traditional housing associations. Among longer-established transfer bodies the incidence of board member payment was higher than the national norm. Evidence from the Second Generation study suggests that the end of the 'promises period has been a time when many organisations have considered board member payment and a significant proportion have opted in favour – albeit usually limiting remuneration to the board chair rather than extending to all members (Pawson et al. 2009).

More recent evidence for the housing association sector as a whole suggests that the incidence of board member payment has continued to grow, with the proportion of associations having opted for payment rising to 39 per cent by 2009 (Insight 2009). Another recent survey found that the paid board member model was especially prevalent among transfer associations. Among associations classed as 'independent stock transfer' bodies 41 per cent had opted for payments by 2008 – somewhat above the national norm of 35 per cent (Ferman and Appleby 2009).

Clearly, the question of board member payment has proved contentious at the national level and it remains controversial within housing associations themselves. Similarly, the sector, as a whole, continues to grapple with tensions between the business efficiency model and the priority on local accountability. The importance of this latter objective has been re-emphasized by the 'trade body' for the sector, the NHF through its In Business for Neighbourhoods initiative which committed adopters to investing in a range of non-housing services and to becoming 'community builders' rather than 'builders in communities'. Important components of the case for housing associations playing a significant role in community-based neighbourhood governance are (a) associations' scale and asset strength relative to other community and voluntary agencies, and (b) associations' long-term financial stake in neighbourhoods. The scale and nature of associations' community focused activity over and above landlord functions is reflected in a recently published analysis (NHF 2008b). 'Community regeneration' activity stimulated by stock transfers is further discussed in Chapter 7.

Within the cohort of transfer landlords, the 'community accountability' dynamic has tended to be strongest among those established through smaller, urban 'partial transfers' such as those carried through under the 1998–2000 Estates Renewal Challenge Fund (Pawson et al. 2005b), as well as some of the more recent transfers set up on the Community Gateway or

Box 5.2   Castle Vale housing association: governance and accountability features

Castle Vale Community Housing Association (CVCHA) is a community based, resident-led housing association. It was established as part of the succession of the Castle Vale Housing Action Trust (CVHAT) that dominated the regeneration of this peripheral housing estate on the north east of Birmingham between 1993 and 2005. CVCHA was formed in 1997 to manage property built by the HAT's housing association development partners. By 2008, CVCHA was managing some 2,400 homes.

The nature of the association and the way it operates is part of an approach to rebuilding the estate that has its roots in the CVHAT experiment. Relatively early in the life of the HAT there was a focus on a broad approach to social and economic as well as physical regeneration and the CVCHA has been part of this legacy (Sullivan et al. 2000). CVCHA's board has 15 members, eight of whom are elected directly or indirectly from tenants or residents on the estate. Five are elected tenants of the Association, with three being elected members of the Tenants and Residents Association who are delegated to the board. Board members have three-year terms and must stand down after three terms. As a measure of the organization's vitality, the elections of tenant board members have typically been contested.

Community engagement techniques and practices employed by CVCHA have included newsletters, a 'democracy day', a youth council and a tenants and residents forum, as well as capacity building and associated resident training.

A vox pop survey (conducted and designed by residents of the estate) asked other residents 'do you think residents have been involved in improving the estate'; nearly eight out of 10 of 188 respondents said they thought they had. One quote from a range of largely (but not entirely) positive views sums up the changes: 'Residents are not the lapdogs anymore – they are the watchdogs' (Beazley et al. 2004).

Community Mutual models (see above). Many other (mainly larger) transfer landlords have 'given a nod' to such concerns through the setting up of area committees and the like. An example of such a 'community-based' transfer association of

Box 5.3   Glasgow housing association and the role of Local Housing Organizations

While possessing superficial resemblance to a 'group structure' the organizational form determined for Glasgow's 2003 stock transfer was unique. While authorizing the handover of the Council's 80,000 homes to a single body, Glasgow Housing Association, the then housing minister, Wendy Alexander, portrayed the move as just the first step towards a number of 'second stage transfers' . Within a decade, SSTs to CBHAs would replace the Glasgow Housing Association as a landlord body.

The transferred stock was designated into over 60 geographical units supposedly destined for subsequent disposal to new owners – a mix of newly created and existing CBHAs. In the meantime, housing management functions were to be delegated to Local Housing Organizations (LHOs) set up as the putative recipients of second stage transfer stock packages. With their own resident-majority committees, LHOs can be seen as a semi-autonomous lower tier of governance within the overall GHA structure. Formally, their relationship with Glasgow Housing Association as a corporate body is a contractual agreement (under Ministerial direction) to discharge defined management functions.

In a managerial sense, LHO managers' dual accountability to their own committees and to Glasgow Housing Association headquarters management placed them in an unusual position. Regulatory encouragement to LHOs to emphasize their distinct character (consistent with their official status as independent 'management only'

➡

this kind is detailed in Box 5.2. However, perhaps the prime – albeit unique – example of a large organization structured to prioritize local accountability is Glasgow Housing Association – see Box 5.3.

Accountability Impacts

The concepts of governance and accountability are closely linked and, while the preceding discussion has focused primarily on the former, it has raised many implications for the housing associations) is seen as having compounded inherent tendencies for a 'them and us' mentality (where 'them' is GHA headquarters). From a local accountability viewpoint, there have undoubtedly been tensions between LHO committees' desire for influence over modernization programmes and the GHA headquarters priority on maximizing efficiency and speed through bulk procurement and standardization.

Particularly given the long-drawn out process of attempting to progress second stage transfers, the tensions inherent in this structure have proved highly problematic. Crucially, it was made known to the wider public only in 2005 that the original GHA business plan had lacked provision for what were very significant costs associated with second stage transfers. (The underlying financial factors involved here are discussed in more detail in Chapter 3 – see Box 3.3.) Aside from the shortfall in financing, the logistical complexities of implementing SSTs have proved formidable (McKee 2009).

Only in 2009 did the first six second stage transfers (involving some 2,000 homes) take place, following strong support in respective tenant ballots. At this time, 31 organizations managing some 20,000 homes were continuing to progress through the second stage transfers process, with the aim of concluding the resulting transactions by 2011. At the time of writing it remains uncertain whether this will be the end of the process. However, given the apparent impossibility of progressing further second stage transfers without additional public funds it is very difficult to see how it could be otherwise.

latter. In this final main section of the chapter we focus more squarely on accountability issues arising from transfer as they relate to government, to private funders, to local authorities and to residents and communities. These four dimensions of accountability are considered in turn below.

Although stock transfer removes housing from state ownership, the influence of regulation is such that the process can be fairly portrayed as strengthening upward accountabilities to central government (Malpass 2001). Regulation has a pervasive influence on the sector, affecting both day-to-day practice and effecting transformational change. A good example of the former is the emergence of a 'mock inspection' industry enabling associations to align practice prior to Audit Commission Inspections. Regulatory intervention has also been a persistent driver of mergers in the sector (Mullins and Craig 2005). The sector's concerns over the reach and influence of regulation reached a climax in the debate accompanying the passage of the Housing and Regeneration Bill 2008 when critics led by the NHF argued that proposed new regulatory powers could place at risk the associations' legal status as 'non-public sector' bodies.

New accountabilities have been introduced as a result of the significant levels of private borrowing which have funded stock transfer transactions. By 2008, in England alone, transfers had 'levered in' over £19 billion in long-term investment in the form of loans from banks and building societies (Pawson et al. 2009). Lending covenants and credit ratings have become important foci of accountability for business planning and day-to-day operations of associations. Randolph (1993) highlighted the impact of the introduction of private finance for housing association strategies. Mullins et al. (1995) argued that the levels of debt managed by stock transfer housing associations meant that the business plan had become central to organizational life – a finding strongly confirmed by the authors' subsequent research.

Accountabilities to local communities have also been changed by the stock transfer process; many of the landlords created as a result have subsequently become less geographically rooted. For a number of the early transfer associations, this has come about as they have expanded their own stockholdings via 'out of area development' (Pawson and Fancy 2003). Similarly, as discussed above, the organizational evolution of many transfer associations has seen them initiating linkages with previously unrelated, remotely based, housing associations – through group structures or mergers. A specific 'accountability deficit' has become evident here as the absence of procedures for tenants to have a say on such constitutional changes contrasted with their experience in stock transfer ballots (Black, 2006). Concerns have also been raised about the lack of transparency of group parent organizations to tenants (Audit Commission 2001).

As also noted earlier in this chapter, the removal of housing provision from local government control was at the centre of debates about a 'democratic deficit' in local services (Davis and Spencer 1995). Less concern was initially expressed about the weakening local authority strategic capacity; for example, by loss of key intelligence sources such as housing registers, and the process described by one observer as 'intellectual asset stripping' through the running down of the tacit knowledge of local housing issues once held by key local authority personnel. But since 2000 there has been greater exhortation to local authorities to develop a strategic role, albeit without too many levers of power to do so (see Chapter 9).

As discussed in the earlier section on tenant involvement, attempts to enhance associations' accountability to residents have been made through a variety of mechanisms. Increasingly, among transfer landlords no less than traditional housing associations, consumerist approaches appear to be displacing formal representation of residents in governance as the main mechanisms for accountability. However, the value of more direct resident involvement has been reinforced by Audit Commission inspections that 'reality check' service delivery with residents and employ 'tenant inspectors' (Mullins and Murie 2006). In 2006 the Housing Corporation accepted a recommendation of the Elton Committee (2006) that 'as a matter of principle all associations should have at least one resident board member on each board or committee *responsible for delivering services*' (Elton 2006: 55, our emphasis), and that this should not be seen as a substitute for accountability or wider resident involvement. However, concerns previously raised by the Audit Commission (2001) about accountability of group parent boards to tenants suggest that the focus here on service delivery may be a significant limitation.

Chapter conclusions

Stock transfers have resulted in a profound shift in the governance of social housing. While, this involves the end of state ownership the emerging new landlords are certainly not free of state control. Arguably, the reach and influence of regulation and the removal of countervailing municipal influence means that transfer in fact amounts to a centralizing measure. More importantly, transfers are an element within a broader restructuring of the welfare state characterized by fragmentation and commercialization.

Largely in an effort to compensate for the resulting loss of accountability to the local electorate, most transfer landlords have been constituted according to the 'stakeholder governance' model. In this, they share features of other Public Interest Companies such as Network Rail, while being somewhat distinct from housing associations of the traditional kind (Maltby 2003). Emphasizing this distinction, transfer landlords are seen by Malpass (2001) as having little in common with 'third sector' traditions. Rather, they form 'part of a new quasi-public sector' (ibid: 11). This reflects their characterization as part of 'a shadow state apparatus' – i.e. organizations substantially influenced and steered by the state (Malpass 2001). Hence, as seen by Malpass, stock transfer landlords are, in essence, 'hived-off parts of the public sector' (ibid: 11). Therefore, they embody 'a sort of bogus voluntarism in which elected representatives and salaried officials create new, not-for-profit organisations from within the public sector' (ibid: 13). However, an alternative perspective would emphasize the tensions within hybrid organizations between market, state and society influences, and the opportunities provided by stakeholder governance models for these tensions to be worked out (Mullins and Sacranie 2009).

Some of our findings on the ways that the 'stakeholder governance' model has been interpreted in the context of transfer landlords are also likely to be applicable to ALMOs although anecdotal evidence suggests that tenant or councillor board member leadership may be much more common in the ALMO context. Like housing associations, ALMOs have (since 2005) been allowed to opt for board member payment (Wolch 1990) although – like many other aspects of ALMO operation – there is little or no published research on take-up or impacts.

However, it seems highly unlikely that ALMOs have been subject to anything approaching the amount of organizational and governance restructuring which has been seen among transfer landlords as many of the latter have looked to reposition themselves to take advantage of new 'business opportunities'. Many senior managers have become increasingly frustrated by the 'constituency-based' LHC governance model. For example, questions have been raised about the willingness of tenant governors to prioritize the long-term interests of the organization over short-term considerations (ODPM 2005).

Regulatory pressures to 'deliver more for less' have formed an impetus towards larger and more streamlined organizations with the resources and influence to compete and to operate efficiently (albeit the relationship between scale and efficiency is contested). Consequential reshaping of organizational and governance frameworks often amount to a dilution or disassembly of the original stakeholder model. At the same time, however, government has urged associations to become more locally responsive organizations, in touch with communities, providing opportunities for local residents to be at the heart of decision-making and willing to support less well resourced voluntary and community sector bodies and social enterprises. In these ways, the tensions between state, market and society influences are worked through in organizational practice.

The generally increasing accountability of associations to private funders explains the fairly widespread adoption of the scale and efficiency logic, and commercial behaviour such as streamlining of governance and chasing credit ratings. Meanwhile, the variable adoption of the local accountability logic can be related to the weaker and less universal accountability ties of associations to local authorities and communities. The origins of stock transfer associations are important in conditioning their responses to these competing pressures. By comparison with traditional associations (of comparable size), they are more likely to have institutionalized the logic of local accountability through their governance arrangements.

Chapter 6

Organizational and Cultural Change in Stock Transfer Landlords

Transfer as culture change

A powerful narrative depicts stock transfer as a journey from municipal paternalist culture to customer-focused, business-driven, performance culture. This can be seen in national policy documents supporting transfer as 'a substantive change of culture in the management of . . . housing' (DETR 2000b: 63). Albeit primarily motivated by financial drivers transfer is also seen as facilitating 'modernization' to improve service delivery. Mintzberg (1993), a pre-eminent management theorist, argues that an agency's performance failings may reflect a sub-optimal 'fit' between its form and culture, on the one hand, and the demands of its external environment, on the other. Hartley and Rashman (2002) follow this thinking in their work on stock transfer by emphasizing reform of organizational culture as the key to securing performance improvement.

To what extent might one expect transfer to be associated with organizational transformation? One factor which potentially militates against this outcome is the standard structural form adopted for transfers. As noted in Chapter 4, virtually every 'whole stock transfer' carried through in Britain has involved the establishment of a new landlord vehicle to take on ownership of the inherited property portfolio. In the vast majority of cases, these bodies have been set up as 'free-standing' entities controlled by a board with councillor as well as tenant and 'independent' representation (see Chapter 5). Also, as partly dictated by the TUPE regulations, all such new bodies have been initially staffed largely by employees of the former local authority housing department, together with other ex-council colleagues. And, while modern regulatory expecta-

170

tions have required that senior management positions in newly forming transfer housing associations must be subject to competition, founding chief executive officers of most such organizations have been the former local authority director of housing. Additionally, a transfer association remains a social landlord subject to regulatory expectations similar to those faced by a local authority landlord.

Given all of these circumstances, it is entirely reasonable to question whether the new landlord organizations are, in fact, any more than 'local authority housing departments in drag', as has sometimes been alleged. The name, the logo and the staff dress code might have changed but can the new organization be expected to embody a distinct form of organizational culture? Also highly relevant is the argument typically stressed by local authorities to evoke tenant support for a proposed transfer which emphasizes the extent to which the new body will provide continuity rather than change (see Chapter 4).

Early in the stock transfer process it was argued that transfer associations were likely to 'retain the ethos of the local authority housing department' (Cope 1999: 295). More recently, others have contended with greater force that transfer can be a case of 'the emperor's new clothes'. In reference to the 2003 Glasgow City Council transfer to Glasgow Housing Association, for example, it was claimed that the city housing department, 'which over the years invested so disastrously, and failed to manage its own staff...has been bailed out' (Robertson 2003). As a large landlord entity staffed by former council employees and taking ownership of the entire ex-local authority portfolio, Robertson saw the form and structure of the 'new' organization as guaranteeing retention of the ethos that created 'deserts wi windaes'. 'If we're going to put this money in and we're not changing the culture and the organisation which created this disastrous public spending fiasco, then what the hell has it been all about?', he demanded.

Of course, the likelihood is that transfer organizations will closely resemble 'parent' local authority housing departments at the outset, but the big questions are about the extent to which the new landlords evolve in the medium and longer term, and about the directions in which such evolution proceeds. To what extent, after five or more years, would it be true to say that transfer housing associations' ways of working remain highly resonant of municipal habits? Drawing largely on two major studies undertaken by the authors (Pawson and Fancy 2003, Pawson et al. 2009) this chapter analyses evidence on the organizational forms and cultures of transfer landlords and their evolution over time. These sources will be referred to as the 'Maturing Assets' research and the 'Second Generation' study. Both projects involved extensive case study work focusing on the ongoing development of transfer housing associations a few years into their existence. The staff focus group work included in the latter research makes it a particularly rich source of evidence in relation to the issues explored in this chapter.

The chapter is structured as follows. First, we discuss the term 'organizational culture' and its potential relevance to the stock transfer policy. Next, we focus on the ways that transfer housing association reforms to staff management have promoted and contributed to cultural change. This leads to a discussion about the ongoing development of transfer housing associations in relation to the concept of organizational life cycles. In the penultimate section of the chapter we look at two distinct organizational forms which have been developed within the cohort of stock transfer landlords – one emphasizing linkage with local communities and one borne of the high priority accorded to organizational growth and diversification. Finally, we draw together some conclusions about the cultural change implications of stock transfer.

Organizational culture and transfer housing association aspirations

Organizational culture can be defined as 'the basic assumptions and beliefs that are shared by members of the organisation, that operate unconsciously and define in a basic, taken-for-granted fashion, an organisation's view of itself and its environment' (Johnson and Scholes 2002: 45) or 'how things are done round here' (Hartley and Rashman 2002: 6). As characterized by Handy (1993), organizational cultures are 'deep set beliefs about the way work should be organised, the way authority should be exercised, people rewarded, people controlled' (181). An organization's culture reflects a shared view of corporate priorities and is evident from the ways that members behave. 'Strong pervasive cultures turn organisations into cohesive tribes with distinctly clannish feelings. The values and traditions of the tribe are reinforced by its private language, its catch-phrases and its tales of past heroes and dramas. The way of life is enshrined in rituals so that rule books and manuals are almost unnecessary; custom and tradition provide the answers' (Handy 1993: 183).

The importance of organizational culture in reforming public services is crystallized in the slogan 'culture eats structure for breakfast', emphasizing the need for managers of underperforming agencies to focus on changing the corporate mindset rather than solely on reshaping the hierarchy. Nevertheless, as emphasized in government-commissioned transfer guidance, these two concepts are closely linked. In the context of pretransfer planning, local authorities have been advised that organizational culture can be actively shaped by decisions about the structure of the transfer landlord. 'The design of the new organisation can be very significant in conveying messages about how far purposes, values and priorities remain the same or differ from those of the previous organisation' (Hartley and Rashman 2002: 4). Hence, 'the design of managerial structures can convey organisational values about the extent of hierarchy and autonomy, flexibility and management style . . . Flatter, team-based structures help to convey autonomy, delegated decision-making, participation and the promotion of learning' (ibid).

In analysing organizational cultures, Handy (1993) identified four ideal types:

- Power culture – a centralized model in which the culture depends on a central power source. With few rules and procedures 'power is exercised by the centre, largely through the selection of key individuals'. 'It is a political organisation in that decisions are taken very largely on the outcome of a balance of influence rather than on procedural or purely logical grounds' (184). Such cultures are highly dependent on key individuals.
- Role culture – a synonym for 'bureaucracy'. Such organizations operate by logic and rationality. Their strength is derived from their functional components – or departments.

Interaction within the organization is controlled via rules and procedures, with such interaction co-ordinated at the top by a 'narrow band of senior management' (185). Role organizations are effective in a stable environment – where the established rules of conduct can be relied upon to enable it to perform its functions. They are inflexible and poorly equipped for adaptation to changing circumstances.

- Task culture – a job, or product-oriented entity, structured as a matrix or net. The whole emphasis of the organization is on 'getting the job done'. The culture emphasizes 'groups, expert power, rewards for results, merging individual and group objectives' (189), where influence is based more on personal expertise rather than personal position. It is a team culture where the shared enterprise in addressing the key task unifies the group. The model is adaptable and provides individuals with a high degree of control over their work. Centralized control – e.g. where senior management attempts to prescribe methods as well as goals – is antithetical to the norms of the task culture.

- Person culture – a culture which treats individuals as its 'central point'. It prevails in organizations which exist 'only for the people [within them] . . . without any super-ordinate objective' (190). Within such entities control mechanisms cannot be imposed; they are possible only by mutual consent.

In Handy's estimation, most organizations are either 'role cultures' or 'task cultures'. The aspiration to replace a role culture with a task culture has been explicit for many transfer housing association senior managers. This has been especially true among managers in new landlords taking on property (and staff) from the larger, urban authorities which have accounted for an appreciable proportion of post-1997 transactions (see Chapter 2). With its focus on these landlords, the Second Generation research found that senior managers commonly saw their organization as needing to replace a hierarchical, 'command and control' ethos with customer-focused, inclusive ways of working. Much of this could be seen as about adopting aspects of the so-called New Public Management (Walsh 1995, Clarke and Newman 1997). For many transfer housing association senior managers, key aspirations here have included:

- Improved staff understanding of – and commitment to – organizational goals
- Developing a more responsible, motivated workforce
- Promotion of a more business-minded way of thinking throughout the organization
- Adoption of a 'customer service ethic' on the part of front-line staff and managers
- A greater emphasis on 'investing in people' and the development of flatter, less hierarchical structures and more inclusive ways of working.

Hartley and Rashman's (2002) reference to 'the promotion of learning' (see above) alludes to the concept of a 'learning organisation'. An organization qualifying for this title was defined by Reid and Hickman (2002) as one 'embod[ying] an organisational learning culture, and where, on the basis of what is learned by staff about the operational life of the organisation, continuous improvements in the way things are done are encouraged and supported' (897). Referring to Deming (1986), Reid and Hickman argued that social landlord aspirations to become 'learning organisations' were closely linked with the view that improving service quality implied a need for '"learning through feedback" as a kind of collective, company enterprise' (ibid: p.897).

Later in this chapter we explore the ways in which stated aspirations around cultural change as discussed above have been implemented in practice within the stock transfer context. To set this in context, however, we must acknowledge that – within social housing – such goals have not been the exclusive preserve of transfer housing associations. To varying degrees, many such 'cultural reform' objectives have been seen as attractive and relevant by managers of other types of social landlord organizations (including those responsible for 'retained council housing'). Nevertheless, partly because of the stimulus potentially resulting from 'transfer events' and partly because of the greater managerial autonomy enjoyed by senior staff in the housing association context, it seems possible that such changes will have been implemented more quickly and in more far-reaching ways by transfer landlords.

In the next section we look at the ways that the 'cultural change' aspirations as defined above (see bullet points) have been implemented in practice by transfer landlords, and at the extent to which such actions have proved effective.

Implementation of 'culture change' reforms

Securing greater staff 'buy-in'

Echoing Handy's characterization of 'task culture' (see above) it has been widely recognized by transfer housing association senior managers that promoting a common sense of purpose and organizational cohesion is essential in securing greater staff buy-in for corporate objectives. As argued by management strategists, internal communications can have a key role here. For many transfer landlords this has been reflected in a strong emphasis on internal communications – e.g. through staff newsletters, policy briefings, corporate conferences and the like.

At the same time, however, reflecting the interpretation of management theorists, Johnson and Scholes (2002), it has often been appreciated that 'better communication' should be about more than simply the effective top-down promotion of a corporate ideology. Channels for feedback are important so that more junior staff have the opportunity to react to, and communicate with, senior managers about organizational change. Highly relevant here is the Taper et al. (2003) finding that the proportion of transfer landlord staff reporting their employer as providing them with opportunities to articulate 'how they feel about how things affect them at work' was 21 percentage points higher than the public sector norm, and 19 per cent higher than the comparable figure for local authority staff (ibid: 26).

As demonstrated by both the Maturing Assets and Second Generation research, the management style described by Johnson and Scholes as 'walking the talk' has been observed in many transfer landlords, with the visibility and accessibility of senior officers often greatly increased as compared with pre-transfer norms. Revealingly, the Second Generation research showed that in post-1997 transfer housing associations it had generally become standard practice for staff (no matter how junior) to address managers (no matter how senior) on first name terms. One staff interviewee commented on the contrast with the pre-transfer experience of being expected to address the Borough Treasurer as 'sir'.

All of this connects with the aspiration to foster a more inclusive, bottom-up culture where workforce consultation is a standard element of the policy development process and where staff are encouraged to think creatively and to (constructively) criticize existing organizational practice. Again, evidence from frontline staff focus groups convened in the Second Generation research suggests that such objectives have been substantially realized by many transfer landlords. By comparison with the situation under former local authority control, staff felt they were more liable to be asked their opinions (and listened to) by senior management, as well as being more encouraged to think more creatively and 'outside of the box'. In a number of transfer organizations, staff reported being called on to suggest organizational and policy changes and, where these were implemented, being rewarded for innovative thinking.

For a number of the Second Generation case study landlords an important aspect of creating a more cohesive organization had involved the post-transfer integration of blue collar staff into the existing white collar structure of employment terms and conditions. In some cases, this led to the replacement of traditional craft operative bonus-related pay frameworks with fixed salaries and contractual terms comparable with those of office-based staff. An important implication of such changes was the replacement of a model largely reliant on pay incentives to maximize operational performance with one stressing the primacy of professional management. Changes of this kind were seen as posing a degree of risk because of staff resistance to change as well as the possibility that they might lead to reduced productivity. At the same time, however, it was believed that such reforms could demonstrate the organization's commitment to its employees and help to create a more cohesive body by addressing the 'them and us' relationship which has traditionally pervaded the interaction between housing management and repairs staff.

Most Second Generation staff focus group participants saw their organizations as significantly more cohesive and less fractured than their council housing department predecessors. However, such stresses had not entirely disappeared. In a small minority of the case studies a sense of 'them and us' (management vs. staff, headquarters vs. local offices) reportedly remained significant. In one organization, in particular, tension between headquarters and outlying offices was reported as not only remaining evident but to have become significantly sharper since transfer and this was associated with a prevailing view that (unlike all other landlords in the study) the transfer housing association in question had become more secretive and more 'political' than the former city council housing department. Nevertheless, the unusual circumstances in which this association operated and its unique structure help to explain these observations and limit their relevance for stock transfer associations in general.

Other research evidence appears to confirm a typically substantial degree of 'staff buy-in' for corporate objectives within transfer housing associations. As reported by Taper et al. (2003), transfer landlord staff had a 'high degree of understanding of their employer's objectives' (2003: 9) with 69 per cent stating that these were understood (31 per cent higher than the local authority norm and 16 per cent higher than the norm for the public sector, as a whole).

A key factor in all this is the distinction between a transfer housing association and a local authority housing department in that the former is a single purpose organization with a clearly defined remit (especially in its initial 'promises period'), whereas the latter is part of a larger body with a wide range of responsibilities and subject to a wide range of pressures – both political and financial. This aspect of the switch from local authority to housing association employment has been viewed as attractive by many of the managers and staff concerned. One interpretation would be that this reflects perceptions of the improved scope for professionalism and clarity of purpose under the post-transfer framework – hence, the higher incidence of staff understanding and identifying with 'corporate objectives'. However, in policy terms at least, the advantages of single purpose organizations have been increasingly questioned as the growing regeneration focus of transfer policy and action consequent upon the spread of transfer to more challenging areas (see Chapter 7) which has emphasized joined up governance, whole systems thinking and 'place leadership' (Gibney et al. 2009) rather than function-based silos.

Motivating and up-skilling the workforce

Linked with the aim of securing greater staff commitment to organizational goals, many transfer housing associations have sought to evoke greater workforce motivation. In securing improved performance in delivering a complex service, better adherence to instructions and rules will never be enough. Many of the transfer housing association senior managers interviewed in the Second Generation study professed to place greater value on staff management and on the organization's staff as its key resource (by comparison with the pre-transfer scenario). As in the Maturing Assets research, many senior managers asserted that their association's commitment to management (as well as staff) training was substantially greater than that of the pre-transfer local authority (see below). This could entail a more inclusive approach to decision-making, more trusting relationships between managers and staff – e.g. allowing staff to make responsible use of office telephones for personal calls (officially outlawed under council management), and abolishing inflexible rules for compassionate leave.

To a much greater extent than is typical in a local authority setting, managerial leadership has tended to play a key role in motivating staff in many transfer housing associations. This reflects the linkage drawn by management theorists between the quality and style of leadership and an organization's culture. Schein (1992) argued that culture and leadership were 'conceptually intertwined', emphasizing the critical role of strong leaders in the early phases of an organization's existence, when its ways of thinking and its commonly held assumptions are being defined and developed. While these observations were made in relation to start-up private companies, they nonetheless appear relevant to the stock transfer housing association case.

Schein identified six 'culture embedding' mechanisms associated with leadership:

- what leaders pay attention to, measure and control on a regular basis
  how leaders react to critical incidents and organizational crises
- observed criteria by which leaders allocate scarce resources

- deliberate role modelling, teaching and coaching
- observed criteria by which leaders allocate rewards and status
- observed criteria by which leaders recruit, promote, select and excommunicate organizational members (ibid: 231).

Part of this is about recognizing the potential significance of leadership as a key aspect of the manager's role – something which has perhaps been traditionally downplayed in the local authority context. Many interviewees in the Second Generation research referred to the inspirational lead given by their own organization's chief officer – as exemplified by the statement that 'the HARCA is the personification of the chief executive'.

In keeping with the 'managerialist' model, most transfer associations have introduced or further developed frameworks linking organizational goals with individual staff member targets – as defined and monitored through employee appraisal systems. Taper et al. (2003) reported that such systems were in place in 97 per cent of transfer associations, with almost half of these systems having been introduced since transfer. However, while personalized targets may in many cases contribute to motivation, they can also provide clear benchmarks for judging when a staff member's performance falls below what is 'satisfactory'. In some Second Generation case studies, landlord interviewees reported that – by comparison with pre-transfer norms – management practices encompassed both greater rewards for (or, at least, recognition of) success as well as reduced tolerance of 'failure'.

Another factor relevant to staff motivation is pay. With many transfer associations emphasizing their identity as 'commercial businesses' it might be anticipated that there would be a general move away from nationally negotiated pay bargaining and towards locally agreed settlements, perhaps incorporating performance-related pay. Less than a fifth (17 per cent) of the transfer landlords included in Taper et al.'s (2003) research continued to set all staff pay in line with nationally-based local government pay agreements. (See also Box 6.1 on the implications of stock transfer for trades union membership and activity.) However, more recent evidence from the Second Generation study suggests that – at least among the larger,

TABLE 6.1   *Transfer association staff: views about employment terms post-transfer*

	Rating of post-transfer terms and conditions as compared with pre-transfer local authority employment		
	Better (%)	Same (%)	Not as good (%)
Pay and conditions	23	53	16
Training	43	36	13
Work content	26	42	23
Overall	32	35	24

Note: Base: 475 staff employed in transfer housing associations and with previous experience as local authority employees.

Source: Taper et al. (2003)

urban transfer associations – many have chosen to remain subject to local government annual settlements.

Associated with the aim of engendering a more motivated workforce has been the commitment professed by many transfer landlords to organizational development and staff training. Organizational development is 'the theory and practice of bringing about planned change' (Hartley and Rashman 2002: 6). Although hard figures are very difficult to find, there does seem to be convincing evidence to underpin the managerial claim that transfer associations have prioritized staff training to a greater extent than had been true in the pre-transfer local authority. For example, Taper et al. (2003) found that whereas 43 per cent of transfer association staff rated their training opportunities as 'better' post-transfer, only 13 per cent felt they were 'not as good' – see Table 6.1.

Perhaps to some extent reflecting a more general trend within social housing, the Second Generation research found that, as well as growing in volume (by comparison with predecessor housing departments), transfer landlords' staff training activity had also tended to change in nature. Rather than focusing primarily on qualification training – e.g. to achieve Chartered Institute of Housing (CIH) membership – a much more diverse range of training activities has typically been offered. Examples have included short specialist courses and bespoke training packages, sometimes delivered on-site. Investment in blue collar staff development has in some cases been evidenced by apprenticeship programmes.

Organizational culture is clearly affected by recruitment practices, since the easiest way to change the culture may be to replace the staff. Although stock transfer landlords initially mainly employ former local authority employees, most also hire some 'outsiders' at the outset and others will be recruited over time. Where the new organization adopts different recruitment criteria to its housing department predecessor, the influx of such new recruits is likely to speed the process of cultural change. Among the initial senior management team members, the position of finance director has almost universally involved external recruitment (Mullins et al. 1995). Such individuals have often brought with them financial acumen and 'hard-headed' perspectives to refresh the upper echelons of the organization.

Second Generation case study evidence suggested that transfer housing association practice here has often departed to some extent from what would have been typical among pre-transfer local authorities. Structured approaches (e.g. open advertising rather than head-hunting) generally continued to be the norm. In their selection criteria, however, some transfer landlords had moved away from council traditions in terms of the emphasis often attached to 'commercial experience' or a 'business-minded' approach. Some senior management interviewees referred to 'hiring for attitude' in the sense of assessed receptiveness to a customer service ethic.

So what is the evidence about workforce morale and job satisfaction within the new organizations? Interviews with middle management and junior staff members in the Maturing Assets research portrayed the experience of working for the new landlord in a largely positive light. Work was generally seen as more rewarding, if often also more demanding than had been the case pre-transfer. Similarly, Taper et al.'s (2003) study found that transfer association staff had a 'generally positive attitude about their current employment, their employer and line managers' (ibid: 25).

Perspectives on job satisfaction among Second Generation staff interviewees were somewhat more mixed. In some cases it was clear that job satisfaction had improved, partly due to greater resources making it possible to respond positively to tenants' requests. In addition, the management style of the new organization was generally seen as positive and empowering, and this contributed to higher rates of employee satisfaction. It was, nevertheless, clear that a small proportion of transferring staff had found the new working environment uncongenial and had resigned their posts within a relatively short period. Also, some remaining staff had found changes in working practices, and perhaps particularly the pace of change, both stressful and threatening.

Partly thanks to the politically controversial nature of certain transfers (see Chapter 4), some of the new associations have found their activities closely scrutinized by a local media hungry for any hints of 'scandal' or 'failure'. Associated public criticism of landlord activities has sometimes been keenly felt by many staff – demonstrating what Handy described as the 'clannish' instincts of the 'task culture' organization (see above).

Promoting more business-minded thinking

A key aspect here has been the managerial emphasis on the primacy of the organizational business plan and the encouragement of an ethic among staff and managers that suggestions for alterations to operational practice must be accompanied by a 'business case' for proposed changes. For some former local authority employees, these messages were novel. A middle manager in a 1999 transfer association covered in the Maturing Assets research commented 'I had never heard the term "business plan" when we were part of the council' (Pawson and Fancy 2003: 20).

Also connected with the aim of promoting more business-minded thinking throughout the organization, transfer landlords have tended to delegate budgetary responsibility to middle and junior managers to a substantially greater extent than had been true in the former local authority housing department.

In some organizations, another important contributor to cultural change under this heading has been through recruitment decision-making, where greater emphasis has been placed on

Box 6.1   Implications of stock transfer for trades union membership and influence

Opposition to stock transfer by certain public sector trades unions may have been partly a reflection of concerns about the possible impact of the process on their membership and influence. Indeed, Taper et al. (2003) confirmed that trades union membership within transfer housing associations was considerably lower than among local authorities. Moreover, nearly a third (32 per cent) of the associations surveyed in the Taper et al. research recognized no trades union for collective bargaining purposes – the comparable figure for pre-1995 associations was 56 per cent).

Consistent with later evidence from the Second Generation study, Taper et al. also found that 'one of the reasons for the decline of trade union membership in the [transfer associations] was because the unions had been associated with high profile campaigns against the transfer. Staff had witnessed what some union representatives had said about the transfer and had subsequently decided, after the transfer had gone through, that the union could not appropriately represent them' (ibid: 33). Nevertheless, our research has demonstrated that in some instances local trades union representatives have played a more pragmatic game than their national headquarters colleagues. Part of this stems from an awareness of the need to avoid falling out of step with many local authority staff who have supported transfer, recognizing it as the only realistic way to access greatly needed investment.

→

applicants' commercial experience than had been normal under local authority landlordship (see above).

Customer-focused operation

Alongside the enhancement of tenant influence on organizational governance (see Chapter 5), perhaps the most critical 'culture change' aspiration for many transfer housing association senior managers has been to engender a more customer-focused ethos. The bullish approach of some newly created associations here is

The Second Generation research found that union membership rates in urban transfer landlords remained at around 50–75 per cent. Nevertheless, while these levels had fallen, there was little evidence of any general decline in trades union influence. There were instances among the case studies where local Trades Union staff saw their unions as having more say in organizational decision-making than had been true pre-transfer.

The continuing – and in some cases increased – influence wielded by trades unions post-transfer partly reflects the typical managerial commitment to a more 'inclusive' organizational culture (see above). In several instances covered in the Second Generation research it was reported – both by senior managers and trades unions – that the two parties had developed significantly more trusting relationships than those existing between unions and local authority employers pre-transfer. In relation to Glasgow Housing Association, for example, the association's 2007 inspection report commented: 'Since transfer, GHA [Glasgow Housing Association] has significantly improved its industrial relations, and it now has a strong working relationship with the unions, who are involved from an early stage in its change projects' (Communities Scotland 2007a: paragraph 9.1).

Union representatives, generally consulted on policy decisions at an early stage, were seen by managers as 'more professional' in their approach than pre-transfer and were treated more as partners than adversaries. Trades union interviewees pointed out that, having access to the employer's business plan, they were in a position to know what was 'affordable' to the organization in terms of salary increases.

exemplified by the mission statement adopted by one early transfer association covered in the Maturing Assets research: 'We aim to provide a service which is not just excellent, but legendary'. With their organizations newly endowed with long-term funding, managers have expected frontline staff to respond more positively to service user preferences and demands than had been the rule prior to transfer. Beyond this, staff interaction with tenants has been seen as needing to reflect a respect for 'the customer' which would demand – for example – that requests should be sympathetically heard and where impossible to fulfil, the reasons patiently explained.

Senior managers in a number of Maturing Assets case study housing associations stressed the challenge posed by the need to re-educate transferred staff in a new way of thinking. 'Our constant message to staff', commented one interviewee, 'is that "tenants are customers and it's the tenants that pay the wages"'.

There is also some evidence to support the managerial claim to have replaced a paternalistic local authority culture with a customer-focused ethos. Operational staff interviewed in the Maturing Assets research asserted that a key aspect of this change was the replacement of a 'No' culture with a 'Yes' culture; in one association the culture change was depicted as having changed to a 'let's find a reason to say yes rather than no' ethos. Frontline staff interviewees in the Second Generation study contrasted this kind of approach with what was described as a typically 'unsympathetic' response to tenant preferences and concerns which had prevailed under former local authority landlordship. Reportedly, there had been little sense that accountability to tenants demanded that, where requests could not be satisfied, a helpful explanation of the reasons was appropriate.

Symptomatic of such change in many transfer associations has been the adoption of the language of 'customer care'. Organizational practices seen as demonstrating a consumerist ethos and introduced by a number of Second Generation case study landlords included repairs by appointment, extended office opening hours and choice-based lettings. In supporting this agenda, some landlords had also adopted devices such as the designation of 'customer champions' within each operational team, or awards for staff initiatives effective in 'making a difference' to service users.

Most – if not all – transfer landlords would probably claim to operate in a more customer-focused way than their local authority predecessor. Relevant operational initiatives or practices cited by associations participating in our research have included:

- More customer friendly officers and staff (e.g. children's play areas, staff wearing name badges, advertising of direct staff telephone lines/email addresses, removal of screens, etc.)
- More opportunities for tenants and residents to participate in shaping services (developing menus of opportunity from

Board Membership to estate boards/local panels, use of tenant inspectors to evaluate services, involvement of tenants in service specifications, etc.)

- Better access to services by the introduction of longer opening hours and the introduction of regular road shows and surgeries
- Improved information and communications (newsletters, website information, leaflets, etc., with these being made available more widely in communities)
- Within staff training programmes, more emphasis on the role of tenants and residents in shaping policies.

It should, of course, be acknowledged that the consumerist ethic has been gaining ground in the local authority housing sector over the past 10–15 years – not least in response to 'top-down' pressure exerted through the requirements of the Best Value regime (DETR 1998, 2000b). According to our research evidence, however, transfers have often ushered in a step change in this aspect of organizational culture. Similarly, the widespread awareness of business plan imperatives seems likely to have inculcated a perception of tenants as consumers to an extent unlikely to be paralleled among housing staff of remaining landlord local authorities.

Organizational life cycles

If the view that functioning in a changed environment requires organizational adaptation is accepted we would expect to find different patterns of adaptation at different stages. Hartley and Rashman (2002) put forward a three-phase model of life after transfer as shown in Table 6.2. Key milestones during this period often include moving out of local authority accommodation and into non-municipal offices. The symbolic significance of such moves should not be underestimated. For some landlords, similar importance has attached to securing re-financing (see Chapter 3).

As demonstrated in both the Maturing Assets and Second Generation research, it is also clear that the end of the 'promises period' (usually five years after the transfer) is also liable to form a critical milestone in landlords' organizational evolution.

TABLE 6.2   *Phases of post-transfer organizational evolution*

	Timing/duration	Phase characterized by...
Phase 1	First 6–18 months post-transfer	Recuperation, psychological repair, a focus on performance but with little outward sign of change
Phase 2	6–24 months post-transfer	Initial review of organizational structure and design
Phase 3	Starting 2–3 years post-transfer	Growing recognition that the organization requires substantial transformation

Source: Hartley and Rashman (2002).

Having completed the property investment programme presented as the main reason for the organization's creation, questions inevitably arise as to corporate objectives for the medium and longer-term future. Not least because without the development of replacement business activities, the organization is likely to be operating on a lower budget and to risk losing its most motivated staff as the task scales down. Practical imperatives 'forcing the pace' of managerial decision-making at this point in a transfer landlord's existence have often included considerations about securing 'new business' to underpin the continuing employment of development (and other) staff. For many early transfer associations, this dilemma was resolved by exploiting opportunities to develop new social housing both in the 'home local authority' and further afield (see Pawson and Fancy 2003).

Illustrating the uncertainties likely to arise at this time, staff in some of the post-1997 landlords included in the Second Generation research expressed concerns about the possible impacts of 'post-promises' organizational restructuring. Such anxieties stemmed from a recognition that, at this juncture, senior managers were likely to see a need to consider potentially radical options for the way ahead. For example, there were worries about diluting what was believed a successful 'brand' by allying with currently separate organizations or reducing the association's autonomy through changes in existing relationships with linked bodies.

More recently, post-promises strategies have also included diversification into other fields of activity – e.g. care home management, provision of development services to commercial and public sector clients, and 'parenting' of new stock transfers. Particularly for smaller transfer landlords, post-promises choices are also likely to include decisions on the extent of autonomy to be retained. For example, an organization established as a free-standing association may perceive that a corporate aspiration to access social housing development funding could necessitate a move to become a subsidiary of a larger parent body (see Chapter 5). Clearly, such choices have critical implications for the evolving culture of the organization.

Intra-sector diversity

Impacts of changing government priorities

In much of this chapter – and in the book as a whole – we draw on research evidence in an attempt to generalize about the form, activities and evolution of Britain's new social landlords. However, in relation to organizational culture no less than other aspects, there is a degree of diversity across the new landlords coming into existence since 1988. Part of this reflects managerial choices and associated decisions made subsequent to set-up, but much results from different organizational origins.

Differences in transfer landlords' organizational structures have, in some cases, been a direct consequence of Ministerial decisions. For example, the unique framework adopted for Glasgow City Council's 2003 transfer to Glasgow Housing Association was strongly influenced by Scottish Ministers and the impacts of this decision on Glasgow Housing Association's organizational culture have continued to be prominent, several years down the track.

More broadly, the policy initiative or era under which transfers have been progressed has had both immediate and lasting effects on both structure and culture in the new organizations. In establishing a new landlord body, the predecessor agency has needed to abide by centrally-defined rules on issues such as organizational size and accountability arrangements (such as those laid down in the Westminster government's transfer manual (e.g. ODPM 2004c)). A locally-focused, community-based ethic was strongly embedded in the ex-Scottish Homes transfer programme (Gibb et al. 2005) and this has been reflected in the ethos of the thirty-plus organizations created through the process. The emphasis on the need for transfer landlords to contribute to 'community regeneration' in the 1998–2000 Estates Renewal Challenge Programme (Pawson et al. 2005a) had a similar impact. Likewise, different patterns of post-set-up adaptation have occurred in different eras of transfer policy reflecting changing regulatory pressures.

Contrasting organizational forms and cultures

This penultimate section of the chapter focuses on two distinct organizational forms emerging from the transfer process – local community orientated organizations and large group structures. These illustrate the tensions faced by housing associations in the current environment, between local accountability and focus, on the one hand, and strategies driven mainly by aspirations for economies of scale and organizational growth, on the other.

Figure 6.1 shows the profile of stock transfer landlords in relation to the size of their stockholdings as at 2008. Around half of the Scottish contingent owned less than 2,000 dwellings, while in England the vast majority had larger portfolios. Nevertheless, a 'localist' strand remains intact within the transfer housing association cohort. In part, this relates to the organizations set up under the Scottish Homes divestment programme and the Estates Renewal Challenge Fund scheme in England (see above). At least in Scotland, the CBHA ethic – and the organizational culture it incorporates – is descended from the estate-scale transfers made by Glasgow City Council (and some other Scottish local authorities) in the 1980s and dubbed 'community ownership' (Clapham and Kintrea 1994). Emphasizing tenant control, the focus here was on collective resident empowerment and local accountability rather than professionalization or modernization.

Inspired partly by the decentralized housing management model popularized by Anne Power, the ERCF housing associa-

FIGURE 6.1   Stock size profile of transfer associations in England and Scotland, 2008

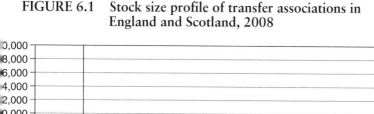

Source: Tenants Services Authority, Scottish Housing Regulator.

tions also stressed the virtues of accountability to residents and embeddedness within the local community. Although the ERCF programme was relatively short-lived, a stream of partial stock transfers has continued in urban England and some of these have involved newly created landlords which have espoused similar models. The 'localist' ethic has also been kept alive since 2000 via the development (and occasional implementation) of new governance frameworks emphasizing collective tenant influence – see discussion on the Community Gateway model in Chapter 5.

At least as far as English associations are concerned, however, Figure 6.1 does not tell the whole story. This is because, while it takes as its basic unit the individually registered transfer housing association, the majority of such associations are in fact subsidiaries within group structures (see Table 6.3). Groups are legal frameworks structured as 'group parent' and 'subsidiary' bodies. Some housing association groups involve only a single landlord body which co-exists within the group alongside other legally autonomous entities with specialist roles – e.g. construction, development and management

TABLE 6.3   *English transfer associations and group membership, 2007*

Transfer type	Transfer housing associations operating as group subsidiaries			Not in group	Total
	Mixed group**	Transfer group***	All in groups		
Partial	21	1	22	13	35
Whole stock*	36	44	80	75	155
Total	57	45	102	88	190

* Including 'split transfers' – i.e. where a whole stock transfer was split between two or more recipient associations.

** Groups containing housing associations formed via stock transfer alongside traditional associations.

*** Groups containing two or more transfer housing associations only.

Sources: authors' analysis of RSR data; kind assistance also provided by former Housing Corporation regional office staff.

of homes for low cost sale. More commonly, however, groups bring together two or more registered housing associations – for example, under a group parent body which undertakes 'corporate functions' such as personnel management on behalf of all group members. Groups vary substantially in the extent to which subsidiary bodies enjoy autonomy. In some, group members are bound by common policies and procedures across a wide range of activities. Effectively, such groups operate as single entities rather than loose alliances of autonomous bodies.

The relevance of all this here is partly that the profile of English transfer associations shown in Figure 6.1 obscures the fact that some of the landlords depicted here as separate entities are, arguably, simply divisions of larger organizations. While most originated as 'freestanding bodies' (see Chapter 2), many transfer landlords have subsequently allied themselves within (or set up) groups. This process of 'agglomeration' is part of a longstanding trend within the housing association sector driven primarily by financial considerations (Mullins

2000, Pawson and Sosenko 2008). If Figure 6.1 treated groups as entities, the typical 'entity size' would rise, compounding the dominance of those with more than 4,000 properties.

As shown in Table 6.3, transfer associations which have become group members can be differentiated between those allying with other transfer organizations and those joining with traditional housing associations. To the extent that entities of the second type are forming, the distinction between transfer landlords and traditional housing associations is becoming eroded, and with it any argument that there remains a 'transfer landlord culture' clearly distinct from mainstream 'housing association culture'.

Irrespective of the origins of counterpart landlords, the integration of transfer bodies within multi-landlord group structures is symptomatic of strategic choices which both follow from and have implications for organizational culture. It speaks of a corporate emphasis on growth and diversification rather than local accountability and identification. In these respects it is in tune with trends dominant across the housing association sector, as a whole.

Adapting a typology applied to social landlords by Gruis (2008), housing associations' business strategies could be characterized in terms of the distinction between 'prospectors' and 'defenders' (Miles et al. 1978). Prospectors are organizations which actively search for market opportunities, while defenders are agencies 'which have a narrow product-market domain [and] do not tend to search outside their domains for new opportunities' (ibid: 29). Whether a transfer landlord evolves into a prospector or a defender will have significant implications for the future development of its organizational culture. For example, the former path will imply more of an outward orientation and a commercial ethos within the organization. The latter suggests more of a focus on managerial professionalism.

Chapter conclusions

There has been understandable scepticism that stock transfers can necessarily be expected to bring about cultural change in the management of social housing. Doubts of this kind are encouraged by the purely opportunistic motives articulated some local politicians and senior housing officers in justifying their decisions to promote transfer proposals. Such views are exemplified by the local authority housing director statement reported by Rollo (2008):

> the deal that we eventually negotiated ... [with Central Government] was so good, that we felt we got to give it our best shot to try and sell it to tenants ... the main reason we were doing it was just financial. There was no desire to change the service or to change the organisation – in fact our whole strategy was sort of minimum change. So it was basically because we were we were going to get a lot more money and could do the things that we needed to do a lot more quickly. (Ibid:19–20)

Given the somewhat instrumental perspective underlying these comments, it is perhaps unsurprising that the relevant local authority failed to evoke majority tenant support for the proposed transfer.

Research findings suggest that an explicit aspiration to use the stock handover process as a vehicle for cultural change has been more in evidence within the cohort of more recent transfer landlords. Nevertheless, even among earlier transfers where such reform was not commonly a recognized objective at the outset, it has been shown that substantial cultural change has typically resulted. Several years post-transfer, the organizations managing former council housing have typically been functioning in ways significantly distinct from their housing department predecessors. Having moved away from a role culture and towards a task culture, the new landlords have, as a rule, become substantially more cohesive, customer-focused and inclusive in their organizational style. They have also become substantially more businesslike, with a business ethic embraced much further down the management hierarchy than formerly. Under a managerialist ethos there has been an emphasis on replacing the previous 'command and control' style of operation with a stress on staff motivation and empowerment, and on the encouragement of innovation.

None of the trends identified here are unique to transfer housing associations. All could be seen as consistent with the tenets of New Public Management which have been embraced in varying degrees by every class of social landlords over the past two decades. To an extent, therefore, it might be that the aspirations, strategies and impacts outlined in this chapter represent a microcosm of post-1988 changes across the entire social housing domain. Unfortunately, there are no comparable 'cultural evolution' studies of continuing local authority housing departments, traditional housing associations or ALMOs which could serve as a benchmark for comparison. Our judgement, however, is that – at the very minimum – transfers have stimulated and accelerated rates of change for the organizations involved. Such changes may also have served as something of a blueprint for other types of landlords perceiving a need to 'modernize' their operations. As organizations spawned by transfers become increasingly integrated with traditional housing associations, this could prove another means by which culture change experience is disseminated across the sector.

Chapter 7

Impact on Housing Stock, Tenants and Communities

With stock transfer being a well-established policy there is now a considerable body of evidence on its medium and longer-term effects. Chapters 5 and 6 have investigated impacts on the ways that social housing is governed and the ways that social landlords operate. This chapter draws on findings from evaluation studies and other sources to assess impacts 'on the ground'. First, we discuss the effect of transfer on housing stock condition. To what degree have transfer-triggered capital works remedied long years of constrained local authority investment opportunities and what challenges have transfer housing associations faced in keeping their spending plans 'on track'?

Next, we look at the consequences of transfer more from a tenant perspective – how has the change of landlord affected rents and tenants' rights? Has transfer been simply a device to secure investment rather than a change with significant effects on day-to-day housing management services? Are transfer landlords – as asserted by some critics – typically driven by their business orientation to adopt a 'hard-nosed' approach to housing management?

In the final section, we examine the impact of transfer on wider communities. Over and above upgrading individual dwellings, to what extent have transfers contributed to broader neighbourhood regeneration? A closely related issue – the consequences of transfer for social housing replacement – is also addressed here. More generally, this section discusses transfer impacts in relation to both the physical and social renewal of run-down areas. How does stock transfer connect with community participation and local governance and involvement of hard to reach groups, such as certain Black and Minority Ethnic (BME) communities?

Housing refurbishment

Particularly since 1997, the need to access private finance to upgrade council housing has been the main stated motivation for stock transfer (see Chapter 3). By 2008, transfers in England had facilitated 'private finance' investment totalling £19.3 billion in repairs to the stock of former local authority housing inherited by new landlords since 1988 (Pawson et al., 2009). As discussed in Chapter 3, however, a substantial proportion of post-1997 transfers have been able to proceed only with the aid of explicit public subsidy. In total, therefore, the capital finance committed to transfers by 2008 (in England, alone) exceeded £24 billion.

The sharply reduced average unit value of homes transferred after 1997 (see Figure 7.1) indicates that more problematic stock was now being transferred e.g. in terms of its outstanding repair needs. (Relevant here is the property valuation method used within the stock transfer context – see Chapter 3.) The extent of investment needs of recently transferred stock is also highlighted by the estimate that a majority (51 per cent) of dwellings transferred since 2001 (up to 2007) failed the Decent Homes Standard on at least one count (CLG transfers dataset).

FIGURE 7.1   Stock transfers in England, 1988-2008: average price per dwelling

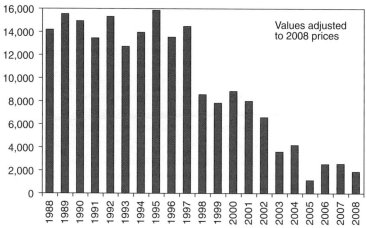

Source: CLG stock transfers dataset.

In some transfers, the incidence of 'non-decent' property was much higher – for example, the overwhelming majority of stock in some large transactions involving Walsall (94 per cent), Wirral (73 per cent) and Wakefield (68 per cent). The typically somewhat poorer quality of transferred stock in 'urban' transfers is indicated by the fact that in post-2001 transactions involving such authorities, 56 per cent of homes were 'non-decent', as compared with only 45 per cent in other transfers.

As discussed in Chapter 4, proposed transfers must secure ballot endorsement from a majority of tenants affected. Tenants must cast their votes in relation to a specific package of commitments made by the local authority on behalf of the proposed transfer landlord. Ballot prospectuses have usually included pledges under the following headings:

- Investment in property repairs and modernization
- Rent levels
- Improved housing management services
- New housing development and/or area regeneration
- Protection of tenants' rights.

At least among post-1997 transfers, pledges on property investment have usually dominated commitments made to tenants (Pawson et al. 2009). Such promises have tended to be about making good disrepair resulting from past underinvestment ('catch-up repairs'), as well as specifying proposed improvement and modernization of tenants' homes (such as upgrading of kitchens and bathrooms).

Although the national quality standards (Decent Homes Standard, Scottish Housing Quality Standard, Welsh Quality Housing Standard) provided stock improvement baselines for post-2001 transactions, most transfers taking place since that time – in practice – incorporated criteria superior to those officially prescribed. However, local authorities seeking to transfer their housing stock are required to draw up local plans in consultation with tenants. This has usually involved establishing local property modernization standards which enhance, to some degree, official criteria. Consequently, in almost half (45 per cent) of the 'second generation' transfers surveyed in Pawson et al. (2009) local stock modernization standards were reported to be 'much higher' than the official thresholds (see also NAO 2010). In particular, this often involved the installation of security features, the adoption of more demanding energy efficiency ratings and investment in environmental improvements. Some modernization proposals also allowed for the routine replacement of kitchen and bathroom fittings even where this would not have been required under the relevant quality standard (because existing fittings did not exceed the maximum allowable age).

It is apparent from Table 7.1 that second generation transfers have seen property investment promises delivered on time in almost all cases. This is in line with findings relating to other transfer cohorts (NAO 2003, Pawson and Fancy 2003, Gibb et al. 2005) although defective stock condition surveys as well as inaccurate assumptions about interest rates, right to buy receipts and other factors have caused difficulties in many cases (PIEDA 1997, Pawson et al. 2005a; Gibb et al. 2005). In some cases, this led to extensions of the period over which stock improvements were completed. Occasionally, other measures such as sales of vacant stock and staff reductions have been needed to 'square the financial circle'. In a few cases, transfer landlords have subsequently joined larger housing association groups to meet unexpectedly large repairs and modernization costs (Mullins et al. 1995) – see also Chapter 6.

Property investment commitments were particularly important for the Estates Renewal Challenge Fund (ERCF) programme which facilitated transfers of individual estates in run-down inner city areas in the late 1990s and early 2000s (see Chapter 2). Here, obstacles to on-time delivery of promised repair and improvement works included cost overruns due to defective pre-transfer stock condition surveys, the need to extend the main works programme to accommodate higher unit costs caused by rising tender prices, and post-transfer decisions to implement certain works at standards higher than originally anticipated. In a few cases, problems arose from the need to carry out significant demolition and replacement – particularly where consent was required for higher than expected levels of clearance. Delays also resulted from the shortage of decanting resources and from the need to secure planning consent (Pawson et al. 2005a).

The Scottish Homes stock handover programme involved transfer housing associations contracting with the former land-

TABLE 7.1 *Transfers 1998–2004: delivery against 'property investment' promises, 2008*

Subject of undertaking	No promise made	Promise . . .					Total respondents
		. . . not met	. . . delayed	. . . on schedule	. . . fully met	. . . exceeded	
Catch-up repairs	2	0	0	8	24	13	47
Other property modernization	0	0	0	12	13	22	47
Other works	4	0	1	14	17	10	46

Source: Pawson et al. (2009) – postal survey. Data cover Great Britain.

lord to carry out a specific works programme. For each transferred dwelling, contracted investment and routine maintenance over 30-year business plans averaged £26,800 or £892
p.a. Generally, the works envisaged involved planned programmes of component renewals though some included demolition and replacement (Graham 1999). In practice,
post-transfer works packages tended to involve the installation
of double glazing, heating improvements, kitchen replacement
and re-wiring. In some cases, promises had also included
'purely cosmetic improvements designed to make tenants in the
newest and most recently refurbished houses feel that they
would get something from the process if they voted "yes"'
(Gibb et al. 2005: 43). The scale of 'catch-up repairs' under the
programme was comparatively modest because – unlike many
local authorities – Scottish Homes had been adequately
resourced to maintain its properties in reasonable condition.

More recently, however, it has become clear that a significant
proportion of ex-Scottish Homes transfers were under-funded
to deliver compliance with the (subsequently defined) Scottish
Housing Quality Standard. For example, Glasgow City Council
has raised concerns that some associations managing former
Scottish Homes properties in the city face unfunded commitments in this respect. Reportedly, a common condition problem
for the homes concerned is attainment of prescribed energy efficiency standards. This could lead to unanticipated demolitions
and consequential demands on already-stretched affordable
housing investment resources (Glasgow City Council 2007a).

Impact on Decent Homes compliance

Transfer landlords have been generally successful in implementing property upgrade programmes. By 2007, about half of
the transfer associations established in England before 2002
were reporting Decent Homes compliance rates of over 90 per
cent (unpublished Housing Corporation Regulatory &
Statistical Return data). By April 2008, this was also true of 12
of the 69 ALMOs (Audit Commission Best Value Performance
Indicator data). Casting these figures within a broader context,
Table 7.2 shows that Decent Homes investment – whether
through stock transfer, ALMO funding or local authority prudential borrowing – had, by 2008, reduced the sector-wide

TABLE 7.2   *Incidence of non-decent local authority housing:*
national trend, 2001–2008

	Local authority % of total stock	Housing association % of total stock	All social % of total stock
2001	52.5		
2002	49.4	17.1	37.6
2003	47.6	20.7	36.5
2004	44.5	18.6	33.3
2005	41.2	18.2	30.5
2006	36.2	15.3	26.1
2007	31.3	12.6	21.8
2008	26.6	10.6	18.0

Sources: Local authority data from BPSA returns; housing association data from RSR returns. Figures originally published by CLG (2009c).

non-compliance rate from 38 per cent to 18 per cent over a six-year period. The housing association figures shown in Table 7.2 reflect both the inflow of large numbers of non-decent properties via local authority stock transfers, as well as the activity of transfer and traditional associations in remedying defects, funded from reserves and new borrowing.

The dramatically improved position portrayed in Table 7.2 may be seen as one of the most important achievements of stock transfer and ALMO activity. However, the Decent Homes standard has been criticized as a relatively low benchmark, especially in relation to energy efficiency, and in terms of its exclusive focus on buildings as opposed to their immediate surroundings (Somerville 2004). It is also important to recognize that 2008 local authority forward projections suggested that non-decent dwellings would continue to account for around 12–14 per cent of total council stock in 2010. Taking into account some remaining non-decent properties in housing association ownership by that time, it seemed likely that around 10 per cent of all social housing stock would remain non-compliant at that time. Particularly with the impact of sub-sequent cuts to Decent Homes spending plans, it is clear that the Ministers' 2006 aspiration to achieve 95 per cent compliance with the Standard across the entire sector by 2010 (House of Commons Library 2009) has become unachievable.

Impact of stock transfer on tenants

Rents

As noted in Chapter 3, fears of local authority rent rises were a significant factor motivating interest in transfers in the early days of the process. The possibility that post-transfer rents could increase steeply has always been seen by local authorities as a legitimate tenant concern and one liable to exploitation by anti-transfer campaigners. The deployment of anti-'privatization' rhetoric (see Chapter 4) has often given this a particular edge. In early transfers a key feature of promotional materials was the suggestion that rents would increase even more steeply if tenants voted to remain with the Council (Mullins et al. 1992). Transfer proposals invariably include assurances on post-transfer rent levels (although, particularly in the early years, these promises were confined to existing tenants, see below). Such 'promises' have usually limited annual increases to inflation plus 1 per cent. As a rule, these undertakings have tended to run for five years, though in Scotland 'guarantee periods' among ex-Scottish Homes transfers ranged from 3 to 30 years (Graham 1999). Similarly, in Glasgow City Council's 2002 transfer, existing tenants' rents were to rise at RPI only for the first five years, with subsequent increases 'guaranteed' at RPI+1 per cent for years 6–30 (except for year 11) (Gibb 2003).

It is, however, important to recognize that in some cases rent guarantees have been qualified to allow for the fact that post-transfer works programmes usually involve significant 'betterment' of individual dwellings (e.g. installation of new heating facilities). Dwellings subject to such improvements may legitimately attract supplementary rent increases over and above those implied by the generally applicable formula – e.g. RPI+1 per cent (Gibb et al. 2005). The implementation of rules in this area has, in some cases, proved controversial in that tenants

Box 7.1   'Betterment' adjustments in post-transfer rent structures: Gentoo-Sunderland

One of the key pledges made in the course of the 2001 Sunderland stock transfer was that rents would rise at 'no more than RPI+1 per cent for first five years'. Then 'For the following 25 years your local housing company would aim to keep any annual increase to within the same rate'. However, the transfer housing association also proposed to retain the Council's existing rent structure whereby rents were set partly according to property quality. 'A' grade properties attracted an extra charge of £7.00 on the basic rent. For tenants living in homes upgraded from 'D' grade to 'A' grade, the rent would therefore rise in that year by RPI+1 per cent+£7.00.

While transfer promises on rents were honoured, the adoption of the former City Council rent structure resulted in actual increases substantially greater than RPI+1 per cent. According to Housing Corporation figures, over the first five years after the transfer, estimated actual rents for a two-bed property rose by £12.08, some £3.11 more than the figure produced under the simple RPI+1 formula (see table below). In effect, rents rose by almost RPI+2 per cent over the period. A 2004 Board report noted that annual rent

→

affected may not have fully appreciated the qualified nature of the rent guarantee. In aggregate terms, therefore, such rules have provided scope for rents to rise at rates somewhat in excess of those implicit in headline ballot commitments (even within the promises period), without any technical breach of undertakings – see Box 7.1.

Another significant feature of undertakings on post-transfer rents is that these have sometimes related only to existing tenants – i.e. those in residence on the transfer date (and, hence, qualified to vote on the transfer proposal). New tenants taking up assured tenancies after the 'promises period' were often charged rents at significantly higher levels for identical properties. As noted by early research, 'rents for these tenancies [those created post-transfer] were calculated in a quite different increases at RPI+1 per cent had been factored into the business plan up until 2012/13, with rises at RPI+0.5 per cent for the remainder of the business plan period.

Gentoo-Sunderland rent increases 2001/02–2006/07

	Estimated avg rent charged (£)*	Avg rent increase (%)	RPI (%)**	Avg rent assuming increase at RPI+1 (£)
2001/02	44.78			
2002/03	45.98	2.7	1.7	45.99
2003/04	48.01	4.4	2.9	47.78
2004/05	51.28	6.8	3	49.69
2005/06	54.72	6.7	2.8	51.58
2006/07	56.86	3.9	3.2	53.75
Difference	12.08			8.97

* Estimate for 2-bed properties across the Group, calculated as simple average of Housing Corporation figures for each of the five LHCs. ** Figures for calendar years.

Source of 'rent charged' figures: Housing Corporation performance indicators.

way [to those of existing tenants] and were not widely publicised' (Mullins et al. 1992: 41). Particularly in some early transfers, the difference between 'promises period' rents charged to new and existing tenants was sometimes very substantial. In one 'first wave' transfer, for example, rents for new tenants were set 50 per cent higher than those charged to existing tenants and in another it was projected that by the end of the promises period new tenants' rents would be nearly double the level of pre-transfer tenants. Hence, a two tier rent structure was being operated during the 'promises' period with pre- and post-transfer tenants' rents subsequently being brought gradually into line from Year 6 onwards.

Comparing transfer housing association rents with those of similar but non-transferring local authorities, subsequent research found that the implementation of rent promises had left pre-transfer tenants better off but new (post-transfer) tenants worse off than their local authority tenant counterparts (Mullins et al. 1995). This reinforced widespread patterns for new tenants to be less satisfied with their housing than longer-standing tenants (Mullins and Simmons 2001).

In practice, rent guarantees have almost always been seen as sacrosanct (Gibb et al. 2005) – given their highly tangible nature, any breach would be apparent to all. Confirming the evidence from the Mullins et al. evaluation, subsequent studies have found no evidence of rent promises to existing tenants being breached (NAO 2003, Pawson and Fancy 2003, Pawson et al. 2009).

As to the longer-term future, transfer housing association business plans have commonly incorporated an assumption of continuing modest real-terms increases in rents (reflecting regulatory norms of RPI+% increases) through the (normally) 30-year length of the plan, an assumption at variance with the deflationary climate of 2009 when for the first time rent regulation was expected to produce rent reductions of around 2 per cent. As a rule, however, such projections have not been explicitly incorporated within transfer promises and – at least in the early phase of the English transfer process – were 'seldom communicated to tenants' (PIEDA 1997: 17).

The 'going rate' for business plan assumptions on long-run rent increases has varied over time. Early transfers tended to work on the basis of continuing rises of RPI+1–2 per cent, with 2 per cent becoming more common during the mid-1990s in England as the process began to encompass more problematic housing with higher rates of disrepair and/or outstanding debt. With the introduction of the Westminster government's national rent restructuring programme from 2001, however, pressure to restrict post-transfer rent rises has been exerted (see below). As part of the process for securing Ministerial consent, local authorities will have needed to demonstrate that future rent levels built into transfer business plans were consistent with national rent restructuring targets (see below). In common with all social landlords in England, transfer housing associations have consequently seen their freedom of manoeuvre on rents being much reduced (see below).

Whether or not in keeping with pre-transfer projections, the NAO's 2003 survey found that one in six longer-established transfer landlords had imposed post-guarantee rent increases in excess of Housing Corporation guidelines (NAO 2003). Overall, nevertheless, there is evidence that transfer housing association tenants are particularly likely to see their rent as providing 'good value for money'. An NHF analysis of residents' satisfaction survey results across 80 landlords showed that 76 per cent of transfer housing association tenants took this view as compared with 73 per cent of local authority tenants and 72 per cent of traditional housing association tenants (NHF 2002a).

In Scotland, there have been concerns that the pre-transfer Scottish Homes rents used as a base for 30-year rent projections were already rather high compared with other social landlords and there must be some concern that the standard formula for future increases may perpetuate and even accentuate this (Graham 1999). Such a trend could prove very problematic for transfer housing associations working in areas of falling demand where social landlords face a growing need to compete with one another for potential tenants (Pawson and Mullins 2003).

Since 2001, English stock transfer landlords have been affected by the increased central government control of housing association rents under the 2002–2012 national rent restructuring programme (DETR 2000c). The programme's general assumption that housing association rents would henceforward rise at no more than RPI+0.5 per cent has significantly changed the financial planning basis for post-2000 transfers. Moreover, while 'rent capping' may seem welcome from a tenant perspective, it is highly problematic for many established transfer landlords whose longer-term income predictions have had to be squeezed in consequence. 'If forced to comply with rent restructuring in the next 10 years then our business plan is bust', commented one transfer housing association finance director in early 2004. 'This means we will have to sell off property and land, severely curtail investment in the remaining properties, significantly cut back on services ... and not undertake any work in form of new development and regeneration' (Hawkey and Birch 2004). Unsaid by the interviewee cited here is the possibility that financial stresses resulting from the rent restructuring regime could also have hastened the incorporation of formerly independent transfer housing associations within more resource-rich associations via group structures or mergers (Pawson and Sosenko 2008).

FIGURE 7.2   Housing association rents, 2003–06

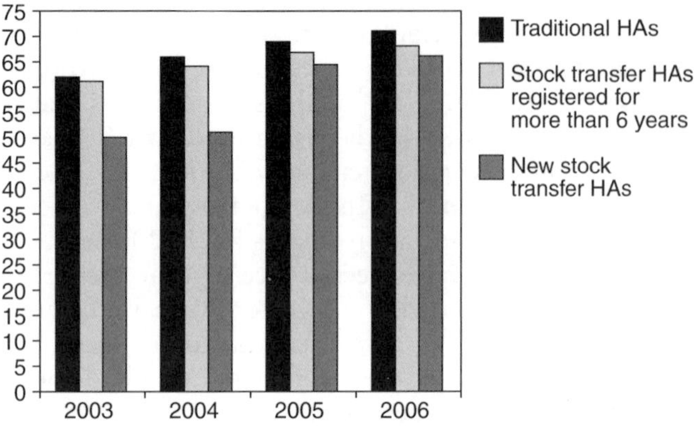

Source: Housing Corporation performance indicators, 2006.

An early and well-publicized casualty of the new regime was 1066 Housing Association which had inherited the stock of Hastings Borough Council in 1996 with a business plan assuming long-term rent rises at RPI+2 per cent. To stave off financial meltdown the association opted to merge with a stronger partner, Amicus, itself the product of a transfer that had encountered some financial difficulties in early years but had subsequently emerged as a regional group structure. Others have sought 'special case' dispensation for limited relaxation of the rent restructuring regime in an attempt to avoid having to impose the kind of 'business plan adjustments' described above.

On average, rents charged by transfer housing associations have tended to lie somewhat below those levied by traditional housing associations. As shown in Figure 7.2, however, there is a significant contrast between recently-set-up housing associations (which will still be subject to post-transfer rent guarantees) and their longer-established counterparts. This pattern has been explained as reflecting a tendency for post-guarantee transfer housing association rents to rise towards the sector norm (Malpass and Mullins 2002).

As noted in Chapter 3, the centrally-controlled 'rent restructuring' regime in place for all social landlords in England since 2001 has substantially reduced landlords' freedom of action. In doing so, it has so far largely avoided the charge often intimated by critics that subsequent transfers would generate long-term costs to tenants in the form of rents at levels substantially higher than charged by other social landlords for comparable properties. For the longer term, and particularly in response to the threat of below-inflation rent increases, there have been arguments for reducing regulatory controls on rents to provide associations with greater control over their main income stream.

Housing management, access to housing and tenants' rights

Overall, research evidence suggests that councils planning transfer have generally sought to reassure tenants by pledging continuity rather than change as far as housing management policies are concerned. However, there have been some specific promises to upgrade repairs and other services by most pre-1998 transfer housing associations in England (NAO 2003) and by virtually all ERCF landlords (Pawson et al. 2005a). More recent research focusing on urban transfers implemented 1998–2004 found that the typical transfer prospectus envisaged enhanced repairs services and/or more effective action to tackle anti-social behaviour but often couched in rather unspecific terms and rarely as a key argument for transfer.

Figure 7.3 illustrates the kinds of 'service enhancements' reportedly delivered by transfer housing associations in the ERCF programme (see Chapter 2). To some extent, however, these should be seen as characteristic of the locally-based intensive housing management styles typically operated by ERCF housing associations (Pawson et al. 2005a). Broader themes of change in relation to housing management approaches by post-1997 transfer landlords have included:

- A more customer-focused style of operation (as already discussed in Chapter 6)
- Growing interest in neighbourhood management – connected with increasing engagement with 'community regeneration' activity (see later in this chapter)
- More 'active' housing management; that is, a more interventionist, preventative approach to problems such as rent arrears and anti-social behaviour.

FIGURE 7.3   Housing management 'service improvements' instituted by ERCF associations

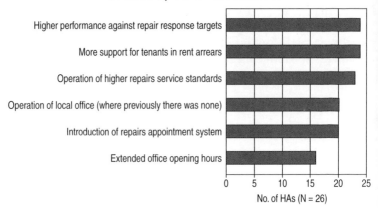

Source: Data from Pawson et al. (2005a).

As far as 'customer focus' is concerned, there is a sense that, as organizations outside the public sector and needing to operate in a businesslike fashion, transfer housing association staff are more inclined than their local authority counterparts to see tenants as 'customers' and to treat them accordingly (see Chapter 6). This may be reflected by the finding from tenants' satisfaction survey analysis that 'transfer organisations . . . (are) significantly more highly rated by their tenants as regards responsiveness (compared with other social landlords)' (NHF 2002a: 2). This referred to tenant responses to questions such as:

- when you last had contact with your landlord, was getting hold of the right person easy, difficult or neither?
- did you find the staff helpful, unhelpful or neither?
- (was the staff member) able to deal with your problem, unable to deal with your problem or neither?

Given their typically highly indebted circumstances and the need to honour high profile pledges on spending and rents, it might be supposed that transfer landlords would adopt a hard-nosed style of housing management. Critics assert, for example, that rents and evictions rise following stock transfer (DCH

FIGURE 7.4   Eviction rates by social landlord class

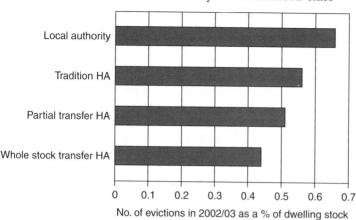

No. of evictions in 2002/03 as a % of dwelling stock

Sources: CIPFA Rent and Benefits Statistics, Housing Corporation CORE and RSR data.

2004b). There is also the view that housing associations, as bodies increasingly exposed to risk, are collectively moving 'from comfort to competition' as they increasingly adopt 'property-centred' rather than 'welfare-centred' approaches (Walker 1998). If risk exposure is proportional to indebtedness, one might expect such trends to be particularly marked among transfer housing associations and to have a noticeable effect on housing management style. Qualitative research evidence has also found that many transfer housing association staff see their organization as operating a 'firmer' approach to rent arrears than the predecessor local authority, with stricter procedures, the establishment of specialist arrears control teams and benefits advice to help resolve problems when they arise (Pawson et al. 2009). However, statistical evidence disproves any suggestion that transfer housing associations are more prone to evict tenants than other classes of social landlord (see Figure 7.4). This seems to suggest that the typically more proactive approach to arrears management adopted by transfer housing associations is effective.

Questioned about their rent arrears policies, most of Pawson and Fancy's 12 case study transfer housing associations reported that these were little changed from those of predecessor landlords (local authority or Scottish Homes), although three reported that they were operating a tougher approach. Two of these associations had changed the threshold for issuing a Notice Seeking Possession from six weeks' to four weeks' rent. It may have been significant that two of the three 'more hardline' associations were partial transfer landlords having inherited run-down estates with what senior managers saw as an ingrained 'culture of rent non-payment'. 'Both of these housing associations saw the need to change this culture as a key challenge and one that required a clear demonstration of the landlord's resolve' (Pawson and Fancy 2003: 34).

How does stock transfer impact on the way that new tenants access social housing? For 'whole stock' local authority transfers the extent of the change depends mainly on how administrative responsibilities are divided between the transferring local authority and its transfer housing association partner – an issue discussed more fully in Chapter 9. Transfers have often triggered the setting up of common housing registers, in some cases reflecting local authority aspirations to retain a central role in the local housing system in a non-landlord role. Common housing registers are arrangements where all (or most) of the landlords operating in a given geographical area adopt common procedures and processing machinery so that applicants for social housing in that area can access it through a 'single gateway' (Mullins and Niner 1996). By 2001, common registers had been established in more than half (55 per cent) of all transfer local authorities as compared with only 21 per cent of non-transfer local authorities (Pawson et al. 2001).

Concerns have been raised that transfer housing associations – with an overriding need to meet often demanding business plan targets – may be more inclined than local authority predecessors to avoid taking on apparently 'risky' tenants. As registered housing associations, however, transfer landlords have to operate within highly regulated frameworks (e.g. as set by the Tenant Services Authority in England) which severely limit the scope for major deviations from the approaches of predecessor local authorities. Hence, while transfer housing associations commonly abandon rules requiring that housing applicants have a 'local connection' (specifically to comply with regulatory rules) there is little evidence to show that whole stock transfer has generally resulted in more restrictive 'new tenant selection' approaches unsympathetic to vulnerable households.

Some partial transfers have, however, brought at least temporary departures in allocations policy as successor landlords have sought to de-concentrate deprivation and dispel sometimes ingrained 'sink estate' images. Some inner London ERCF housing associations, for example, secured local authority agreement for time-limited relaxation of nomination expectations (Pawson et al. 2004). The stated justification here was to develop more 'balanced communities' as advocated by Page (1993, 1994). Estates where pre-transfer vacancies had been overwhelmingly let to homeless and other deprived households were, in consequence, opened up to more economically active groups such as key workers. Another tack was to introduce 'community lettings' policies under which family or other connections with the estate would enhance an applicant's re-housing priority. From the landlord viewpoint, such initiatives were seen as a vital component in wider strategies aimed at promoting long-term sustainability and community cohesion.

The impacts of stock transfers on access to social housing have been discussed in more detail elsewhere (see, for example, Pawson and Mullins 2003, Taylor 2008, Pleace et al. 2008).

How does transfer affect tenants' rights? Transfers in England have involved tenants exchanging their local authority secure tenancy for a housing association assured tenancy. As highlighted by transfer critics, assured tenancies are ostensibly inferior because they confer less security (the landlord has wider repossession powers), because succession rights are more limited and because there is no statutory Right to Buy (DCH 2004b). This might well be expected to reduce the attraction of transfer from the tenant perspective; a problem for councils promoting 'yes' votes.

To neutralize this potential difficulty, transferring tenants have generally been offered a contractual guarantee that their statutory rights as local authority tenants on such matters would be legally preserved after transfer by agreement. A particular issue here has been the commitment often incorporated in ballot promises that the new landlord will forgo the option of using powers under Ground 8 (Housing Act 1988, Schedule 2). This power, which may be used in cases of substantial rent arrears, entitles a housing association to mandatory repossession of an Assured Tenancy. Hence, unlike most possession

actions by associations (and all those entered by local authorities), there is no opportunity for judicial scrutiny on 'reason-
ableness' grounds (Citizens Advice, 2008). Survey evidence
suggests that transfer associations indeed make relatively little
use of Ground 8 (Pawson et al. 2010). It may be that the small
numbers of instances of evictions under Ground 8 by such
landlords reflect actions taken against tenants who acquired
their home subsequent to the transfer and who were technically
not covered by any commitment to desist from use of this
power.

In any case, however, housing associations (traditional and
transfer landlords alike) have generally tended to offer, by contract, a greater range of rights than those available to assured
tenants under statute. In Scotland, for example, it was found
that 'the great majority' of housing associations had taken this
course (Mullen et al. 1997). In this sense, then, the contrast
between secure (local authority) and assured (housing association) tenants' rights has been less marked in practice than
might have been expected when the assured tenancy legislation
was established in 1988 (see Chapter 2).

In certain important respects, however, transfers create two
classes of tenants under successor landlords. Firstly, as noted
above, transferring tenants are typically offered a post-transfer
'rent guarantee' which often does not apply to households
becoming new tenants during the relevant period. Secondly,
and more importantly in the longer term, new tenants do not
enjoy the Right to Buy retained (as the Preserved Right to Buy)
by pre-transfer tenants moving across to the new landlord.
Instead, new tenants have to make do with the much less
financially attractive Right to Acquire. With the ongoing
effects of tenancy turnover, of course, post-transfer assured
tenancies eventually become the norm so that the Right to Buy
as it is carried over into the stock transfer housing association
world gradually withers on the vine. Early studies also suggested that, as well as enjoying fewer rights and paying (often
considerably) higher rents, new (post-transfer) tenants tended
to be less satisfied than existing (pre-transfer) tenants (Mullins
et al. 1995).

The belief that concerns on 'loss of statutory rights' might
have undermined tenant support for transfers is widely thought
to have motivated the Scottish Executive's introduction of a

unified social tenancy regime under the Housing (Scotland) Act 2001 (Kintrea 2006).

Housing management performance

With one official evaluation describing transfer housing associations as 'a new breed of dynamic RSLs (Registered Social Landlords)' (Cobbold and Dean 2000: 6) it might be assumed that transfer generally delivers a demonstrable premium in terms of housing management performance. However, while this is typically asserted by transfer housing association senior managers, the statistical evidence is not clear cut. Attempts to measure impacts in this area have been complicated by the absence of common performance indicators for local authorities and housing associations and by the problem of differentiating between transitional and longer-term impacts.

Partly in recognition of such difficulties, the Mullins et al. (1995) study could only conclude cautiously that 'LSVT has not brought about any obvious deterioration in housing management performance. Indeed, in many areas there has been an improvement' (ibid: 113). Less positively, Graham (1999) found that Scottish Homes transfers brought no immediate improvement in management performance.

One earlier study looking at the very distinct Scottish experience of small-scale 'community ownership' transfers, however, firmly concluded that the initiative had boosted management performance across the board. Clapham and Kintrea's (1994) evaluation focused on six Glasgow City Council estate transfers to community based housing associations and co-operatives undertaken in 1986 and 1987. Comparing 1988/89 statistics recorded by the six transfer landlords and by Glasgow City Council and Scottish Homes, it was found that 'the management effectiveness of all of the small, locally-based landlords was better than that of the large, traditional landlords' (ibid: 233). Given that improved performance appeared to have been achieved without higher spending on repairs or management, Clapham and Kintrea attributed the CBHAs' success in this area to 'better organisation through small scale and increased resident involvement' by comparison with Glasgow City Council as predecessor landlord). Indeed, it was argued that stock transfers would bring performance enhancement only where they involved handovers to small organizations since 'there is no evidence that larger landlords of any type perform well as housing managers' (ibid: 241).

An attempt to track, longitudinally, the performance of land-lords whose status changes from local authorities to housing associations is set out in Table 7.2. The analysis focuses on the performance of the relevant local authorities as recorded in the 1998/99 Audit Commission dataset and the performance of the respective transfer housing associations in 2005/06. The comparison here is necessarily very narrow, reflecting the very small number of comparable performance indicators available. On the re-let indicator, there was a slight performance deterioration across the entire local authority cohort over the seven-year period – with the typical period for re-letting empty properties rising from 35 days to 37 days. However, whilst non-urban transfer housing associations bucked this trend, urban transfer housing associations registered a larger deterioration – from 43 days to 51 days (see Table 7.3). As regards day-to-day repairs services, the median proportion of urgent repairs completed on time by both sets of transfer housing associations in 2005/06 was an improvement on the 1998/99 figure for predecessor local authorities (see Table 7.3). Nevertheless, this was of a marginally smaller magnitude than the performance improvement recorded across the local authority sector as a whole.

Generally, the evidence here is rather inconclusive. Whatever the benefits of stock transfer might be, there is no indication from this analysis that these typically include a significant boost to routine housing management performance.

A related issue is the extent to which transfer housing associations focus on improving routine housing management performance as opposed to a dominant focus (to begin with, at least) on capital works programmes. As noted above, transfer promises tend to play down aspirations for better day-to-day services. Also, particularly by comparison with the Arms Length Management Organization regime (see Chapter 8), it could be argued that there is little regulatory incentive for transfer housing associations to achieve 'excellence' on day-to-day services. The reference to the ALMO regime here relates to

TABLE 7.3 *Comparison of housing management performance 1998/99 and 2005/06*

Performance indicator (median scores)	1999–2004 urban 'whole stock' transfers		1999–2004 other 'whole stock' transfers		All local authorities	
	1998/99 (LA)	2005/06 (HA)	1998/99 (LA)	2005/06 (HA)	1998/99	2005/06
Average re-let interval (days)	43	51	30	29	35	37
Percentage of 'urgent repairs' completed on time	89	94	89	95	89	96

Notes: (1). Columns 2 and 3 relate to the 22 'urban' local authorities making whole stock transfers 1999-2004 for which data was available. (2). Columns 4 and 5 relate to the non-urban (district council) whole stock transfers 1999–2004 for which data was available – 40 transfers in the case of void management and 30 transfers in the case of urgent repairs. (3). Column 6 relates to all 285 local authorities which retained a landlord function as at that date. Column 6 relates to the 222 local authorities which retained a landlord function in 2005/06. (4). Where authorities (e.g. Bradford, Sunderland) transferred to a group structure, mean 'groupwide' figures have been calculated to facilitate pre- and post-transfer comparison.

Sources: Local authorities – Best Value PIs (Audit Commission website), HRA Business Plan Statistical Annex returns (CLG website); Housing associations – Housing Corporation performance indicator data.

TABLE 7.4 *English housing association performance trends, 2002/03–2006/07*

	Traditional HAs	First generation transfer HAs*	Second generation transfer HAs**	
			Non-urban	Urban
(a) Performance, 2002/03				
Voids available for letting (%)	0.9	0.7	0.8	1.2
Re-let interval (days)	34.3	24.5	31.4	44.9
% of routine repairs on time	94.8	93.0	90.1	94.1
(b) Performance, 2006/07				
Voids available for letting (%)	0.7	0.5	0.4	0.5
Re-let interval (days)	38.3	29.4	30.9	37.5
% of routine repairs on time	96.0	95.0	97.0	96.0
(c) Performance change, 2002/03–2006/07				
Voids available for letting (%)	-0.2	-0.2	-0.4	-0.7
Re-let interval (days)	4	4.9	-0.5	-7.4
% of routine repairs on time	1.2	2	6.9	1.9

* Associations established via 1988–97 transfers.
** Associations established via 1998–2002 transfers.

Source: Housing Corporation Performance Indicators dataset.

the fact that, as explained in Chapter 8, ALMO funding has been conditional on the achievement of 'management excellence'. Having secured business plan funding and tenant backing, transfer housing associations, by comparison, could be seen as in a relatively 'comfortable' position.

Table 7.4 analyses performance change over time, in relation to the 312 housing associations in the Housing Corporation's performance indicator dataset for 2006/07 and which were also in existence in 2002. The table compares the median scores for different classes of association with respect to three performance indicators, two connected with empty property management and one with responsive repairs. Table 7.4(c) shows that, over the relevant period, traditional housing associations slightly reduced the proportion of their dwellings classed as vacant and available for letting and also improved the proportion of 'routine' repairs completed on time. Speed of re-letting empty properties, however, declined. Second generation transfer associations, however, substantially improved their performance on all three measures. This analysis seems to cast doubt on the suggestion that recently-established transfer associations need not prioritize the enhancement of routine housing management services.

Standard performance indicators are, of course, rather narrow measures and tend to emphasize efficiency rather than effectiveness. Regulatory inspection judgements provide a broader-based assessment of social landlord services, as well as factoring in the local circumstances within which a landlord operates. Table 7.5 presents an analysis of Audit Commission inspection results for 177 housing associations in the four year period to March 2008. As shown here, 31 transfer housing associations were rated 'good' or 'excellent'. This represents 42 per cent of transfer housing associations inspected – substantially higher than the 31 per cent of traditional associations assessed during the relevant period and similarly judged. Among urban transfer housing associations, the 'good/excellent' rate was still higher at 54 per cent.

Unfortunately, however, it is not possible to broaden the comparisons set out in Table 7.5 to the local authority/ALMO sector because regulatory inspections of the latter are no longer undertaken according to a rolling programme.

TABLE 7.5 *Analysis of English housing associations inspections 2004/05–2007/08*

	Housing management services assessed as . . .				Total
	Excellent	Good	Fair	Poor	
Post-1997 urban transfer housing associations	1	12	10	1	24
Other transfer housing associations	1	17	29	3	50
All transfer housing associations (subtotal)	2	29	39	4	74
Traditional housing associations	1	31	57	14	103
Total	3	60	96	18	177

Note: Where an organization was inspected more than once during this period the most recent inspection was taken as the organization's score unless it is a re-inspection (because re-inspections are, by their nature, liable to lead to higher scores than initial inspections).

Source: Data from Audit Commission (2008).

Tenant satisfaction

Research evidence on tenants' satisfaction has been cited as supporting the contention that transfers have generally led to better landlord performance – irrespective of whether they have involved the 'breakup of local monopolies'. Cobbold and Dean (2000), for example, found that overall 'satisfaction with landlord' rates were considerably higher among transfer housing association tenants than among local authority tenants (85 per cent as compared with 79 per cent). Perhaps more tellingly, 38 per cent of transferring tenants in their study believed that post-transfer housing management was an improvement on what had gone before whilst only nine per cent thought the opposite.

However, Cobbold and Dean were careful to acknowledge that a 'feel good factor' associated with the major catch-up repairs programmes implemented in the immediate post-transfer period tends to affect tenants' satisfaction scores at this time. 'There is evidence that tenant satisfaction ratings among LSVT tenants may decline once initial (and frequently expensive) improvements have been made to homes' (ibid: 5). Likewise, some transfer housing associations report that extensive housing refurbishment and more responsive management in the early post-transfer phase tends to push up tenants' expectations, with the longer-term effect that it becomes very difficult to maintain the higher satisfaction ratings achieved in this 'honeymoon' stage.

Nevertheless, as shown in Table 7.6, survey evidence suggests that – with the exception of those established via post-1997 urban transfers, transfer housing associations tend to enjoy an edge over both traditional housing associations and local authorities/ALMOs in terms of satisfaction ratings. However, the second generation urban transfer housing association score on 'satisfaction with opportunities for participation' matches the all-landlord norm (see Table 7.6(a)). This is perhaps significant because many of the landlords concerned will be operating in metropolitan settings where there is likely to be a stronger tradition of tenant involvement and, arguably therefore, higher expectations in this respect.

Impacts on neighbourhoods and communities

Overview

As noted above, housing stock transfer has been one of the strategic options available to local authorities to deliver investment in the fabric of the housing stock so as to meet official property quality standards by set target dates. At the same time, transfer and the investment needed to achieve and sustain these standards has increasingly been seen as a potential catalyst for the wider regeneration of neighbourhoods – both physi-

TABLE 7.6 *Tenant satisfaction ratings compared*

(a) Proportion of respondents satisfied with service, accommodation and area							
Satisfaction with …	First generation transfer HAs*	Second generation transfer HAs**		Traditional HAs	LA/ALMO	All	Sample size
		Urban	Non-urban				No
	%	%	%	%	%	%	
Overall service	81	73	79	75	78	77	240,733
Accommodation	86	80	86	81	84	83	233,843
Neighbourhood as a place to live	81	71	83	75	79	77	227,447
The way landlord deals with repairs and maintenance	78	65	73	72	75	74	229,730
Opportunities for participation	57	54	55	54	53	54	231,064

Aspect	First generation transfer HAs*	Second generation transfer HAs**		Traditional HAs	LA/ALMO	All	Sample size
		Urban	Non-urban				
	%	%	%	%	%	%	No
Rating for being told when workers would call	81	77	78	77	79	78	135,747
Rating for attitude of workers	92	89	92	89	91	90	127,006
Rating for overall quality of repair work	85	81	85	80	83	82	127,978

(c) Satisfaction with communication – proportion responding positively

Aspect	First generation transfer HAs*	Second generation transfer HAs**		Traditional HAs	LA/ALMO	All	Sample size
		Urban	Non-urban				
	%	%	%	%	%	%	No
Easy to get hold of right person at last contact?	73	65	75	67	70	69	152,990
Staff found helpful at last contact?	85	79	86	80	82	81	152,494

* Associations established via 1988-97 transfers.
** Associations established via 1998-2002 transfers.

Source: Analysis of NHF STATUS tenants survey database as at summer 2007.

cally and socially. The relevance of neighbourhood renewal and community regeneration objectives became much greater after 1997 when transfers began to take place in inner city and other urban areas seriously affected by economic decline and social deprivation (see Chapter 2). This was also a period in which the 'wider role' played by many housing associations in neighbourhoods and communities was transformed from a perceived risk and distraction from core business requiring close regulation (Housing Corporation 1999) to an expectation as part of the government's sustainability agenda (ODPM 2003f), and the industry's identity 'in business for neighbourhoods' (NHF 2003).

Since 2000, government guidance for local authorities considering transfer in England has required authorities to 'consider how transfer could contribute to the regeneration of [the] area' and stipulated that 'Investment to improve social housing should be properly planned and part of a wider neighbourhood renewal strategy' (ODPM 2004c: 14 and 20). Further, the housing transfer process and the associated investment are seen as representing 'an important one-off opportunity for local authorities, residents and other stakeholders to improve community well being' (ibid: 20). In order to secure Ministerial consent, therefore, authorities have been expected to incorporate within transfer proposals credible plans to promote regeneration in relation to work and enterprise, crime, education and skills, health, housing and the physical environment. This new holistic focus is quite contrary to earlier views that a key benefit of transfer was to separate housing from other local services (see Chapter 5). This was sometimes portrayed as beneficial in helping to avoid distractions from improving landlord services, and in rendering impossible the local authority practice of siphoning off rental income to meet wider corporate goals. It could be argued that this shift in tack represents learning the benefits of 'joined-up governance' as well as reflecting the shift of the stock transfer programme to 'more difficult' neighbourhoods and authorities.

Alongside this shift there has been an increasing emphasis on putting 'residents at the heart' of option appraisal processes and long-term governance of transfer landlords. This has helped to stimulate greater attention to resident-led models such as community gateway in England and community mutual in Wales (see Chapter 5) and on engaging 'hard to reach residents' in these processes (Mullins et al. 2004).

For several years from 2002, these new more 'bottom-up' perspectives on transfer were promoted by the Community Housing Task Force, a Westminster Government team working with local authorities to support the options appraisal and ballot processes. Such approaches now seem attuned to the 'new localism' being advocated across the political spectrum which some have seen as challenging the top-down model of transfer in which decision-making has shifted away from local bodies to large regional and national housing groups. Indeed, recent speculation has suggested that 'localism one of the [Conservative] Party's key policies – is most easily pursued when local services like housing are council-controlled' (Stothart 2009).

Housing development and replacement

Transfer is classically seen as a device for upgrading rundown stock and transfer landlords are therefore characterized as being typically focused on the enhancement and management of their inherited assets. Alongside these roles, however, many of the more than 200 housing associations created via stock transfer have also become housing developers on a significant scale. In recent years this has tended to be linked with 'regeneration' activities where new housing is constructed in the course of demolition and replacement programmes. Before considering this in detail, however, we first review the rather different housing development activity associated with pre-1997 transfers.

Among the early transfer associations, interest in housing construction was often motivated largely by managerial ambitions to expand property portfolios or, at least, to offset stock losses resulting from sales under the Preserved Right to Buy (see above). It was recognized that, over time, stock shrinkage resulting from sales (and, in some instances, demolitions) would push up unit management costs, eventually placing organizational solvency at risk. Another impetus – to some extent shared with more recently-established transfer landlords – was the wish to exploit staff skills and experience built up during the intense post-transfer phase of catch-up repairs and modernization work. Perhaps partly for this reason, management boards as well as senior staff have often been eager to identify and exploit development opportunities arising as initial catch-up repairs and modernization programmes have neared completion.

By 2002, transfer housing associations established pre-1997 had constructed more than 50,000 homes (Pawson and Fancy 2003). The extent and pattern of this activity (mainly involving landlords based in English shire districts) was partly a product of a peculiar combination of economic and public policy circumstances in the early 1990s. These included:

- falling construction costs (resulting from the property market recession affecting London and the South at this time)
- general inflation at moderate levels and an absence of rent control
- expanding public funding for social housing development (until 1993/94)
- the Housing Corporation's contemporary competitive ethos (involving certain transfer housing associations being 'steered' into new local authority areas to provide competitive bids and influence existing housing association bidding behaviour).

Many earlier transfer housing associations also benefited from receiving relatively high value stock from local authorities with relatively small residual housing debts. In these circumstances, transferring local authorities were often able to 'recycle' at least part of the net transfer receipt into new social housing development, with the transfer housing association as a rule selected as the delivery vehicle.

An important feature of housing development by first generation transfer housing associations development was its geographical distribution. Nearly half of all homes built by pre-1997 transfer housing associations prior to 2003 involved sites outside the association's 'home authority'. A few of the 1988–93 landlord cohort quickly asserted themselves as major regional players, with stockholdings accumulated across numerous local authority areas. Prominent examples included Bedfordshire Pilgrims (home authority: Bedford Borough

Council), Sovereign (Newbury District Council) and Magna (West Dorset). By 2006, Housing Corporation data showed six of these associations each managing stock in more than 20 local authority districts. Landlords spawned by more recent transfers, however, have tended to focus their typically more limited new development activities more squarely within their original areas of operation. Case study evidence has suggested that transfer housing associations' increasingly local focus also reflected the post-1996 governance model, with the newer, more tenant- and councillor-influenced, landlords tending to be less enthusiastic about geographical diversification (Pawson and Fancy 2003). Nevertheless, the earlier period of expansionism sowed the seeds of growth of some of the larger housing association groups that have since become increasingly dominant in the sector.

More recently, English transfer housing association aspirations to secure development funding have been adversely affected by two new developments. First, by the withdrawal of the Local Authority Social Housing Grant scheme which had allowed local authorities to reclaim this grant from the Housing Corporation, effectively facilitating grant 'recycling' and 'double subsidy'. Second, by the Housing Corporation's 'Re-inventing Investment' policy under which, from 2004/05, the majority of the programme was allocated to 'partnering housing associations' able to assemble annual programmes of more than £10 million, thereby excluding many newly developing transfer associations.

Since 1997, as transfer has increasingly engaged with urban areas containing substantial numbers of problematic and/or highly dilapidated buildings so the task facing transfer landlords has increasingly come to involve demolition and replacement – estate and neighbourhood regeneration – rather than 'simple' housing refurbishment. For example, Housing Corporation data shows that associations created by transfers in England in the period 1998–2003 demolished over 2,000 properties in 2006/07 – over 0.5 per cent of their stock at the start of the year.

Housing Corporation figures also show that, in the ten years to 2006/07, transfer housing associations demolished more than 22,000 dwellings in England alone (see Table 7.7). Notably, the average annual number of transfer housing associ-

TABLE 7.7 *English housing association demolitions and construction, 1997/98–2006/07*

(a) Demolitions

	Traditional HAs	Transfer HAs	Total	Transfer HAs %
1997/98	1,074	602	1,676	36
1998/99	1,244	716	1,960	37
1999/00	2,068	1,206	3,274	37
2000/01	789	1,849	2,638	70
2001/02	2,798	1,925	4,723	41
2002/03	1,496	2,099	3,595	58
2003/04	1,555	4,445	6,000	74
2004/05	1,499	3,557	5,056	70
2005/06	1,294	3,017	4,311	70
2006/07	1,330	2,662	3,992	67
Total	15,147	22,078	37,225	59

(b) New build completions

	Traditional HAs	Transfer HAs	Total	Transfer HAs %
1997/98	27,515	2,811	30,326	9
1998/99	22,978	2,916	25,894	11
1999/00	20,345	3,464	23,809	15
2000/01	19,075	3,665	22,740	16
2001/02	19,132	4,112	23,244	18
2002/03	17,531	3,717	21,248	17
2003/04	15,890	5,479	21,369	26
2004/05	17,489	5,542	23,031	24
2005/06	18,630	5,922	24,552	24
2006/07	20,419	6,485	26,904	24
Total	199,004	44,113	243,117	18

Source: Data from Housing Corporation RSR dataset.

ation demolitions in the five years to 2006/07 – some 3,200 – was nearly three times the number in the previous five years. Under the Glasgow City Council 2003 transfer it was envisaged that some 19,000 (mainly sub-standard) homes would be demolished by 2015 – a figure equating to around a quarter of the entire transferred stock (GHA 2006). While this instance is something of an 'extreme case' among whole stock disposals, many partial transfers involving run-down inner city housing have facilitated substantial clearance activity. Of the 45,000 homes transferred to housing associations under the ERCF, for example, some 10 per cent had been demolished within five years of transfer, with another five per cent due for clearance within the next five years. Some housing associations, surveyed in 2004, anticipated that more than 50 per cent of their transferred stock was likely to have been demolished within 10 years of its acquisition (Pawson et al. 2005a).

Evidence suggests a tendency for actual levels of clearance to exceed those anticipated at transfer. Among 45 'second generation' transfer associations surveyed in 2007, almost half (22) reported that the extent of demolition had turned out to be greater than what was originally expected. In only six instances was the opposite true (Pawson et al. 2009). Post-transfer decisions to expand clearance have sometimes reflected improvements in the quality of stock condition information, recognition of changing (low) demand for particular types of properties in specific locations or the introduction of more systematic and rigorous assessments of housing conditions. Some associations have reported that involving tenants in the decision-making process (e.g. through area committees or scheme panels) had made increases in the numbers of proposed demolitions less controversial than might otherwise have been the case (Pawson et al. 2009).

Housing demolition and replacement stimulated by transfer, has provided opportunities to alter the mix of housing types, and in some cases tenure, at a local level, with a view to underpinning long-term neighbourhood sustainability. In some instances (e.g. Glasgow) the freedom of the transfer landlord to undertake such schemes has been constrained by a requirement to hand over cleared sites to the local authority or to repay to central government capital receipts generated by site disposals to private developers. Significantly, in parallel with actual versus planned demolitions, the numbers of new homes being built by second generation transfer housing associations surveyed in 2007 was usually reported as higher than originally planned (Pawson et al. 2009). This was true for both new build for rent and for sale, and especially marked for urban transfers. In this sense, it could be said that these transfers are 'delivering added value' in relation to what was originally expected.

In some large urban transfers, housing association clearance and construction activity has been largely associated with major area renewal projects planned in partnership with the local authority. Perhaps the largest of these has involved Glasgow Housing Association and Glasgow City Council who defined seven 'transformational regeneration' projects in 2004 (GoWell 2007). In total, these schemes were expected to involve up to 9,000 demolitions, with a similar number of new build homes being developed – roughly two thirds of these being for private sale. Collectively, these schemes have been described by Professor Alan McGregor as 'one of the most ambitious urban regeneration programmes in the UK' (Glasgow City Council 2007b: paragraph 2.7).

Another large-scale example has involved the participation of Gentoo Group (formerly Sunderland Housing Group) in an area Renewal Plan which envisaged the demolition of 4,100 dwellings, with 3,750 replacement homes being constructed. As in Glasgow, the plans had been developed in consultation between transfer housing association and city council. Unlike Glasgow, however, the process had been largely driven by the former, with the latter having a more passive role. The model for regenerated estates was for mixed tenure neighbourhoods with rented and for-sale properties fully integrated in a pepper-potted layout where tenure could not be identified from house design. From the business viewpoint this was recognized as costly because values of for-sale properties would be compromised by proximity to rented homes. However, this was seen as justified by the social benefits of community integration. In addition, recognizing that house buyers with choices would weigh up Gentoo houses against those provided by private developers in 'more exclusive' areas, new homes to be developed for sale under the plan were to be 20 per cent larger than comparable new private sector dwellings.

Social, economic and community regeneration

The notion that social and economic renewal of deprived communities could be an important spin-off from stock transfer was first advanced in the wake of the ERCF programme, with its focus on run-down local authority estates in inner cities and other urban areas (HACAS Consulting 2002). Here, the term 'community regeneration' is defined in terms of non-housing initiatives concerned with community sustainability, 'activities which are additional to core housing management services' (ibid). The importance attached to such activities rose alongside the enhanced post-1997 official commitment to tackling social exclusion (e.g. Cabinet Office 2001).

The growing linkage between stock transfer and community regeneration is to some extent attributable to 'top-down' pressure from central government – e.g. as transmitted through central government's specification for transfer proposals (see above). However, with transfers increasingly involving less popular and sometimes highly problematic housing, many transfer landlords are also likely to be motivated by enlightened self-interest: the perception that 'sustainable communities [are] . . . essential to the long-term viability of investment in the area' (HACAS Consulting 2002: 28). Hence, for one case study partial transfer housing association investigated by HACAS, the need to combat low demand was a key driver for its interest here whilst for another the issue was the 'manageability' of the inherited stock. All three HACAS case study housing associations were 'convinced that [their] investment in community regeneration [was] essential to business plan viability and . . . important in obtaining private sector funding' (ibid: 55).

Whole stock transfers dominated by particularly run-down and/or low demand housing are also likely to be seen as central to broader regeneration strategies. The Glasgow transfer, for example, was seen by Gibb (2003) as a key plank in the Council's wider plans to restore confidence in the city, thereby stemming long-term population decline. 'Improving social housing [as part of a large-scale co-ordinated effort] . . . can lead to better residential environments that help to encourage families back into the city' (111). In this way Gibb argued that the council's longstanding aim of increasing family home ownership might, ironically, be 'achieved in part by investing in hitherto neglected social housing'.

Evidence from the National Housing Federation's Neighbourhood Audit (NHF 2008c) suggests that, in the five years to 2007/08, 'second generation' transfer associations invested some £56 million in 'community capital projects', with the majority of the relevant funding originating from associations themselves (Pawson et al. 2009). For more than half of these associations such activity included contributing to (or managing) the development of community facilities.

Perhaps of even greater importance is the evidence from the NHF survey on the 'added value' being contributed to neighbourhoods by housing associations. For example, over and above housing management activity, post-1997 transfer housing associations were estimated as having provided such 'additional services' to the value of £81 million in 2006/07. More than £50 million of this was provided through direct funding and the (non-chargeable) contribution of association staff time (Pawson et al. 2009). As shown in Figure 7.5, the activities most commonly involved youth provision of various kinds. Most urban transfer housing associations were also involved in community capacity building, IT training and sports activities. A key finding of the Pawson et al. (2009) research was that urban transfer housing associations had typically come to be involved in 'community regeneration' activities to a far greater degree than had been originally anticipated.

High rates of 'community regeneration' activity among post-1997 urban transfer housing associations partly reflects the inclusion within this cohort of some associations established under the Estates Renewal Challenge Fund programme. ERCF transfers incorporated an explicit neighbourhood renewal emphasis through specific covenants – or obligations – written into some transfer agreements by transferring local authorities. The importance of community regeneration objectives in the programme was also reflected – at least for some of the schemes – in funding for such activities being built into government grant awards. Even so, much of the community regeneration activity under ERCF was financed through other public sources – e.g. Single Regeneration Budget, European Social Fund, Home Office grants and the like (Pawson et al. 2005a).

FIGURE 7.5 Neighbourhood services provided by English housing associations, 2006/07

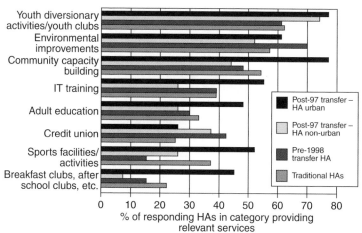

Source: Data from NHF Neighbourhood Audit 2008.

While housing associations established through Scottish Homes transfers have some features in common with English partial transfer landlords, it appears that these organizations have been somewhat less active in the community regeneration area. Research reviewing the Scottish Homes transfer programme confirmed that recipient associations had undertaken a variety of 'community regeneration' projects. However, 'without exception, all the wider action activities (implemented by case study transfer landlords) were small scale and housing remained by far the most important activity of the associations' (Gibb et al. 2005: 51). Similarly, 'In the case of the organisations which existed prior to the Scottish Homes stock transfers, it is clear that the transfers *have not* been instrumental in them developing a wider role' (ibid: 51 – italics added).

Many second generation transfer housing associations have incorporated provision for community regeneration spending within their business plans (with such commitments being necessarily reflected in the transfer valuation agreed with the local authority). Poplar HARCA, for example, structured its business plan to generate £2 per week per tenant for years 1–3 and £1 per week per tenant for years 4–30 (HACAS Consulting 2002).

Similarly, Trafford Housing Trust was able to develop an innovative programme of community investment work with young people by securing an inflation proofed 'endowment' of £700,000 per year to fund wider regeneration activities as part of the stock transfer transaction, as Box 7.2 illustrates. Whilst such provision is believed to be unusual, growing numbers of transfer housing associations are 'maturing' to the point where they pass their 'peak debt' year and begin to generate surpluses. There is evidence that these surpluses are seen by at least some of the associations concerned as facilitating an expanded level of activity in this area (Pawson and Fancy 2003).

Involvement of BME communities and the role of BME housing associations

Stock transfer's progressively more urban character post-1997 has meant the process has increasingly affected areas with significant black and minority ethnic (BME) populations. As recently as 2004, however, government remained concerned that 'despite experiencing some of the worst housing conditions, BME communities have not benefited to the same extent as other communities from the funding released by stock transfer for improvements to housing and neighbourhoods' (ODPM, 2004c: Appendix E, paragraph 2).

There was an anxiety that, without specific attention to the issue, BME communities could be insufficiently involved in stock transfer planning and that overcoming this problem could require the involvement of BME-led advice agencies. This concern was strengthened by the requirement for all stock-holding authorities to undertake an option appraisal by 2005 to decide how they would meet the Decent Homes Standard by 2010. This policy was actively promoted by the Community Housing Task Force, the requirement for tenants to be 'at the heart' of the process and to engage 'hard to reach groups' (ODPM 2003c)

While all tenants may be seen as 'hard to reach' in relation to consultation on stock options, involving some BME tenants may present particular challenges due to, for example, language barriers or mistrust of the local authority as an organization (Mullins et al. 2004).

Box 7.2   Funding community investment from transfer funding: Trafford Housing Trust

'Our near housing activity is funded mainly through our Community Fund. This was established as part of the stock transfer and so sits in our business plan for the next 30 years. An inflation proofed £700,000 per year, it is used for social, environmental and economic improvements outside residents' dwellings.

The Community Fund also has a positive impact on other potential donors, since it ensures the sustainability of our neighbourhood working. Our major lender was sufficiently impressed by our commitment to building social capital that they offered a six-figure matching donation to be used with their agreement on activities we want to pursue. Our vision is to create the grant that goes on giving by using the fund in ways that delivers efficiencies in what we do now so that these targeted interventions lead to repeatable year on year savings in current activities , leaving more money for new innovations.'

Source: Matthew Gardiner (Chief Executive) of Trafford Housing Trust: cited by Wadhams (2009) and included with permission.

Concerns about transfer ballot defeats and criticisms of the absence of real choice for residents (summarized later by Centre for Public Services 2004) may explain the emphasis on 'options' and on resident consultation and 'reach' in an attempt to boost legitimacy. The early stock transfer programme had tended to bypass areas with significant BME communities, but the focus after 1996, and particularly after the 2000 Green Paper (DETR 2000c), on tackling the investment backlog inevitably brought the investment process into localities with much greater ethnic diversity. Add to that the emphasis of the modernization agenda on democratic renewal and public participation (Newman 2001), the requirements of Best Value for meaningful tenant involvement and the proactive approach to involvement in transfers stimulated by the Community Housing Task Force, set up in May 2001 to support local authorities working on decent homes options, and the need for 'good practice' on BME involvement becomes clear.

Each stock investment option provided opportunities for high levels of involvement for small numbers of residents through membership of governance and consultative structures. Both stock transfers and ALMOs typically had a third of the governing body recruited from residents, while PFI contracts were tendered and managed by resident-led steering groups (RSGs) which demanded high levels of commitment. In one case study the RSG had been meeting fortnightly for 4 years before the PFI contract even started to operate. The community gateway model for stock transfer (CIH 2002b) also provided for high-level involvement. This sometimes raised 'representativeness' questions about the relatively small numbers of active tenants and there were suggestions that targets be set in relation to BME representation on governing bodies.

Surveys of authorities on the stock transfer, ALMO and PFI programmes (Niner and Rowlands 2003) demonstrated some success in securing ethnically 'representative' governing bodies. 80 per cent of sample authorities who had completed transfers (between 1988 and 2001) in areas where BME communities made up more than 3 per cent of the population had at least one BME board member, and BME members made up 18 per cent of all board members in these transfer landlords. BME board members were more likely to have been recruited through the tenant and local authority constituencies than through the independent route, where BME 'representatives' might have been more easily 'headhunted'. However, in many authorities formal tenant consultative and governance structures remained white dominated, sometimes failing to reflect the diversity of the tenant population (for example nearly two thirds of authorities on the 2001/3 transfer programmes had no BME shadow board members). In situations of ethnic diversity, for example, with many new migrant groups adding to long-standing BME communities, it became apparent that boards could never be truly 'representative' but should set out to 'reflect' the diversity of their communities.

Informal methods had greater potential to overcome the mistrust that had plagued attempts to engage BME communities and other residents in plans to improve homes and communities. But these only worked where certain conditions were met. Successful authorities employed staff to reflect the communities they served, staff and tenant representatives used their own networks to make contact with 'hard to reach' tenants, these networks were extended to include the places and organizations where 'hard to reach tenants' were likely to be contacted. These included shopping, community and leisure venues such as supermarkets, specialist 'ethnic' food shops, barbers, faith groups, schools and nurseries and community organizations (Mullins et al. 2004).

Successful involvement tended to be associated with new approaches to engagement, often using informal networks alongside more formal structures. One PFI scheme was developed in an area where formal representative structures (tenant and resident associations (TRAs), tenant liaison committees (TLCs) and community forum) had failed to adapt to the growing ethnic diversity of the area. In this case, the Residents Steering Group (RSG) was treated as a new institution, and innovative approaches were used to recruit tenant and leaseholder member. Door knocking, 'Fun Days' and 'headhunting' proved effective in attracting new blood and in achieving wider participation in the RSG than in other forums in the same geographical areas. Networks were being built between the RSG and the wider voluntary sector, including BME community groups, to ensure that would continue to be open to new members (Mullins et al. 2004).

Central government also at that time supported the idea of BME-led housing associations playing an active role in the stock transfer process and urged transferring local authorities to consider how such organizations could be involved. Possible mechanisms could include 'second stage' transfers from 'mainstream' transfer housing associations or BME housing associations taking on management of ex-local authority stock under contract (ODPM 2004c: Appendix E, paragraphs 37–8). Research in four case study areas (Campbell Tickell 2005) explored some of the ways in which BME-led housing associations had been engaged in transfer processes. Approaches found to be effective included collaboration between BME associations, the local authority and the stock transfer landlords, engagement with BME communities and various forms of research. However, only Spitalfields HA appeared to have been actively involved as a prospective transfer landlord. It was cited as having repositioned as a 'community association' as part of Tower Hamlets Housing Choice programme covering just 1 per cent of the council's stock. Other BME associations in Tower Hamlets 'had come under pressure from Defend Council Housing and withdrew from Housing Choice' (Campbell Tickell 2005: 18). Generally, the study found little evidence of BME association involvement in stock options appraisals, ill-informed concerns about BME associations' capacity and a general strategic vacuum.

After 2005, the tide had appeared to turn against BME associations for a variety of reasons, particularly the community cohesion agenda which brought a presumption against the funding of organizations working with specific ethnic groups and an increasingly competitive financial environment in which the relatively recent acquisition of stock and high debt ratios of most BME associations counted against them. A rash of mergers with mainstream associations, the well publicized collapse of Ujima HA and supervision of Presentation HA, two of the largest BME housing associations, made further discussion of direct involvement in stock transfer increasingly unlikely.

Chapter conclusions

Stock transfer has levered substantial investment into social housing, increasingly to the benefit of areas with seriously dilapidated property. In virtually all cases, transfer housing associations have found it possible to deliver (typical) five year commitments on stock repairs and modernization. In this way, the programme appears to have avoided the fate of other high profile public sector infrastructure renewal projects (e.g. railway upgrading) often plagued by cost overruns and delays. Despite some reservations, it can be claimed that this has enabled a significant and rapid improvement in the condition of social housing towards the Decent Homes Standard (and equivalent standards in Wales and Scotland).

Being relatively unencumbered by poor quality stock, many English 'first generation' transfer housing associations exploited opportunities to become major developers of new housing both within and beyond the boundaries of their original 'home areas'. For most transfer landlords, however, stock losses through continuing sitting tenant sales and (in some cases) demolitions have been well in excess of additions through new construction. More recently-established landlords are, for various reasons, unlikely to emulate their first wave counterparts in this respect and for them the most likely route to significant organizational growth is likely to come in the form of follow-on transfers or mergers rather than new development.

Central government's post-2001 'rent-capping' policies blew a hole in the business plans of some transfer housing associations, leaving them with difficult choices between unpalatable service cutbacks, asset sales or a potential loss of local identity and control resulting from merger with a stronger partner. More recent threats of rent reductions to reflect falling RPI have placed further potential strains on the model.

Hard evidence that transfer has generally improved housing management performance is fairly thin on the ground, though part of the problem here is the continuing inconsistency of monitoring frameworks applicable to local authorities and their housing association counterparts. Within the housing association sector, however, it seems clear that transfer landlords tend to set standards which traditional housing associations would do well to emulate. It may be that their typically rather compact geographical form confers advantages over traditional housing associations of similar size both in terms of housing management costs but also in being in a better position to engage with local communities. Equally, the focus on achieving demanding business plan targets is certainly a key organizational driver, at least in a transfer housing association's early pre-peak debt phase, though there is no evidence that this generally translates into a tough (as opposed to a tight) management style.

Rather than undermining the rights of existing tenants, transfer could be seen as compromising the position of new tenants who generally lose access to the Right to Buy (which would be available to new tenants being housed by a local authority).

As the transfer process came to involve deprived inner city areas, so central government has made clear an expectation that it must deliver significant 'regeneration' benefits – in terms of both the physical and social fabric of neighbourhoods. This has tended to reverse the earlier focus on transfers as creating 'stand alone housing organizations' and to promote the importance of holistic contributions to neighbourhoods; increasingly by involving communities in decision-making and governance and by promoting a 'new localism'. At the planning stage, such objectives have often been couched in fairly cautious terms, although there are good examples of organizations that have made an early contribution to community investment by making budgetary provision in transfer transactions and revenue budgets. Many new landlords operating in urban settings have also quickly come to adopt an 'enlightened self-interest' attitude in this area and have become involved in community regeneration activities to a much greater degree than originally anticipated. Some transfer associations have benefited from budgetary provision for ongoing community regeneration activity from within the transfer business plan. In most cases, however, it has only been as associations' business plans have matured and finance has become available that some are choosing to spend on community investment and regeneration. At the time of writing, however, it is too early to say how effective these will prove in helping to secure transfer landlords' viability and, more broadly, reviving neighbourhoods in social and economic terms.

Chapter 8

ALMOs: Short-Term Expedient or Long-Term Alternative?

By 2009, almost 1.2 million homes had been transferred from councils to housing associations in England (see Chapter 2). However, this represents the cumulative impact of a process unfolding for two decades. The portfolio of homes managed by local authority Arms Length Management Organizations – ALMOs – grew to over 1 million in just six years from 2002–2008. By the end of this period, more than half of the housing remaining in council ownership was being run by ALMOs rather than directly by local authorities. Created ostensibly as 'delivery vehicles' to oversee property upgrading to meet the government's Decent Homes Standard, there are mixed signs as to whether ALMOs will become an enduring component of England's social housing landscape.

This chapter explores why ALMOs were formed, looks at how they are structured and operate and discusses how they might become part of the long-term future after council housing. It should be acknowledged at the outset that while ALMOs have attracted substantial press coverage there has been relatively little in-depth research on their activities and that, therefore, this chapter necessarily represents only a pre-liminary assessment of the ALMO story.

ALMO Origins and Purpose

Usually constituted as a company limited by guarantee, an ALMO is a non-profit organization established by a local authority to manage and improve all or part of its housing stock. Unlike stock transfer, the ALMO option has not been available to local authorities in Scotland or Wales – though the possibility of Scottish ALMOs was floated by the SNP Edinburgh administration in 2007 (Scottish Government

2007). Hence, unlike other chapters in this book, this chapter is exclusively about England.

The key feature of ALMOs is that, while the local authority remains property owner, legal landlord and normally sole shareholder, housing management functions are contracted to a new 'arms length' body. As the name implies, ALMOs are intended to operate with a significant degree of autonomy from council control. For local authorities, the critical aspect of the post-2002 ALMO regime in England is that 'high performing' ALMOs qualify for public funding over and above what would be available to a stock-owning local authority directly managing its housing. In the period 2002–10 central government estimates that £5.7 billion will be channelled to ALMOs in this way (CLG 2009d).

The ALMO archetype is arguably descended from the local housing company concept advocated as an alternative to the stock transfer model of the early 1990s (Hawksworth and Wilcox 1995a). Drawing on the Swedish municipal housing company regime, consideration was given to a re-definition of public debt to exclude borrowing by separately managed public corporations (see Chapter 3). When this was ruled out by Treasury after 1997, Ministers decided that their aspiration for leveraging external finance into social housing would continue to be achieved through housing associations whose loans were not counted in 'public sector net borrowing' (PSNB). The later development and take-up of the ALMO concept was achieved following its inclusion as one of several possible options for restructuring council housing in an influential report by Zitron et al. (1999) and its further exploration by a working party convened by the Westminster Government whose work informed the drafting of the 2000 Housing Green Paper.

The Green Paper acknowledged that a considerable body of England's social housing had fallen below acceptable standards in terms of its state of repair, its facilities and its energy efficiency. To achieve what was defined as a 'decent' standard (see Chapter 3 for details), investment of some £19 billion would be required (DETR 2000c). As noted in Chapter 3, Ministers set a target for the complete elimination of 'non-decent' social housing by 2010. Every stock-owning local authority was faced with the need to undertake a certain amount of investment in order to achieve the Decent Homes Standard. For some, the rel-

Box 8.1   Stock transfer or ALMO?

	Stock transfer	ALMO
Form	Asset ownership and management passes to housing association	Asset ownership and control of Housing Revenue Account remain with local authority but housing management delegated to arm's length organization under contract (some ALMOs also manage the HRA on behalf of their parent authority)
Relationship with local authority	Council normally nominates 1/3rd of board. Otherwise operates independent of local authority	Council owns assets, agrees funding through management contract and appoints at least 1/3rd of board
Staffing	Staff performing housing management-related functions within local authority transferred to transfer housing association under EU TUPE regulations	Staff performing housing management-related functions within local authority transferred to transfer housing association under EU TUPE regulations
Funding	Long-term (often 25–30 year) private finance in place at formation. Debt profile specified in business plan	Annual HRA funding subject to negotiation with local authority
Sustainability	Able to access funding to develop new properties to compensate for stock losses under Right to Buy (RTB also limited to transferring tenants)	Management contract to be re-negotiated every 5 years. Very limited opportunities to develop new homes. Right to Buy sales may reduce portfolio size – no limitation on RTB in relation to tenancies granted after ALMO setup

ative scale of disrepair and their own resources meant it was possible to envisage Decent Homes Standard compliance without the need to consider radical options for altering the governance and/or ownership of their stock. For the others, however, the Green Paper set out three alternative possibilities for accessing additional investment.

Setting up an arm's length management organization or ALMO was one of these three possible 'alternative management' options (alongside PFI transactions and stock transfer). Some of the key features of these three approaches are compared in Box 3.2 (Chapter 3). The 'fourth option' of increased public funding for local authority housing, traditionally managed, (as advocated by groups such as Defend Council Housing – see Chapter 4) was ruled out by successive Housing Ministers.

In practice, most local authorities needing to supplement mainstream resources to fund Decent Homes compliance have had to decide between stock transfer and ALMO. Building on Box 3.2 these alternatives are compared in Box 8.1, Whilst the initial structure of the two organization types have similarities, for example in board structure, in the longer term, differences may emerge. Stock transfer housing associations are mainly funded through long-term mortgage finance and there is a clear incentive to carefully manage stock over the term of the loan. ALMOs have a clear mandate for five years – the period of their initial management contract and target timescale for achieving the Decent Homes Standard. Beyond this period, ALMOs may have diminishing income due to attrition of stock through Right to Buy sales, and this may limit their ability to maintain housing stock to a high standard.

The Politics of ALMOs

As noted in Chapter 2, combined with the introduction of the local housing company governance model in 1996, the election of the Blair government in 1997 somewhat diminished the extent of hostility to stock transfer on the part of Labour-controlled local authorities. Recognizing the scope for accessing greater investment, some Labour-held local authorities began to advocate transfer and most were successful in obtaining ballot endorsement from tenants. Ministers will, however, have been aware that political antipathy to transfer remained entrenched in some areas – especially some larger urban authorities, often with substantial housing investment needs. Transfer fundability was also an issue in many such areas, with heavy levels of outstanding council housing debt. If Ministers were to credibly espouse the upgrading of all poor quality council housing, a new mechanism was needed to operate alongside transfer. This would need to be capable of being presented (to the Treasury, as well as the outside world) as part of the government's public service reform programme, and yet attract greater approval from local authorities than stock transfer. Hence, the ALMO model was born.

Nevertheless, like the Right to Buy and stock transfers, the ALMO policy has been contested and controversial. The *critical* view put forward by Defend Council Housing, who have provided support and lobbying for local opponents to both LSVTs and ALMOs, is that ALMOs 'are the government's strategy for a two-stage privatisation ... they are simply a short term attempt to get round tenants opposition to stock transfer' (DCH 2004a: 1). Whether most ALMOs will morph into housing associations has yet to be seen and, even if this occurred, whether it would amount to 'privatization' remains arguable (see Chapter 4). There is a danger that rhetoric in this debate can be exaggerated. For example, Cowan and McDermont (2006: 81) assert that 'the [Decent Homes delivery] options open to local authorities all require relinquishing autonomy and control to the private finance sector'. At least as far as ALMOs are concerned, this overstates the position.

More credibly, the critical perspective sees ALMOs as less accountable to tenants than directly managed council housing because of ALMOs' partial insulation from the influence of elected local authority members and the influence gained by 'independent' ALMO board members who are not subject to the electoral process. While tenants usually account for a third of ALMO board members (see below), Defend Council Housing correctly points out that tenant board members (although elected) are constrained by company law and cannot directly represent tenant interests.

Critics view ALMOs as wasting money that could otherwise be invested in additional social housing. Certainly, pursuing the

ALMO option involves both initial and ongoing costs which would not be incurred if a local authority chose, instead, to retain direct control of housing management. Set-up costs often include substantial legal and consultants' fees. For example, according to Defend Council Housing (2004a), these amounted to £2 million in the case of Ashfield Homes (although exactly what was included within this figure is not stated). Then there are the publicity costs associated with informing tenants about an ALMO proposal and paying for the required consultation (possibly including a formal ballot). It is claimed, for example, that Camden Council spent £500,000 unsuccessfully promoting a 'yes' vote during the Council's 2004 ballot (Centre for Public Services 2004). The creation of a new organization to sit alongside a council's residual housing department usually involves the creation of new senior management posts, some of which may be a net addition to the overall establishment. Here, again, ALMOs are potentially vulnerable to the charge that they are not a 'value for money' solution.

In contrast, the *official* view from successive Housing Ministers is that (like stock transfers) outsourcing operational tasks to an ALMO can be highly beneficial because it enables a local authority to concentrate on strategic housing responsibilities and in this way 'provides a strong incentive for better performance, ensures a sharper focus on the two distinct housing functions, and helps to guarantee tenants a greater role in the future management of their estates' (Hansard 2003). It was also contended by government that formalizing the split between strategy vs. delivery via the ALMO model could be advantageous in facilitating:

- involvement of a wider range of people, including tenants, in decision-making, and helping to encourage innovative thinking; and
- a more businesslike approach to managing the stock, concentrating on delivering high quality services offering value for money and responding to the needs of tenants (ODPM 2004b: 15).

Having delegated housing management functions to ALMO partners, Councils are supposedly freed to coordinate the various social housing providers operating within their area, and to facilitate the development of additional affordable housing. At the same time, housing managers are partially insulated from competing (potentially distracting) priorities and are expected (by government) to achieve improved service delivery. Some vindication for this view is provided by the fact that most ALMOs have been judged by the Audit Commission to have significantly improved their service delivery and via the quantitative analysis which demonstrates that ALMO local authorities have improved their performance to a greater extent than their non-ALMO counterparts over recent years (see Table 8.4 below). However, most observers would probably see such improvements as having resulted mainly from the incentive effects of performance-based resource allocation rather than from structural reform. It cannot be known, whether – as argued by Defend Council Housing – a similar transformation could have been achieved if similar levels of funding had been made available for traditionally managed council housing.

The final view can be described as *pragmatic*, that ALMOs were the 'least worst' option for local authorities who wanted to retain some control and democratic accountability while securing the necessary investment to improve housing quality. Such an argument was often used by local authorities in selling ALMOs to tenants. Some councillors backed the ALMO option, believing it to be only a short-term expedient, with management responsibility being retrieved once the Decent Homes investment programme had been completed. What is clear is that establishing ALMOs can only be understood as part of a financial scenario where local authorities had to meet Decent Homes standards by 2010 but were prevented from doing so by significantly increasing borrowing or raising rents. In the pragmatic view of ALMO politics, the logic for this type of organization ends when the repairs are completed and tenants have shiny new kitchens and bathrooms.

Councils weighing up the possibility of establishing an ALMO were faced with a complex, as well as politically charged, decision. As indicated in Box 3.2, the benefits of more generous funding and the possibility of new affordable housing development through stock transfer and PFI options needed to be balanced against the lower political risk with an ALMO which preserves council asset ownership and the potential to recover direct control over housing management. Case study research from north-east England reveals various motives at work. In Hartlepool, stock transfer was thought able to leverage more funding to both achieve Decent Homes standards and tackle other local problems such as anti-social behaviour. In nearby Stockton-on-Tees, Tristar ALMO was set up, according to one interviewee, as 'a way of securing money without the council losing control' (Gibb and Trebeck 2008: 9).

ALMO formation and profile

As with stock transfer, central government can encourage a local authority to consider the ALMO option, but the decision to proceed lies with councillors. Official guidance required an options appraisal process with 'tenants at the heart' (see Chapter 3). In practice, public participation has sometimes been restricted mainly to discussing the way a local authorities' preferred option will be developed. ALMOs differ from LSVTs in that there is no Ministerial expectation of a tenant ballot, though under section 105 of the 1985 Housing Act tenants need to be 'consulted' (House of Commons 2003). This distinction was important for Stockport council whose 2003 LSVT ballot proposal was defeated but could establish an ALMO in 2005 after 'extensive consultation' (Stockport Council 2006). Of the authorities testing tenant opinion on ALMO establishment in the period up to 2006, 21 held a ballot and 33 'used other methods to test opinion' (Hansard 2006). Bolton Council, for example, established an ALMO in 2002 after neither ballot nor survey: a tenants conference was held where all present voted in favour (Audit Commission 2003b).

For local authorities opting for a ballot to test opinion, approaches have been diverse in the absence of prescriptive official rules. Councils have had discretion in wording the ballot question: Derby in 2002 asked 'are you in favour of the management of your home by Derby Homes?', whereas Leeds in 2003 implied the new company would be aligned with the local authority: 'are you in favour of a Council run ALMO in Leeds running housing services in the future?' Interestingly, both ballots returned an 88 per cent 'yes' vote.

Not every test of tenant opinion on ALMO set-up has met with clear approval. Lambeth proceeded to form an ALMO in 2007, claiming majority tenant support when, in fact, only 42 per cent of survey respondents had voted in favour – the council controversially excluded the 'don't knows' from responses to a survey which evoked a response rate of only 27 per cent (Ellery 2007). Such mathematical dexterity could not have saved Camden's 2004 ALMO ballot where, after a strong campaign by Defend Council Housing, 77 per cent of tenants voted against the proposal (Weaver 2004). This was the exception, as ALMO ballots have been more consistently in favour of change than LSVT transfers, with the average vote in favour of ALMOs where local authorities held a ballot in Rounds One to Four was 86 per cent (Hansard 2004). This may reflect either the emotional attachment of tenants to council stock ownership or a fear that this was their last chance to secure much-needed property investment.

As with stock transfers, the expansion of the ALMO sector has been a process controlled and regulated by central government, featuring annual 'bidding rounds', with local authorities pitching for a share of annually released ALMO funding. An authority's submission set out plans for separating housing strategy and management and its investment needs consistent with eliminating non-decent properties within a specified period. In compiling submissions, local authorities needed to demonstrate compliance with official guidance on the split between delegated and retained functions. This indicated that it would be appropriate for an ALMO to undertake:

- All tenancy management functions (e.g. rent collection, void management and enforcement of tenancy conditions)
- Management of day-to-day repairs
- Stock investment decisions
- Leasehold management.

It was recommended that, for its part, an ALMO-sponsoring local authority should retain responsibility for housing needs assessment as well as for policy on lettings, control of anti-social behaviour and homelessness. Operational responsibilities should be retained with respect to housing advice and Housing Benefit administration. Management of council house sales could legitimately be undertaken by either party. Homelessness administration could be contracted out but a local authority would, in this instance, retain responsibility for ensuring that such functions were discharged satisfactorily. Last, but by no means least, while the authority might devolve management of its Housing Revenue Account (HRA), ultimate control over the HRA had to remain with the local authority (ODPM 2004b).

Having had its ALMO bid accepted, an authority received an offer of funding conditional on a satisfactory Audit Commission inspection having been completed (ODPM 2004b). Figure 8.1 plots the expansion of the sector as it grew, following the six ALMO bidding rounds from 2002–2007. With Ministers having advised that this process is at an end, the size of the sector will not increase unless new grant monies are made available (CLG 2006d) – or unless the option is made available in Scotland or Wales. However, a new generation of 'development ALMOs' was foreseen by the 2007 Housing Green Paper, apparently as vehicles to facilitate house building on local authority-owned land (CLG 2007a).

In practice, Round One bids helped to shape model rules and procedures widely used throughout the programme. For example, Round One local authorities developed standard documents such as a Memorandum and Articles of Association, and Management Contract between the local authority and ALMO. These templates were subsequently used for most ALMOs with only minor modification (MacKenzie 2007). Contracts have typically been of five years duration with an option to renew, although Ashfield Homes in 2002 agreed a 25 five-year agreement with five-year break clauses (Audit Commission 2006: 13). A five-year term had a logic linked with the common expectation of completing Decent Homes upgrade programmes within this timeframe (as has also typically been the case for stock transfers).

By 2007, most of the Round One ALMOs had reached a stage where their contract was due for renewal, presenting the sponsoring local authorities with a strategic choice on whether to recover full control or – in negotiating an extension to the ALMO's existence – acknowledge the organization's legitimate role above and beyond the delivery of Decent Homes. Given that, in the event, all contracts have been extended rather than ended, there has been an opportunity to negotiate a clearer def-

FIGURE 8.1   Growth of the English ALMO sector, 2002–2008

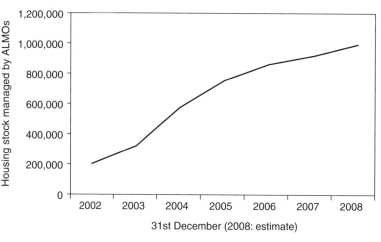

31st December (2008: estimate)

Source: Data from National Federation of ALMOs (NFA).

inition of the roles and responsibilities of each party, the ALMO's permitted activities and geographical areas in which it can work.

As legally constituted entities, ALMOs assume the role of employer when they take on housing management responsibilities. As in any situation involving public service outsourcing, staff transferred from council to ALMO have retained their original employment terms and conditions under Transfer of Undertakings (Protection of Employment) Regulations or TUPE. Unlike with stock transfers, the local authority continued to act as landlord and residents continued their secure tenancies.

By 2009, there were 69 'live' ALMOs operating in 66 local authority areas. They ranged in size from United Residents Housing, a Tenant Management Organization (TMO) in Lambeth with 2,500 properties, to Sheffield Homes with 42,000 homes. Just under two thirds of ALMOs are larger than the 12,000 upper size limit suggested in the early Rounds. With the median ALMO having 12,700 properties (see Figure 8.2), they are typically much larger than stock transfer housing associations (median stock size, 2006: 4,100 (RSR data)). However, direct comparisons may be inappropriate since many transfer

FIGURE 8.2   ALMO size by managed housing stock, October 2008

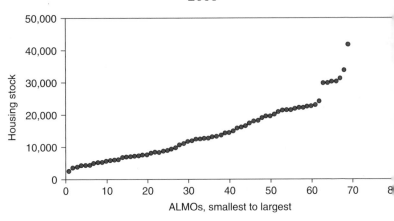

Source: Data from NFA.

housing associations are linked with other associations via group structures (see Chapter 5).

There is an uneven geographic spread of ALMOs across England, with most based in the north and London (see Table 8.1). Even within regions, there are concentrations as most northern ALMOs cluster around the cities of Manchester, Leeds and Newcastle. This probably reflects locations of retained council stock needing most investment to achieve the Decent Homes standard, as well as the 'bastions of resistance' to earlier stock transfers. More northern ALMOs were funded under Rounds One to Three, compared to most London boroughs in Rounds Four to Six.

Importantly, the proportion of local authority owned stock delegated to ALMO management is much greater than implied by the 19 per cent of all authorities with ALMOs (see Table 8.2). This is because (a) stock transfers mean that approximately half of all English authorities are no longer landlords, and (b) the average social housing stock of stock-owning authorities opting to set up ALMOs has been substantially larger than that of authorities retaining ownership and management on the traditional model.

While ALMOs have had to be established in compliance with official guidance, those established between 2002 and 2008 are

TABLE 8.1   *ALMOs by English region, 2008*

Region	Local authority areas		Total ALMO stock, 2008	
	With ALMOs	% in region with ALMOs	Number	% of all council owned stock
London	20	61	365,753	81
Yorkshire & Humber	7	33	194,117	78
North West	12	28	135,196	65
North East	8	35	108,809	71
East Midlands	6	15	68,337	33
West Midlands	3	9	64,587	30
East	4	8	37,105	20
South West	4	9	18,911	16
South East	2	3	13,543	7
England	66	19	1,006,358	51

Sources: NFA, unpublished data supplied to the authors. In calculating these figures it has been necessary to refer to local authority stock data for 2007 rather than 2008 (because the latter are not yet available). Consequently, the percentage figures cited here will slightly underestimate the true proportion.

far from uniform in design or scope. For example, Westminster's ALMO manages all local authority housing stock, Leeds divided its stock between a number of ALMOs (originally six, merged into three in 2007) and Manchester has a mixture of an ALMO and several stock transfers and PFIs. Bolton's ALMO, Bolton at Home, is closely involved in neighbourhood regeneration and is aligned to the Council's wider Bolton Community Homes partnership; others like Colchester Borough Homes have pioneered environmental initiatives. Contrasting fortunes of two organizations established in 2002 in neighbouring Greater Manchester boroughs are illustrated in Box 8.2. Bolton's highly rated ALMO continues to efficiently manage stock previously run by a highly rated council – with predominantly the same staff. Neighbouring Salford tells a story of what can go wrong: critical Audit Commission reports, senior staff departures and a policy reversal leading to

Box 8.2   A tale of two ALMOs

BOLTON: top marks for a well run 'housing department in exile'?

Bolton MBC in Greater Manchester, with a population of 261,000, has been under minority Labour Party control for two decades. Although England's 50th most deprived local authority, it has avoided neighbourhood abandonment common in some other Northern post-industrial towns. The Audit Commission's inspection of the council's management of 21,000 homes in April 2002 assessed repairs and maintenance as 2-star ('good') with excellent prospects for improvement, and customer involvement as 2-star, though with uncertain prospects.

As a well-performing local authority, Bolton set up a combined housing management and regeneration ALMO 'Bolton at Home' in December 2002, having successfully bid for Decent Homes funding in ALMO Round Two. ALMO staff subsequently moved out of their former Housing Department offices. Bolton at Home's unpaid board was set up consisting of 15 members with equal representation for tenants, council nominees and 'independents'. ALMO meetings have been open to all Bolton residents and with minutes published on Bolton at Home's website. Founding Chairman, Noel Spencer MBE, remains a Labour Party councillor and was previously Chair of Housing at Bolton Council. Chief Executive George Caswell, previously a regeneration consultant, draws a salary in excess of £110,000.

The initial Audit Commission inspection of Bolton at Home followed in October 2003, rating the organization as 2-star with excellent prospects – sufficient to unlock Decent Homes funding. A subsequent inspection in September 2005 demonstrated further improvements, making Bolton at Home the first landlord in the north-west to achieve the coveted 3-star rating as well as being judged to have promising prospects for further improvement.
Bolton at Home achieved the Decent Homes standard for all its properties two years ahead of schedule in 2008 after spending £250 million on housing and environmental improvements. Yet despite this success, the ALMO's long-term future remained in doubt and as discussed below Bolton Council was, in 2009, envisaging the possibility of stock transfer to a housing association.

SALFORD: zero star rating causes ALMO to implode

Though bordering Bolton to the south, Salford's ALMO experience has been far less straightforward. The city is the 15th most deprived in England, its population of 216,000 contains a relatively high proportion of elderly and disabled residents and much

→

of the 26 per cent of the City Council's housing stock is high rise and low demand. Salford was an earlier adopter of the ALMO concept, and one of the local authorities selected in 2000 to work with the government on standard documentation.

'New Prospect' was duly established in September 2002 as a Round Two ALMO for Salford's 29,000 council properties. However, the Audit Commission inspection report published the same month awarded a 'poor' [zero star] rating, and Salford's application for Decent Homes funding was withdrawn. A proposed second funding application in Round Four in 2004 also failed to proceed as a further Audit Commission inspection had rated housing management services as only 'fair with uncertain prospects for improvement'. The Audit Commission (2004c: 4) noted 'the relatively low base from which the ALMO and the council is starting to improve its service in comparison to other ALMOs in metropolitan areas'.

Alongside these developments it was recognized that the initial estimate of funding required for Decent Homes compliance had been unrealistic. Instead of £53 million, the shortfall would be £315 million. Combined with the failure of New Prospect to achieve the ALMO-funding performance threshold the local authority found itself forced to adopt a complete change of approach. New Prospect ALMO was progressively dismembered. First, management responsibilities for 10,500 properties were transferred to Salix Homes, a Round Six ALMO. Second, following a 73 per cent 'yes' vote by tenants, the remainder of New Prospect's 14,800 homes were transferred in October 2008 to City West Housing Trust, a new housing association. A final chapter, as envisaged at the time of writing, will involve 2,000 units of the most problematic stock managed by Salix Homes being passed to a PFI consortium. Both Salix Homes and City West Housing Trust have had been set up with an equal mix of tenant, council and independent board members.

Salford will fail to meet the Decent Homes standard by 2010, probably by many years: City West Trust expect to complete by 2014, followed later by Salix Homes and the PFI entity. It is difficult to know whether the troubled history described above resulted mainly from intractable housing conditions, from poor management, or a combination of both. New Prospect's Chief Executive John Townsend who had previously worked for the council's housing department was removed in July 2003 after the disappointing Audit Commission inspection. Their Chair, tenant Hilary Peat, resigned in 2006 and was subsequently cleared of damaging allegations that she had over-claimed disability benefit.

Sources: Audit Commission (2003b, 2005, 2008, 2004c); Bolton at Home (2008a, b); City West Housing Trust (2008); New Prospect (2008); Personal interviews; Salix Homes (2008).

England's first transfer of local authority-owned stock from ALMO to housing association.

Finance, regulation and governance

ALMO finances

As noted above, the additional investment finance made available to councils with qualifying ALMOs was a key factor incentivizing ALMO establishment. As a body autonomous from its local authority parent, rather than independent of it, an ALMO's finances are inextricably linked to the council's Housing Revenue Account (HRA). All income and expenditure relating to a council's housing stock must pass through its HRA. Under the ALMO regime, capital expenditure for house construction and major repairs (including Decent Homes improvements) is funded by government borrowing, with interest and capital repayment debited to the HRA. A local authority responsible for a funded ALMO benefits from additional *supported borrowing*. The counterpart to this additional supported borrowing is the *ALMO allowance* – the element of the HRA Subsidy to cover the debt charges incurred by an authority on its borrowing for its ALMO.

Since 1989, HRAs have been tightly ring-fenced from the local authority's General Fund to prevent local authorities cross-subsidizing public housing from general income, or vice versa (Garnett and Perry 2005). Local authorities must sign-off a business plan for their HRA with government, regardless of whether they have set up an ALMO. However, while these general principles of HRA operation are seen as 'logical and efficient' (Housemark 2007: 59), the way that the subsidy system works for ALMOs is seen as more problematic. HRA Subsidy is the annual financial support provided by government where a council's (notional) rental income is less than (notional) HRA expenditure. In the ALMO context, each year the management fee paid by the local authority to the ALMO is adjusted according to the level of HRA Subsidy received from government. This 'annuality' hinders long-term planning. Also, because an ALMO is funded through a local authority's HRA it has limited ability or encouragement to diversify income sources and in this (and other) respects does not operate on a level financial playing field with housing associations. The HRA Subsidy mechanism is unpopular with both councils and ALMO managers who see it as complicated and restricting local decision-making. As discussed later in this chapter, the HRA Subsidy system is under review at the time of writing.

In most cases, ALMO-sponsoring local authorities have retained operational management as well as ultimate control of their HRA (CLG 2007b). ALMOs sometimes face tough negotiations with councils on management fees and the division of capital receipts can also be contested (Reid et al. 2007: 17). As they would see it, ALMO staff are well-placed to judge whether it is cost-effective for houses to be modernized or demolished and replaced. Although the government has announced that ALMO funds can be used for demolition, the HRA Subsidy regime does not allow capital receipts to be fully re-invested and therefore dwellings cannot readily be replaced. The bottom line is that ALMO managers have no authority for capital investment decisions outside those agreed with the council in their delivery plan.

The performance threshold

As noted above, local authorities can access earmarked funding only once their ALMO has been established and has met the specified performance threshold. As originally proposed, ALMOs would have been required to achieve an 'excellent' (3-star) Audit Commission inspection rating before Decent Homes funding would be granted. In practice, however, the threshold was set as 'good (2-stars) with good prospects for improvement'. The Audit Commission gives credit to an organization that 'manages its stock well, treats its tenants well and delivers value for money' (Audit Commission 2003a: 7). More specifically, inspection judgements are based on the extent to which the landlord is assessed as meeting the standards set out in the Commission's Key Lines of Enquiry (Audit Commission 2003a). Their two-dimensional scoring system rates service (with stars) and prospects for improvement.

Before handing over responsibility for tenancy management to its newly-established ALMO, an indicative inspection of the council's housing service was encouraged. This was seen as enabling local authorities to set a realistic timescale for remedying any identified areas of weakness before the all-important inaugural ALMO inspection. Under the system which has applied to local authorities since 2001 and housing associations since 2003, all Audit Commission inspection findings are openly published as well as being communicated to the key stakeholders directly concerned. In the ALMO context, this can be incendiary if the organization's performance is judged as falling below the Decent Homes funding threshold. As in Salford (see Box 8.1), the position of senior ALMO post-holders is likely to be placed in jeopardy. In most such cases, the authority has opted for a follow-up inspection which, it is hoped, will judge that previously identified weaknesses have been fully addressed.

ALMOs awarded 'good' or 'excellent' ratings must be re-inspected 2–3 years after the initial review to ensure standards are maintained. An ALMO unable to demonstrate this, risks having its access to Decent Homes funding suspended. Initially, such ALMOs have been placed under review and an action plan agreed to enable them to restore acceptable standards within twelve months. Continuing poor performance could lead to a suspension of funding, though this would be as a last resort (Audit Commission 2008). Falling ratings happen and have major impacts on AMLO managers. Tristar, Stockton-on-Tees's ALMO, fell from 'good' in 2002 to 'fair' when re-inspected in 2005. This led to the resignation of the Chair, Chief Executive and the departure of many senior managers. New procedures were introduced to recover the focus on high quality tenancy management rather than just property improvements. The 2006 inspection restored Tristar's 'good' rating, hence ending the organization's crisis (Gibb and Trebeck 2008). Funded 2-star ALMOs may also request re-inspection at any time if they aspire to access Social Housing Grant – a status requiring an 'excellent' (3-star) rating. However, financial risk attaches to such requests as the Audit Commission charges up to £50,000 per inspection.

Performance-related resource allocation is not an entirely new phenomenon in social housing. The Housing Investment Programme system, as operated for English local authorities from 1991, also rewarded what was judged as 'efficient and

TABLE 8.2 *ALMO inspection ratings as at March 2009*

Number of ALMOs in each category:		Service			
		Poor	Fair (*)	Good (**)	Excellent (***)
Prospects for improvement	Excellent			5	16
	Promising		6	21	4
	Uncertain		1	4	
	Poor		1		
Totals		0	8 (14%)	30 (52%)	20 (34%)

Source: Data from Brandon (2009). Data relate to most recent Audit Commission inspection report. 11 ALMOs not yet inspected.

effective' authorities by awarding additional borrowing consents (Bramley et al. 2004). However, the integration of the ALMO-funding performance threshold was one of the most far-reaching decisions in the design of the ALMO regime. Apart from anything else, this differentiates ALMOs from stock transfer housing associations who, having developed a funded business plan at the outset, have less direct incentive to maintain high performance in day-to-day service delivery. As seen by informed observers of the sector (e.g. McIntosh 2002), the single minded goal of an ALMO is to secure and retain a favourable Audit Commission rating. Setting high standards, at least in relation to those facets of services that are inspected, has been a significant factor in driving up performance. Of the 58 ALMOs inspected to March 2009, only eight failed to reach the funding threshold. Table 8.2 identifies the 50 ALMOs eligible to receive Decent Homes funding, 60 per cent rated 'good' and 40 per cent 'excellent'. Comparing Audit Commission inspection ratings awarded in the year 2007/08, three quarters of ALMOs received two stars or above compared with only one third of housing associations (Brandon 2009).

Other evidence exists to demonstrate the effectiveness of the ALMO performance threshold in pushing up service delivery standards. Table 8.3 shows that authorities having established ALMOs had, indeed, recorded performance improvements in

TABLE 8.3 *Housing management performance change in ALMO and non-ALMO LAs*

	ALMO LAs		Non-ALMO LAs		Difference 2002/03-2007/08	
	2002/03	2007/08	2002/03	2007/08	ALMO LAs	Non-ALMO LAs
% rent collection	96.7	97.9	97.4	98.3	+1.2	+0.9
% rent arrears	3.00	2.47	2.46	2.01	-0.53	-0.45
Avg relet interval (days)	43	32	36	30	-11	-6
% urgent repairs on time	93.0	97.0	92.4	97.0	+4	+4.6
Avg time to complete non-urgent repairs (days)	16.0	9.6	17.0	12.0	-6.4	-5.0

Sources: Audit Commission Best Value Performance Indicators; Communities and Local Govt Department HRA Business Plan Statistical Annex returns. Figures show median values for authorities in each cohort.

the previous five years with respect to all five performance indicators shown here. More importantly, on four of the five indicators gains by councils with ALMOs were greater than those registered by their non-ALMO counterpart councils. For example, ALMO authorities had cut empty property re-let intervals by 11 days – almost twice as much as other councils.

The statistics set out in Table 8.3 seem to confirm that the financial incentives built into the ALMO regime have indeed contributed to performance improvement across the sector. This is consistent with the argument advanced elsewhere that carrots are more effective than sticks in this context (Housing Quality Network 2005). What might, however, be questioned is how effectively such incentives embed a framework for performance maximization. By comparison with stock transfer, it could be argued that the ALMO regime fails to incorporate incentives for long-term thinking and is therefore no more than a short-term fix, with external regulatory engagement potentially given priority over internal goal setting, a danger apparently recognized by the Tenants Service Authority's recent attention to increasing accountability to boards and tenants and 'less reliance on what the regulator and inspector says' (Source: Tenant Board Member Report of TSA Briefing, September 2009).

Governance, accountability and culture change

ALMOs are normally legally constituted as companies limited by guarantee. Local authorities retain a 100 per cent shareholding in all ALMOs, except Kensington and Chelsea TMO which is owned by its tenants. ALMO governance is exercised through a Board of Directors which must include tenants, council nominees and independent members with relevant experience of social housing, finance or other technical skills. ALMOs, like most LSVTs, typically select one third of their Boards from each of these three categories to demonstrate that no single group is in a majority. Council nominees are invariably councillors and their selection reflects the local political balance. From 2005, ALMOs have been brought into line with housing associations and allowed to pay board members, though appear less willing to do so. A small sample survey in 2008 of social landlords managing over 5,000 properties found that 35 per cent of ALMOs pay Directors compared with 78 per cent of housing associations (Insight 2008).

To ensure that tenant board members are representative of their community, they should be elected by fellow tenants (ODPM 2004b: 12). Whether and how this takes place in practice remains to be researched. The government's agenda is to 'promote greater tenant involvement and accountability for local housing decisions' across all types of social housing providers (CLG 2006a: 8). Two ALMOs are pioneers in tenant-driven models. Kensington and Chelsea TMO was originally established in 1996 under 'right to manage' legislation, transforming into an ALMO in 2002 to access Decent Homes funding. While the stock remains local authority-owned, tenants and leaseholders own all shares in the ALMO and elect eleven of the 21 Directors. Somewhat less radically distinctive is United Residents Housing, a TMO managing four large housing estates in Lambeth established as a Round Five ALMO in November 2006. Here, half the Directors are tenants but the council remains sole shareholder.

Table 8.4 provides some support for the ALMO claim that this organizational model effectively prioritizes tenant involvement. In three of the four broad regions of England, the proportion of tenants 'satisfied with opportunities for participation' was higher, on average, among ALMOs than among local authorities retaining direct management of council housing.

The first Chief Executive of an ALMO has usually been the local authority's former Director of Housing (Reid et al. 2007). This has probably helped to reassure tenants and councillors, as well as providing useful management continuity in the ALMO's early years. However, even by the standards of corporate life, ALMOs have seen an astonishing turnover of CEOs. During 2007 one quarter of ALMO Chief Executives in England were replaced (Hilditch 2008). Some left for new challenges, having achieved Decent Homes standards, perhaps to housing associations where they might have seen greater scope to innovate. Others, such as in Salford and Stockton-on-Tees, were forced out after disappointing Audit Commission ratings. Some appear to have been casualties of tensions between ALMOs and councils, described below. The high attrition rate of ALMO Chief Executives must be seen as reflecting, at least

TABLE 8.4 *ALMOs: % of tenants 'satisfied with opportunities for participation', 2007/08*

Local authorities . . .	London	South	Midlands	North
. . . with ALMOs	60	70	68	66
. . . without ALMOs	56	66	65	66

Source: Data from Audit Commission Best Value Performance Indicators.

in part, ALMOs' somewhat uncertain status and long-term prospects, as well as their incomplete insulation from local authority political machinations.

CLG research has illustrated the need for ALMOs to have a strong management team led by a respected Chief Executive if significant change in organizational culture is to be achieved (Reid et al. 2007). Decent Homes funding can be spent wisely and properties improved, but visionary leadership is needed for customer-centred values to become fully embedded in organizations previously steeped in the bureaucratic paternalist traditions of local government. Exemplifying the potential for such change, Stockport Council was awarded a zero star rating in 2001 for housing management, but in the Audit Commission's 2006 inspection report, one year after establishing an ALMO, achieved three stars ('excellent with excellent prospects'). The Chief Executive attributed the transformation to giving staff more responsibility, engendering a belief that change was good and putting tenants – now called customers – first (McIntosh and Bright 2007). Overall, however, there is a dearth of research evidence on the extent to which such change typifies the ALMO experience.

More clearly apparent across the sector are symbolic changes which parallel the corporate and stock transfer sectors. To emphasize their autonomy, ALMO management generally place considerable emphasis on a move out of former Housing Department offices and this has been a common development in an ALMO's initial phase of existence. Where this is not possible, attempts are sometimes made to create new entrances and rationalize office space to congregate ALMO staff in a single location. New logos and livery have often been developed for customer-facing staff, launch events held for staff and business partners and a new name selected. Most ALMO names incorporate the title of their local authority, though a few organizations have been more creative; for example, St. George's Community Housing (Basildon); Ascham Homes (Waltham Forest) and Six Town Housing (Bury). Nevertheless, and understandably, these new brands have a far more localist feel than the equivalent branding emerging within the stock transfer sector, particularly in the naming of group structures which are generally less locally orientated.

Relationships with local authorities

ALMOs were intended to function at arm's length from local authorities and maintain a clear distinction between the operational focus of the former and the strategic focus of the latter. In its inspection reports, the Audit Commission comments on the relationship between councils and ALMOs and an inspection rating of 'uncertain prospects for improvement' is often symptomatic of perceived problems in this area (Ounsted 2007). To demonstrate proper separation, it is argued that the Board Chair should not be a local authority nominee, councillors on the Board should not set the local authority's own housing policy and there should be no local authority 'interference' in the ALMO's day-to-day running. It is not clear whether these three tests are always met. On a positive note, over half ALMOs have tenants chairing the Board (NFA 2008a) and this is in marked contrast with stock transfer housing associations where such a situation is highly unusual – at least in England (Pawson and Fancy 2003, Pawson et al. 2009). However, this may not be a strong counter-balance if the tenant Chair is inexperienced and Chief Executive is the council's former Housing Director.

Again, the absence of research evidence makes it difficult to assess the generality of relationships between local authorities and ALMOs. However, a casual reading of the housing press suggests there have been a number of negative instances. Underlying some problems of this kind may be the tendency for councils to see ALMOs as their agent rather than partner, continuing to emphasize their role as stock owner and landlord

(Reid et al. 2007). There can also be a tendency to micromanage. In 2007, Rotherham Metropolitan Borough Council despatched staff to help its ALMO resolve financial problems. As noted by an opposition councillor, 'if this is an arm's length management organisation then what are we doing sending in a management team from the council? Just how independent is the organisation?' (Humphries 2007).

In August 2008, both the Chief Executive and Chairman of Doncaster Metropolitan Borough Council's ALMOs were suspended after the Mayor criticized lapses in health and safety procedures (Humphries 2008). The following month, Westminster Council dismissed their ALMO's Chair and Chief Executive, alleging the latter wanted 'more independence and control over housing stock' (Story 2008). For his part, the former Chair asserted that the tensions had arisen from the council's reluctance to allow the ALMO a proper degree of independence. Specific matters of contention had included council-imposed cuts in the housing maintenance budget, a contested decision to recover direct control of the Housing Revenue Account and 'attempts to control the ALMO's Housing Corporation-funded new homes programme' (Rogers 2008: 13). More recently, in September 2009, ongoing tensions between Ealing Council and their ALMO led to an announcement that the management contract would not be renewed in 2011. Instead, the contract will be tendered to the private sector (Hardman 2009).

Many local authorities have continued to provide legal, IT and human resource facilities for their ALMO, governed by service level agreements. There is a question whether such agreements, arguably symbolizing a 'market contractor' ethos, are the best way to manage the complex relationship between local authorities and ALMOs. They are inflexible when government policy shifts or local conditions change, and tend to focus on managing a process rather than working co-operatively towards better local outcomes. As reported by Reid et al. (2007), service level agreements initially drawn up by Round One and Two ALMOs were often quickly drafted and avoided contentious issues, especially components of unit cost and quality control. Chief Executives, having experienced this, subsequently reflected that they could (and should) have driven a harder bargain from the outset. ALMOs in Rounds Three to

Six had the benefit of this experience and appeared more willing to negotiate agreements fitting their business plan requirements (Reid et al. 2007). One result has been that some local authorities have been forced to reflect on the efficiency and productivity of their remaining departments as establishing ALMOs continues the 'hollowing out' of many traditional local authority activities (Centre for Public Services 2004, Reid et al. 2007).

Once more reflecting the currently limited research evidence, there is no clear-cut answer as to whether ALMOs genuinely operate at arm's length from local authorities. Relationships between the two change over time, and personalities make a difference. ALMOs, from the early bidding Rounds, have developed a track record as independent organizations and staff turnover (more pronounced at Chief Executive level) will have brought in new employees who have not worked in the public sector. However, many transferring staff are said to retain a strong public service ethos towards tenants and the local area (Reid et al. 2007). The National Federation of ALMOs (NFA) was established in 2003 at the prompting of a Housing Minister who saw benefits in being able to negotiate with a single sector representative. Funded by its members who comprise all ALMOs in England, this small trade body has played a significant role in lobbying government to develop a long-term and independent future for the sector (NFA 2008b)

ALMO futures

Ostensibly, ALMOs were set up as Decent Homes 'delivery vehicles' whose establishment could be characterized as largely opportunistic on the part of the local authorities concerned. In opting for this approach, authorities were motivated largely or entirely by the prospect of significant additional spending power (while avoiding the need for stock transfer). Implicitly, the transaction costs and additional running costs of the structure were considered 'a price worth paying' in providing access to substantial extra capital funding. Whether the posited 'in principle' benefits of separating strategy from delivery were seen by any authorities as a significant 'attracting factor' is highly questionable. On this basis, it might be anticipated as inevitable that ALMOs having completed Decent Homes upgrade plans would be wound up in short order, returning the stock to directly council control. As yet, however, this has not happened. Some of the possible reasons for this are noted in (d) below.

Much attention has focused on a long-running review of ALMO futures being conducted by central government from 2005. Finally, in 2009, a Ministerial consultation paper on the broader reform of local authority housing revenue accounts (CLG 2009b) looked likely to push the debate forward. As part of this agenda, Ministers re-committed themselves to 'a strong future for ALMOs' and foresaw ALMOs taking on stock management on behalf of other social landlords (CLG 2009b: 42–3).

As long ago as 2005, a report commissioned by NFA and CIH called for local authorities to be given greater control over their Housing Revenue Accounts (HRAs) as a means of facilitating long-term financial sustainability for council housing – ALMO-managed or otherwise (Terry et al. 2005). Following an evaluation exercise (CLG 2006a), this proposal appears to have been accepted in 2009 with the publication of far-reaching proposals to dismantle the HRA system and replace it with a devolved framework for council housing finance (CLG 2009b: 5). The historic HRA debt, a notional figure of past capital expenditure on council housing in each local authority area, would be redistributed across all remaining stockholding authorities. This was portrayed as simplifying local government finance and providing the basis for long-term asset management decision-making.

The scheme drew an initial welcome from the sector's primary trade body as offering 'the potential to reverse decline and to place council housing on a long-term sustainable footing for the first time in well over a generation' (CIH 2009: 12). The proposed settlement was seen as having the capacity to remove the financial pressures otherwise likely to force many authorities to contemplate post-2010 stock transfer as a means of *maintaining* hard-won Decent Homes compliance. Under this scenario, councils with ALMOs would remain free to contemplate retaining such arrangements for the medium and longer term. Nevertheless, the CIH recognized that given the complexity of the proposals it remained difficult to be sure that they were capable of delivering their professed aims. It also appeared possible that it would be difficult to secure the desired universal acceptance from local government, given that councils currently unencumbered by debt might well baulk at being expected to accept new liabilities through the settlement.

But while the wider proposals appeared potentially ground-breaking for council housing, as a whole, likely outcomes remained difficult to predict at the time of writing. Hence, five possible ALMO future pathways are described below. These are not mutually exclusive given the continuing validity of the earlier government statement that 'there will be no single or pre-scribed model . . . Where ALMOs are shown to be popular and working well, there are a range of options for sustaining their role beyond delivery of Decent Homes' (CLG 2006b: 3–4).

(a) No change

ALMOs well-rated by the Audit Commission, and who are still spending Decent Homes funding on stock improvement, face little pressure to change their status. However, continuing to operate within an unreformed Housing Revenue Account straightjacket after the capital funds are spent will prove prob-lematic for some. After achieving full Decent Homes compli-ance, jobs were lost at Hounslow Homes and Derby Homes was forced to close two housing offices to help balance their books (Hilditch 2006). Under the existing HRA system, there is a concern that with the 'no change' option, 'standards and ser-vices will decline' (Housemark 2007: ix).

A specific concern is that continuing Right to Buy sales are leading to a gradual withering of ALMO portfolios. Government policy has, until recently, prevented the construc-tion of replacement properties. However, for ALMOs achieving 'excellent' inspection ratings a small pot of gold at the end of the rainbow was established in 2007 with the announcement that ALMOs could apply for Social Housing Grant (SHG) to build new homes. Along with two local authority housing com-panies, eight ALMOs were enabled to bid for grant funding from 2008 to 2011 (Housing Corporation 2007). The first recipient, Stockport Homes, planned to build 17 new proper-ties (NFA 2009). Hence, early indications were that only modest numbers of new build would be funded through this mechanism; insufficient to replace dwellings being lost through sitting tenant sales. The NFA viewed the measures as half-hearted, complaining that they did not allow its members to compete 'on a level footing' with housing associations for a share of SHG funds (NFA 2008c). However, with new opportunities for local authority house-building announced in 2009 (see Chapter 1), it appeared possible that some ALMOs might benefit from this policy switch.

Nevertheless, a 'no change' future for ALMOs may also face legal risks. The Brixen Judgment in the European Court of Justice has raised questions about whether competitive tenders are required for local authorities outsourcing housing management services rather than uncontested awards to an arms-length body (NFA 2009) – see also (d) below. While the Brixen case may not set a precedent, it could herald the future tightening of European Union legislation (Thorpe 2006). There may also be competition challenges with some of the ALMO diversification strategies discussed in section (e) below.

(b) Stock transfer to a housing association

Recent years have seen reports of ALMOs contemplating a change of status via a full stock transfer. Despite being predicted as a likely scenario by Defend Council Housing, such a transfer has as yet occurred only in the case of the failed Salford ALMO in October 2008 (Box 8.1). In 2009 this situation looked set to change, with four local authorities (Bolton, Oldham, Stockton and Warrington) reportedly having determined, via stock options appraisals, that existing ALMOs should be wound up, and their managed portfolios subject to stock transfer ballots (Stothart 2009). These are in addition to councils in Ealing (see above) and Hillingdon who are not seeking to renew their ALMO contracts, and Rochdale who are reviewing options (Twinch 2009). Taken together, these seven ALMOs hold over 90,000 properties or just under 10 per cent of total ALMO stock.

The driving force prompting consideration of the transfer option has been projected funding shortfalls to maintain the Decent Homes Standard in the medium and longer term under the existing HRA subsidy system (see above). While this position may be set to change (see above) the existing financial freedoms open to housing associations could open up another – possibly more immediate – path to salvation. The 2009 announcement of a deferral of Decent Homes funding for ALMOs yet to achieve a two-star rating has only compounded financial pressures to contemplate transfer by the authorities affected (Orr 2009) .

Conventional wisdom has been that a 'conversion' of ALMO to stock transfer would be unpopular with tenants and councillors, given that original ALMO establishment was often advocated on the grounds that this would be preferable to (i.e. a way of avoiding) transfer. Given that such a transfer could proceed only if endorsed by a tenant ballot, this is potentially critical. The 2008 vote for the Salford transfer (see above) and the move by several other ALMO councils to contemplate a ballot perhaps suggests this belief to be mistaken. Nevertheless, the possibility that councils with ALMOs might opt to pursue stock transfer was thrown into question by the government's 2009 proposals for fundamental reforms to the local authority Housing Revenue Account system as discussed above – and in more detail in Chapter 10.

(c) Transfer to a tenant-led organization

Just as some view ALMOs as a 'half-way house' to conventional stock transfer, thought has been given to other intermediate organizational structures. In 2001, the Housing Corporation funded the CIH to develop a 'Community Gateway' model – a form of 'tenant-led stock transfer' (see Chapter 5). The model, as piloted in Preston and subsequently emulated elsewhere, was reported as evoking significant ALMO interest as an interpretation of transfer consistent with the tenant-focused organizational culture ALMOs have sought to develop (Hilditch 2007).

Tenant and community involvement is an option supported by the NFA, who have proposed various alternative structures including co-operatives and community land trusts (NFA 2009). Although any such model also incorporating transfer would require endorsement by tenant vote, it might be imagined that such an outcome would be more likely if the successor landlord could be structured to reflect 'community-oriented' ALMO values.

(d) Council reversion or contractorization

Most ALMO Management Contracts expire after five years and, therefore, by late 2008, the majority of Round One and Two ALMOs will have had to re-negotiate their contracts. As noted above, given the considerations prompting their initial establishment it might be imagined that such contract extension would be unlikely. As yet, however, while a number of ALMOs have completed their Decent Homes programmes, none has reverted to local authority control (NFA 2008b).

Folding an ALMO back into local authority control would not be straightforward because, as independent organizations, they have acquired an institutional life of their own (Reid et al. 2007). Senior managers have become used to delegated authority, staff generally have better terms than when employed by the local authority and tenants have been motivated through decision-making. Tenants, satisfied with day-to-day management services and living in refurbished homes, might not be willing to vote for a return to local authority control. It should be noted that '[CLG] expects any consultation on a significant change to the local authority's management arrangements with the ALMO to be as comprehensive as that undertaken before the setting up of the ALMO (CLG 2006b: 2).

However, recent developments in Ealing (see above), as well as in Westminster and Hillingdon (Twinch 2009) suggest that ALMO management might morph into another form of 'contractorization'. In striving to retain their current role via a competitive process, ALMOs may come more to resemble non-public bodies such as 'management only' housing associations or even for-profit companies.

(e) Partnerships and diversification

The government is keen to promote Local Strategic Partnerships between local authorities, housing associations, ALMOs, private developers and other service providers to increase affordable rental housing supply and improve community cohesion (Warburton 2008). Partnerships can leverage income from surplus council land, use ALMO tenancy management skills and promote mixed income communities (CLG

2006a: 7). For example, First Choice Homes in Oldham is part of a consortium for the local Housing Market Renewal Pathfinder along with local authorities, housing associations and the private sector. The rationale is that, instead of ALMOs being given more powers, they could partner organizations that have specialized competencies and private borrowing capacity.

Diversification could be in the form of ALMOs managing housing on behalf of other landlords, or improving other neighbourhood services – potentially even beyond their existing local authority boundary. Bolton at Home is an ALMO that already funds improvement to dilapidated private housing stock and runs a network of community centres helping residents access housing and social services (Housemark 2007: 10). Akin to the 'business diversification' strategy, often seen among post-promises transfer housing associations, this approach can provide an ALMO with scope for income-generation leveraged off its existing infrastructure and harvesting scale economies.

The limitations on partnerships and diversification are the potential for contractual complexity and loss of focus on core tenancy management. Housing associations employing an ALMO to manage housing stock or provide other services, would need to pay VAT on the management fee that would probably not be recoverable. Some ALMOs would need to amend their constitutions, and potentially seek Ministerial consent for such new activities or for work extending outside council boundaries.

Chapter conclusions

The most common view on ALMOs when they were first introduced is that they were a political compromise rather than an inherently attractive organizational model for managing social housing in the longer term. However, despite current uncertainties, benefits brought by ALMOs are now more widely acknowledged. Tenant surveys reveal high satisfaction with service quality and the Audit Commission consistently rates ALMOs as high performing housing managers. And, while the Ealing case might lead to an ALMO being terminated through 'contractorization', this might remain an isolated instance. Most ALMOs have developed an autonomous identity and are backed by a broad support coalition of senior managers, staff, an effective trade body, consultants and tenant board members. Arguably, in their operating style – if not in their legal status – longer-established ALMOs have already come to resemble stock transfer housing associations.

While there has been consideration of alternative ALMO futures, the debate has become polarized between opponents of 'privatization' and supporters of public service reform, in part due to a lack of detailed research evidence. Unlike housing associations and conventional local authority landlords, there has been minimal study of ALMO operation. Genuinely evidence-based policy-making on ALMO futures would call for more detailed understanding of ALMO governance, the role of tenants and the relationships between ALMOs and parent local authorities. Research would help clarify whether ALMOs can be fairly characterized as diluted stock transfer housing associations, or whether they have in fact developed distinct approaches which could inform learning by other types of landlord. In any event, a powerful cohort of ALMOs looks likely to remain a part of England's social housing sector for some time to come.

Chapter 9

Local Authorities and Housing After Stock Transfer

Thanks to continuing stock transfers, council housing has now disappeared from half of England's local authorities. In Wales nine authorities had completed or were about to complete whole stock transfers totalling 55,000 homes by 2009. In six of Scotland's local authorities – including the largest city in the land – council housing is no more. In addition, as discussed in the previous chapter, a large tranche of English council-owned housing has been hived off to semi-independent ALMOs. By 2009, only a third of England's local authorities (34 per cent) retained council housing on the traditional model. The local authority housing department of old is, therefore, already very much the exception rather than the rule. Any continuation of existing trends would see such authorities reduced to a small minority by 2015.

This chapter outlines the housing functions remaining a local authority responsibility after stock transfer and looks at how such obligations are discharged. It asks whether there is a principled case for separating housing strategy and implementation and looks at the actual evidence as to whether post-transfer local authorities are more effective housing strategists.

Drawing on research evidence, we then go on to discuss how post-transfer local authorities can exercise influence on the local housing system and what kind of relationships they enjoy with other key stakeholders (including transfer landlords). What are the common interests and the tensions inherent in such relationships?

This leads on to a broader consideration of the impact of transfer (or ALMO set-up) on local housing governance. Can contemporary trends be accurately portrayed as a 'fragmentation' of the established system, has there been a move to 'network governance', and what is the deeper message on how to theorize the operation of social landlords?

Local authority housing functions post-stock transfer

For much of the twentieth century, the construction and management of council estates formed the overwhelming focus of local authority interest in housing. However, these functions were never the sum total of local authority housing responsibilities or activities. Councils' obligations for improving housing conditions and associated public health duties are longstanding. Since the 1970s, local authorities have been tasked with important obligations on homelessness.

In England, official emphasis on the significance of the local authority 'strategic housing' or 'enabling' role dates back for more than two decades (DoE 1987). To begin with, this was widely interpreted as little more than a public relations tactic to mollify councils, resentful at the effective termination of their house-building activities. Through the 1990s, however, the growing emphasis on generating affordable housing via the land use planning system helped to add substance to the continuing official promotion of strategy making as a key housing responsibility. From 1991, the assessed 'quality' of local authorities' annual housing strategy documents also formed an element within the calculation of a council's borrowing approval (DETR 2000c para. 3.26). Hence, housing strategy-making also acquired a financial significance.

As defined in 2000, activities officially considered as aspects of housing strategy include:

- assessing local housing needs and devising plans for tackling problems across all types of housing in the area, via wide consultation;
- identifying, co-ordinating and facilitating the resources and agencies that can contribute to the delivery of the strategy;
- co-ordinating and planning for the provision and development of additional housing, both in the private and social sectors;
- linking housing with wider policies for the social, economic and environmental well-being of the area, including the regeneration of deprived neighbourhoods;

- enforcing and raising standards;
- monitoring and evaluating the success of the strategy.

(Based on DETR 2000c: para 3.26)

More recently, a new and broader role for the local authority strategic housing function has been articulated by the Westminster government. In their discharge of activities under this heading, authorities are now seen as contributing to the delivery of economic growth and prosperity, as well as in 'place-shaping' (CLG 2006c). 'Going far beyond achieving purely housing outcomes, housing is also seen as making an important contribution to both social and environmental objectives such as community cohesion, reducing health inequalities and improving educational attainment' (CIH 2007). These goals are to be pursued within the framework of Local Area Agreements which define a single set of priorities and desired outcomes for a locality. Local Area Agreements, in turn, are seen as the 'delivery plan' for authorities' Sustainable Communities Strategies (CLG 2006c).

What implications does this all have for the housing role of local authorities post-stock transfer? While a (whole stock) transfer terminates council housing as an institution it does not end a local authority's responsibilities in relation to housing matters. Important legal obligations remain, irrespective of stock ownership. As well as housing strategy activities, these include all statutory obligations on homelessness, the allocation of housing and promoting effective management and maintenance of private sector housing.

While post-transfer local authorities retain responsibility for important operational as well as strategic housing responsibilities (see Box 9.1), they have the option of contracting out the day-to-day implementation of functions such as homelessness assessment (an issue further discussed below). All the same, official guidance emphasizes that the ultimate responsibility for the quality of such services rests with the local authority – irrespective of its precise operational role (Pawson et al. 2004). Importantly, this means that in the context of regulatory inspections of post-transfer councils, judgements on an authority's performance in discharging homelessness duties ignore the operational location of the functions concerned. In other words, ultimate responsibility for poor contractor performance will be that of the local authority.

The case for separating policy and strategy

As noted above, official pro-transfer arguments have often highlighted a belief that the housing strategy role may be more effectively discharged by councils which have ceased to operate as landlords in their own right (DETR 2000c, Community Housing Task Force 2004). This is allied to a broader contention that clear separation of policy-making and implementation functions is beneficial to both functions. ODPM's Sustainable Communities plan, for example, emphasized this viewpoint and asserted that 'Best Value reports show that landlord concerns often dominate local authorities' thinking on housing when they should be considering strategies for the whole housing market (ODPM 2003f: 16). The same kinds of arguments have been advanced in support of official statements favouring the establishment of ALMOs.

However, there is a theoretical literature which questions whether separation of policy-making and implementation is necessarily beneficial. Mintzberg (1994), for example, queried whether 'calm detachment' was in fact a pre-requisite for effective policy-making. In Mintzberg's view, such a scenario could result in inappropriate decisions because of the policy-maker being too far removed from the 'shop floor'. More broadly, Mintzberg questioned the notion of a clear split between policy-making and implementation. Where policies are not implemented successfully, 'the real blame has to be laid, neither on formulation not implementation but on the very separation of the two' (285). One of the subtleties of Mintzberg's arguments is his view that formalized separation of policy-maker and implementer places too much reliance on quantitative data and not enough on informal contact between the 'front-line' and the 'back office'.

Applying this to the stock transfer context, we have previously argued the need for wariness of excessive separation between strategy and operations. 'Successful strategies tend to be "emergent" rather than "intended", this means that too

Box 9.1 Post-transfer local authority housing functions

Housing strategy and needs assessment

Stockholding or not, local authorities remain responsible for the periodic production of local housing strategies. A new duty, instituted in 2003 in both England and Scotland, also obliges authorities to produce local homelessness strategies (Homelessness Act 2002, Housing (Scotland) Act 2001). Allied to these responsibilities, local authorities have a longstanding legal duty to consider (aggregate) housing conditions and needs in their district with respect to the provision of further housing accommodation (in England, under Housing Act 1985 S8). Closely linked to these duties, local authorities are also obliged to undertake a periodic review of housing conditions (Housing Act 1985 S605). This is an inspection to be undertaken from time to time to determine the action the local authority will take to address sub-standard residential property.

These functions are closely related to the role of 'housing enabler' which central government has been encouraging local authorities to adopt more whole-heartedly ever since the late 1980s (DoE 1987). Bramley (1993) defined enabling in the housing context as referring to 'that range of activities that makes possible, encourages or facilitates the provision of social housing opportunities by bodies other than the local authority itself' (128). Contemporary thinking would probably see 'housing enabling' as rather wider than this – encompassing, for example, facilitating the development of a wider range of sub-market housing.

Homelessness and housing advice

In relation to homelessness, a post-transfer local authority retains responsibility for all statutory obligations laid on its stockholding counterparts. Under Part VII of the Housing Act 1996 English authorities are therefore obliged to assist homeless and potentially homeless people by:

→

- ensuring the free availability of advice on homelessness and its prevention to anyone needing such help
- giving proper consideration to all applicants for housing, including making enquiries to establish whether the applicant is owed a re-housing duty
- deciding whether applicants are eligible for housing assistance, whether they are homeless, whether they have priority need and whether any act or omission on the applicant's part led to their loss of accommodation
- securing suitable accommodation for unintentionally homeless people with a priority need
- ensuring that other homeless applicants – i.e. those not in priority need or whose homelessness resulted from their own acts (or omissions) – receive advice and assistance to help them find accommodation themselves.

At least until its assessment process has been completed, a local authority must also ensure provision of temporary accommodation for any applicant who it has reason to believe may be unintentionally homeless and in priority need. Similar expectations apply in Wales and Scotland.

Allocations

Conceptually rather less straightforward is the Housing Act 1996 requirement that post-transfer local authorities in England – notwithstanding their non-landlord status – must devise and publish an allocation scheme and allocate housing accordingly. What this means in practice is that households potentially subject to nomination to housing associations by a 'stockless' council should be ranked according to the authority's official prioritization framework.

Councils are no longer legally required to maintain a housing register – again, irrespective of their landlord status. However, it remains customary to do so. Unless contracted out to another organization, a post-transfer authority will retain the management of this list.

much distance between strategy and implementation can weaken performance' (Mullins 2004: 11).

Official policy on retained housing functions, post-stock transfer

Since the late 1990s, central government in England has become somewhat more assertive in emphasizing that local authorities should not see stock transfer as ending broader housing responsibilities or even downgrading their status. Earlier research had confirmed that in planning stock transfers there tended to be an overwhelming focus on setting up the transfer vehicle and the practicalities of ensuring the ownership handover. In some early case studies, authorities made very limited provision for the retained and enabling housing role which was often split between several departments with no clear responsibilities for co-ordination. The low priority accorded to this activity is apparent from the following three extracts from the 1995 evaluation report:

> Immediately after transfer the number of residual housing posts in case study authorities ranged from nil to seven. (Mullins et al. 1995: 86–7)

> Following transfer many authorities disbanded their housing committees. Housing strategy became one of the matters dealt with by committees with wider briefs such as Community Affairs or Environmental Services. (Mullins et al. 1995: 93)

> In the other case members appeared to see the transfer as the end of their housing role. They had not sought to develop a strategic approach and since there had been few complaints from tenants they were quite happy to leave housing matters to the association. (Ibid: 94)

Typically, there was relatively little thought given at this stage to the planning of post-transfer local authority housing services (Aldbourne Associates 1996).

Later official guidance applicable to English authorities intent on transfer, stipulated that the Secretary of State consent will be dependent on an authority demonstrating convincingly that such functions will be operated effectively post-transfer (ODPM 2004c: chapter 14). Indeed, authorities seeking transfer consent are expected to provide evidence of 'post-transfer strengthening of the strategic role' (Community Housing Task Force 2004: 3). Such evidence is supposed to include the financial and staffing resources the authority intends to devote to discharging retained functions (an issue further discussed below).

As far as ALMOs are concerned, government guidance stresses that strategic and stock management functions need to be formally separated with the former being retained under direct housing authority control and the latter being delegated to the purpose-created body (ODPM 2003b). There is a general expectation that homelessness assessment should be seen as a 'strategic' function in this context. Hence, unlike the stock transfer scenario (see below), there is a strong presumption that the function should be retained under direct council control and not devolved or contracted out to the ALMO (see Chapter 8 for a more detailed discussion about the split of responsibilities between ALMOs and their 'parent' authorities).

Managing homelessness and access to social housing post-transfer: the legal and regulatory framework

Irrespective of stock transfer, the legislative framework for co-operation between local authorities and housing associations on managing homelessness and access to social housing (in England) is set out in the Housing Act 1996 s.170. This states simply that 'Where a local housing authority so request, a registered social landlord shall co-operate to such extent as is reasonable in the circumstances in offering accommodation to people with priority on the authority's housing register'. For housing associations, the operational implications of the legal duty to 'co-operate' on lettings were spelled out in Housing Corporation regulatory guidance under which associations are expected:

- to demonstrate their co-operation with housing authorities in homelessness reviews, in the formulation of homelessness strategies and in the delivery of housing authorities' homelessness functions;

- when requested to do so by the housing authority and to such an extent as is reasonable in the circumstances . . . (to) provide a proportion of their stock to housing authority nominations and temporary accommodation to the homeless;
- to adopt criteria (following consultation with housing authorities) for accepting or rejecting nominees and other applicants for housing – and to exclude applicants from consideration for housing only when their unacceptable behaviour is serious enough to make them unsuitable to be a tenant, and only in circumstances that are not unlawfully discriminating;
- to operate lettings policies which are responsive to housing authority duties.

(Housing Corporation 2002: paragraphs 3.6b to 3.6f , IX)

In Scotland, safeguards were instituted under the Housing (Scotland) Act 2001 by creating a new class of 'statutory referrals', along with a fairly heavy duty dispute resolution procedure (Communities Scotland 2002). Although this regime applies to all Scottish authorities, its introduction has been attributed to assuaging concerns over the stock transfer scenario (Kintrea 2006).

In England, the formal expectation is that co-operation between local authorities and housing associations on homeless households and others seeking social housing should be structured via nomination agreements (Pawson et al. 2004, ODPM 2004a). A local authority 'nomination' in this context is where a person seeking housing is referred by a council to be housed by a housing association. A nomination agreement is where a housing association commits to making available a proportion of its lettings to such referrals and to a set of agreed liaison procedures. Housing Corporation guidance stipulated a normal expectation that such agreements should incorporate a housing association commitment to make available 50 per cent of net lettings to council nominees (Housing Corporation 2003). For stock transfer housing associations a stated 'nominations entitlement' of at least 75 per cent has been much more common (Pawson and Mullins 2003: 56).

Post-transfer local authority housing practice

Resources

Linking with the preceding discussion, this section draws on a range of research evidence on post-transfer local authority housing practice. Before looking at the evidence on specific roles and functions, however, it is worth discussing what is known about how post-transfer authorities resource and structure their remaining housing functions.

Mullins (1996) found that, among 27 early transfer local authorities, the majority had retained less than six designated housing staff in the post-transfer context. It should be recognized that this work focused mainly on the relatively small, rural authorities which dominated the early phase of stock transfers. Looking at post-transfer councils in 2001–02, however, the Audit Commission found that a third had less than 10 staff employed to carry out all retained 'housing' functions. One in five had more than 30. The apparent inconsistency with the earlier research is probably largely due to the increasing average size of post-transfer authorities over time.

The Commission, in any case, saw some local authorities as having cut back on their housing staffing to such an extent that 'it is difficult to see how [such authorities] can effectively carry out the role expected in legislation and guidance' (Audit Commission 2002: 18). The survey also seemed to confirm the common tendency for councils to make insufficient provision for post-transfer staffing: a majority of responding local authorities reported having expanded their housing staffing since stock handover. Although, with the passage of time, the Commission's research evidence is now becoming degraded, such concerns continue to be seen as valid. For example, the CIH commented that 'It is widely recognised that the strategic housing function has had a low profile and has been under-resourced for some time in many authorities, *particularly those that are small and have transferred their housing stock*' (CIH 2007: 7, our italics).

In the Scottish context, Taylor (2008) found that, post-stock transfer 'resources for homelessness services had to be identified and won' (summary paragraph 4.1). Transfer had also caused problems because the loss of an authority's landlord function was accompanied by an end to the scope for subsidising homelessness management activities from the housing revenue account.

Housing strategy

Aside from the theoretical arguments about separating strategy from operations, it remains difficult to point to clear evidence that such an approach delivers practical benefits in the housing field. The Audit Commission's study 'Housing After Transfer' judged the evidence here as 'inconclusive' (Audit Commission 2002). This sceptical stance was emphasized in the statement by a highly-informed commentator that 'there is no indication that the 90 authorities who had sold their stock were better at strategic work than the ones who had not . . . I do not think there is any evidence to support the fact that splitting the roles guarantees better performance' (witness statement by Head of Housing Inspectorate: House of Commons 2004: 37).

An analysis of more recent Audit Commission inspection reports, as shown in Table 9.1, also fails to reveal any correlation between stock transfer and assessed local authority 'effectiveness' in relation to housing functions retained after transfer. While no authority was judged 'excellent' in this respect, the proportion of 'good' performers was lower among post-transfer local authorities. Moreover, the average score taking account of both current effectiveness and prospects for improvement was slightly higher (better) for councils retaining a landlord function.

Facilitating affordable housing development

Since the Barker (2004) report, central government in England has taken a renewed interest in housing supply, with the 2007 Green Paper committing to substantial increases in public funding for affordable housing development (CLG 2007a). There have been hints that local authorities would regain a significant foothold as housing developers (ibid: 76–7). In Scotland, a number of local authorities are staging a modest revival in council house-building, financed partly via 'prudential borrowing' (Scottish Government 2008a, b). Overall, however, there is as yet little sign of a broader reversal in

TABLE 9.1 *Audit Commission ratings from inspection reports published 2004–09*

Local authority status	Performance rating				Total	Total	Average score*
	Poor %	Fair %	Good %	Excellent %	%	No	
Landlord	25	44	31	0	100	16	2.7
Post-transfer	32	48	19	0	100	31	2.5
All	30	47	23	0	100	47	2.5

*Combined rating for current effectiveness and prospects for improvement, where ratings were converted to numerical values as follows: poor = 0, fair/uncertain = 1, good = 2, excellent = 3.

Rating covers housing strategy, homelessness and private sector housing functions.

Source: Audit Commission (2008).

housing associations' overwhelming dominance as the providers of new social housing. As since the late 1980s, it continues to be as enablers rather than providers that local authorities can most importantly contribute.

On a practical level, the most significant levers available to a local authority in support of housing 'enabling' activity are its land-use planning powers. Under these powers, an authority can require that a private housing developer makes provision for an element of 'affordable housing' within any planned residential construction scheme. Since 1992, planning authorities in England have been required to develop formal policies on how they will ensure the provision of a sufficient quantity of 'affordable housing'. In part, this reflects central government's growing aspiration to use planning leverage to secure effective subsidy for affordable housing, as well as a belief that traditional sources of land for housing association development were becoming exhausted, and a concern that facilitating housing development for 'key workers' was necessary to underpin economic prosperity in some regions (Bramley et al. 2004: 100–1).

The precise impact of affordable housing policies using land use planning powers is difficult to pin down. Most of the focus here has been on the number of 'additional affordable homes' being constructed thanks to local authority policies in this area. It was, for example, estimated at a relatively early stage in the policy's genesis that it might have the capacity to generate an 'extra' 16,000–22,000 affordable homes per year (Bramley et al. 1995). In practice, it seems that the policy's impact has accumulated only slowly, so that by 2003 estimates suggested that it would be producing an 'additional' 18,000 homes (Crook et al. 2002).

Debate continues on the extent to which affordable housing constructed under 'planning agreements' between developers and local authorities can be fairly characterized as 'additional' in the sense that its costs are cross-subsidized – e.g. through offsetting land value. Monk et al. (2005) found that only nine per cent of affordable homes completed in 2002/03 under planning agreements were developed without any public subsidy. More often, the package involves land being provided at a discounted or nil price, but construction costs still being subsidized from public funds alongside private borrowing (Bramley et al. 2004).

However, rather than generating effective subsidy to underpin the development of affordable housing which would otherwise have remained unfunded, research evidence has shown that the most significant impact of affordable housing (land use planning) policies has been to shift housing association development into areas otherwise 'off limits' because of their high land values (Crook et al. 2002, Monk et al. 2005). In the sense that this has enabled housing associations to make incursions into higher status neighbourhoods, fostering more diverse communities in these areas, affordable housing policies must be counted as having had a powerful impact.

At the same time, whilst local authorities are seen as generally tending to become more assertive in making use of planning powers to facilitate affordable housing development, there is a case for arguing that many have failed to exploit these to their full potential (Bramley et al. 2004). In the stock transfer context, the question arises as to whether such powers are more likely to be used effectively by local authorities which have ceased to be landlords. Ministerial arguments that relinquishing direct provision will foster clearer and more focused local authority strategic thinking (see above) suggest that this would be expected. In practice, however, here is no specific research evidence to show that this is so (see Table 9.1 above). And the sceptical comments of the Audit Commission on the linkage between strategic activity and transfer also suggest that it is unlikely that post-transfer authorities generally make any better use of planning powers than their landlord council counterparts.

Over and above the use of land-use planning powers, local authorities in England have historically wielded considerable influence over housing association development activity via the allocation of public resources. In the initial phase of stock transfer an important aspect of this was the direct capital funding of associations via Local Authority Social Housing Grant. Particularly during the 1990s, when many stock transfers generated a net capital receipt for the local authority (see Chapter 3), some local authorities made good use of the scope for 'recycling' (at least an element of) these funds into housing association development through Social Housing Grant. This contributed to the substantial house-building activity recorded by many early transfer associations (see Chapter 7 and Pawson and Fancy 2003). However, the proscription of Social Housing Grant 'receipt recycling' in 2003 reduced the significance of this funding stream.

More recently, the Housing Corporation (now subsumed within the Homes and Communities Agency) has further strengthened its dominant role in disbursing public funding for housing association development in England. Under this system local authorities retain a degree of influence in that Agency funding decisions should accord with an authority's housing strategy. There is also an expectation of authorities being consulted by the Homes and Communities Agency on proposed funding decisions. However, while local strategies could be portrayed as 'setting the agenda', authorities, in practice, remain very much the junior partners in such exchanges. Indeed, their position was further weakened by the establishment of regional housing boards and the moves toward allocating investment on a 'sub-regional' basis rather than within the framework of local authority boundaries (ODPM 2003f). With the demise of the regional governance experiment, these functions were then aligned with Regional Development Agencies, which in turn appeared to have an uncertain future in the context of the forthcoming election in 2010. Meanwhile, a tide of 'new localism' appeared to provide some prospects of a renewal of the role of local government.

In Scotland, in the immediate wake of devolution central government signalled an intention to promote the strategic housing role of local authorities. As well as requiring local authorities (for the first time) to produce local housing strategies, Ministers also held out the possibility of councils securing administrative control of social housing development funding as a quid pro quo for choosing to transfer their own housing stock. Although it was not legislated in quite these terms, this latter measure was included in the Housing (Scotland) Act 2001. This led to the Transfer of the Management of Development Funding (TMDF) being carried through in 2004 for Scotland's two largest local authorities – Glasgow and Edinburgh. Subsequently, however, official policy was reversed and (stock transfer or not) there appears little prospect of any other councils securing TMDF.

Over and above the provision of explicit funding, local authorities and other public bodies can help to enable housing development by helping to make available construction sites. Many transfer packages have incorporated developable land, with the market value of such assets apparently not always being fully reflected in the transfer price. Subsequent to transfer, an authority may play a continuing role in enabling housing development through ongoing disposal of local authority-owned land or through facilitating site assembly via compulsory purchase.

Managing homelessness and access to social housing: evidence on post-transfer practice

As noted above, post-transfer local authorities retain important legal duties in relation to homelessness and facilitating access to affordable housing. How are these obligations discharged in practice, and to what extent is an authority's ability to do so compromised by the lack of its own housing portfolio?

A particular concern here is that, in the post-transfer context, housing associations' limited ability to reject people nominated to housing association tenancies by a local authority could thwart the authority's ability to discharge statutory re-housing responsibilities to homeless households (Bennett 2001, Taylor 2008). This has led to calls for stronger regulation or legal duties on housing associations to accept homeless nominees, concerns acknowledged by central government (DETR 2000c).

In the interests of preserving housing association independence, neither in England nor Scotland does the legal framework completely eliminate the theoretical possibility of an individual nominee ultimately being denied access to a housing association tenancy. Nevertheless, the actual incidence of such problems appears to be relatively infrequent. Among 32 post-transfer local authorities surveyed by the Audit Commission in 2001, only two reported that homeless (or other) nominees were 'often' rejected by the main transfer housing association – most frequently due to having unpaid rent arrears from a former tenancy with the association. More than a third of responding authorities said that homeless nominees were 'never' rejected by transfer housing association counterparts (Pawson and Mullins 2003). Similarly, an early evaluation of post-2001 'Section 5' regime in Scotland found it to be working effectively (CIH in Scotland 2005). Subsequent research on Scottish transfers observed that 'Households assessed as homeless did not necessarily have good access to permanent housing [managed] by [housing associations]' (Taylor 2008: summary, paragraph 5.1). However, there was no suggestion that post-transfer arrangements were in any sense 'unworkable' in terms of barring access to social housing for a homeless household entitled to a tenancy.

In practice, in the era of choice-based lettings nomination agreements are sometimes seen by practitioners as outdated and obsolete (see Pawson et al. 2006: paragraph 2.26). Choice-based lettings describes the procedure for managing access to social housing where properties available to let are advertised and people seeking a social sector tenancy are invited to 'bid' for (express interest in) those which meet their requirements. Competing bidders are usually ranked, not on a first-come-first-served basis or according to the ability to pay, but according to administrative criteria which combine assessed housing need with the time that the applicant has been registered for a move. Research evidence has demonstrated that in circumstances where all housing association vacancies are advertised, the distinction between 'nominee' and 'non-nominee' lets can be seen as obsolete on the grounds that all partners (including the local authority) have signed up to a common ranking policy (ibid). Nevertheless, in its early manifesto for the 2010 election, the English National Housing Federation indicated that preserving a degree of independence in lettings was still a very live issue. 'Reforming the way social housing is allocated to meet a wider range of needs' was one of the five issues prioritised for its 'tools of success election manifesto pledge card'. The accompanying report explained that 'the way social housing is allocated is not working . . . in some areas only people whose circumstances have deteriorated so much that they are defined as homeless have any chance . . . we propose that local authorities retain their duties to provide a safety net. However our model of allocations and nominations would support the creation of mixed communities... and avoid pushing all of the most vulnerable people into the same area or estate' (NHF 2009: 13).

Housing access and homelessness

An important issue affecting the way that post-transfer local authorities and housing associations work together on nominations is the way that homelessness and housing allocation functions are structured. It is open to authorities to contract out the operational aspects of these functions (Pawson et al. 2004). Survey evidence dating from 2001 showed that, at that time, about half of post-transfer authorities in England had contracted out housing registers, with around a third having outsourced the assessment of homelessness applications (Pawson and Mullins 2003). In Scotland, by contrast, post-transfer councils have tended to retain all homelessness management functions (Taylor 2008).

In the main, local authorities outsourcing these functions have contracted them to the transfer landlord itself, generally on five-year terms. Such decisions often reflect a local authority view that the management of access to social housing is integral to the landlord function, rather than being a strategic activity. It can also follow from a council's 'in principle' objective of minimizing its post-transfer operational involvement in housing activities. At least in the early days of stock transfer, this sometimes reflected a mistaken belief that through outsourcing a function such as homelessness assessment the local authority could shed all responsibility for the discharge of the service.

Another motivation which may have been significant in some councils' calculations is the concern about potentially facing difficulty in discharging statutory re-housing duties, as discussed above. The logic here would be that, through its operational role in making homelessness assessment decisions, a transfer landlord managing this function under contract will be likely to take greater ownership of the need to discharge the (council's) legal duty towards a statutory homeless household. And, hence, the theoretical risk that the local authority might find itself unable to secure re-housing is made more remote.

In cases where there is a split of responsibilities between the stock transfer landlord and the local authority (i.e. where operational responsibility is retained by the authority), there is clearly greater scope for overt conflicts between the agencies. In contrast, in cases where all functions are contracted to the transfer association, these conflicts are hidden. But the interests of homeless people could still be harmed by transfer if this were to lead the new landlord to operate the homelessness legislation in an unduly restrictive way. As the body ultimately responsible for the discharge of these duties, it is up to the 'client' local authority to ensure that this does not happen.

Recent research looked at the division of responsibilities for lettings functions in post-transfer local authorities where properties were mainly let under the choice-based lettings model – see above. The study, which focused on 26 post-transfer authorities where choice-based lettings (CBL) partnerships were established, revealed an even split between local authority-led and transfer housing association-led projects (Pawson et al. 2008). However, the chosen approach varied largely according to the type of authority. In smaller, more rural districts, joint CBL schemes were usually council-run (as in places such as Boston, Kennet and West Wiltshire), whereas in larger, more urban authorities, leadership tended to lie with the transfer housing association (as in Bradford, St Helens and Walsall). Overall, the findings suggested that local authority-led schemes appeared more likely to secure more whole-hearted housing association participation, perhaps because following stock transfer a council can present itself as a neutral actor in this guise.

Where the leadership of a CBL partnership scheme rests with the transfer housing association this is also likely to encompass the management of the local authority's housing register. This may or may not be perceived locally as constituting 'contracting out'. It, nevertheless, has the effect of impeding local authority access to data essential to inform its continuing strategic housing role (e.g. trends in the numbers and characteristics of households being entered on the housing register). One early study viewed this as an important argument for the post-transfer in-house retention of both housing register management and homelessness functions (Aldbourne Associates 1996). Such outsourcing was also seen as undesirable because it could 'result in both officers and [Elected] Members losing their sense of ownership of responsibility for the [housing] enabling function' (ibid: 26).

Official guidance has nevertheless remained generally neutral on the merits of post-transfer outsourcing of these activities. The main thrust of the advice has been that decisions should be taken on an informed basis and in line with Best Value considerations (Pawson et al. 2004). However, the Audit Commission advised that such decisions should be avoided in the immediate pre-transfer period; rather, any consideration of outsourcing should be held over until a transfer has been completed and arrangements have bedded down. The concern here was the perceived risk of decisions made in the run-up to transfer being based on an inadequate appraisal of the options due to the competing priorities involved in delivering the transfer itself. Backing up this line of thinking, Taylor (2008) found that homelessness implications of stock transfer tended to have been given little prior consideration in Scotland. The Commission also noted that inspection findings were inconclusive as to whether homelessness and allocations services were most effectively run by outsourcing or in-house provision (Audit Commission 2002).

There is also evidence of a limited tendency for local authorities which outsourced homelessness assessment and/or housing register management at transfer subsequently recovering direct control of these functions (Pawson and Mullins 2003). This may, to some extent, reflect a recognition that direct control of such functions can facilitate effective strategic enabling activity.

Apart from the relative merits of the outsourcing/in-house options purely in terms of the specific functions concerned, there is a wider issue at stake here; namely the extent to which 'housing activities' retain a profile in a council which has ceased to act as a landlord in its own right. This will depend, in part, on the crude numbers of staff undertaking housing functions who remain in direct local authority employment. The greater the body of 'housing staff', the greater the case for retaining a senior manager with a housing brief who will be in a position to articulate housing concerns and to dispel any impression among colleagues and Elected Members that all housing responsibilities have been jettisoned along with stock ownership.

Partly in sympathy with this argument the Audit Commission argued that, in structuring local authority post-transfer housing functions 'fragmentation' should be avoided: 'it is rarely effective to divide retained housing staff between many different sections – in particular, separating private sector staff from strategy and housing needs staff limits cover and makes it less likely that policies will complement each other as they should' (Audit Commission 2002: 20). In practice, the Commission argued, transfer has often led to intellectual asset stripping.

In concluding this section, it should be re-iterated that significant powers remain available to enable post-transfer local authorities to exercise influence on local housing systems. As yet, however, there is no evidence of any general tendency for stock transfer to facilitate more effective housing strategy and enabling activity. As regards the discharge of re-housing responsibilities to homeless households, it is clear that stock transfer can seriously complicate the job of a stockless local authority. Fears that transfers to constitutionally 'independent' landlords would make the homelessness legislation generally unworkable have not, however, been borne out.

Stock transfer impact on local housing governance

Stock transfer is part of a process which involves 'policy implementation at the local level [becoming] increasingly dependent on collaboration among different and competing organisations' (Malpass 1997b: 93). The shift of social housing out of public ownership inevitably weakens the traditional dominance of local authorities in shaping local housing systems. On the face of it, central government sacrifices some of its ability to transmit influence on housing delivery previously channelled through local authorities.

Accordingly, the transfer process has been interpreted as reducing the utility of the central-local relations and public administration paradigms in theorizing the operation of local housing systems (Mullins et al. 2001). Indeed, the transfer process was highlighted as a case in point, illustrating the increasing importance of inter-organizational networking in the functioning of housing systems (Reid 1995). The key argument here is that the transfer process – even as it has evolved under the more directive Decent Homes regime (and Welsh and Scottish equivalents) – continues to be characterized by an element of negotiation between key players. This is seen in the development of the transfer package, the choice and/or setting up of the successor landlord, and in defining the 'transfer promises' to serve as the basis of the tenant ballot.

As Reid also pointed out, close inter-organizational working continues after stock transfer, both through the formal governance structure of the successor landlord (on which the local authority is normally represented) and through collaboration between the council and its transfer housing association counterpart. Surveyed in 2002, nearly three quarters of transfer housing associations perceived that they continued to enjoy a 'special relationship' with their founding local authority (Pawson and Fancy 2003). By implication, these relations remained closer than those between local authorities and 'traditional' housing associations. Neither do such ties necessarily weaken over time: the incidence of perceived special relationships was the same among transfer housing associations established 1988–96 as among those set up post-1996.

A 'common-sense' explanation of perceived local authority/transfer housing association special relationships might highlight the typical pre-eminence of the latter as the largest social landlord in the locality, or the representation of council nominees on transfer housing association governing bodies (still relatively rare among traditional associations). However, research evidence confirms that this is far from the whole story. In particular, many transfer landlords remain functionally integrated with their founding local authorities in ways quite distinct from the relationships between councils and traditional housing associations. This may involve local authority outsourcing of functions such as homelessness assessment and housing register management (as discussed above). On the other side of the coin, some transfer landlords continue to contract services from founding local authorities – e.g. repairs, grounds maintenance and information technology (Pawson and Fancy 2003).

Historically, close relations between councils and transfer housing associations have also sometimes reflected preferential treatment in the distribution of Local Authority Social Housing Grant. However, with fewer post-2000 transfers generating net capital receipts and with the 2004 abolition of Local Authority Social Housing Grant the significance of this factor has declined. Instead, access to council-owned developable land has become more significant.

Within the context of the more urban transfers, increasingly seen since 1997, relations between transferring local authorities and their stock transfer housing association counterparts have often been coloured by the council's recognition that the new landlord is by far their most important partner agency in delivering area regeneration objectives. Because many transfer landlords come to embrace regeneration objectives as vital to their own long-term organizational prospects (see Chapter 7) there can be rivalry over the leadership of the local regeneration programme. Here, much depends on the assets conveyed in the transfer. Where – as in Glasgow – the terms of the deal were carefully specified to exclude handover of any developable land, it is easier for the authority to retain control of such activities. Nevertheless, the need for a newly-established landlord to demonstrate its 'consultative' credentials can extend the lead-in time for schemes involving clearance and replacement of transferred stock and, in this way, spark frustration on the local authority side. Albeit far from typical, strained relations between Glasgow Housing Association and Glasgow City Council in 2009 demonstrated the extent to which rival agendas on regeneration can contribute to tensions between local authorities and transfer landlords (Braiden 2009).

Research evidence demonstrates that the operational relationships between post-transfer councils and their transfer housing association counterparts also have the capacity to generate inter-organizational tensions. These may involve client/contractor stresses concerning local authority functions outsourced to the successor landlord. Sometimes such stresses have reflected defective contracts – e.g. agreements unrealistically costed or failing to properly specify performance targets, penalties and incentives (Pawson et al. 2004). Other tension-inducing scenarios have included cases where the original contracting or outsourcing decision was accepted only reluctantly by the transfer housing association (e.g. where the successor landlord was obliged to take on the local authority's in-house repairs service) or where the new landlord subsequently came to perceive delivering a local authority function (e.g. homelessness assessment) under contract compromised its independence or exposed it to financial losses.

Another difficulty stemming from council/transfer housing association functional inter-relationships relates to accountability. As noted by the Audit Commission (2002), the perceptions of tenants and other service users need to be carefully managed to promote understanding of a potentially confusing post-transfer inter-organizational division of responsibility for services such as homelessness.

Setting the local governance implications of stock transfer in a wider context, Lowe sees the phenomenon as part of the 'streamlining' of social housing. This, in turn, 'dovetails into the newly modernised local authority governance with centralised executives, cabinets and executive mayors in parallel with a reduced role for local councillors whose role is to act as conduits of information in a clearly top down system' (Lowe 2004: 52).

The preceding discussion has been predicated on the fact that stock transfers have, for the most part, replaced a unitary local authority with a single post-transfer social landlord and on the observation that at least up until 2008, the majority of such organizations created in England continued to exist as independent or autonomous entities. Nevertheless, even among those established through whole stock transfers, around half had by this time begun to alter their organizational identity by joining or setting up 'group structures' involving other associations. Over time, it is highly possible that ongoing sector restructuring will progressively involve the complete absorption of transfer landlords within regional or national organizations. This process is likely to have profound consequences for local housing governance and may well mean that the observations outlined above will come to be seen as describing no more than a passing phase.

Chapter conclusions

Local authorities have important housing-related roles which are quite independent of whether they continue to operate as landlords in their own right. However, while central government argues that divestment of direct provision has the capacity to trigger more effective strategic policy-making, organizational theory suggests this is, at least, debatable. And, in practice, there is little evidence of any general tendency for transfer having improved performance in this area. Indeed, it is clear that at least until recently, a proportion of transferring authorities erroneously believed that in offloading stock ownership, other housing responsibilities could be similarly jettisoned.

Among the most important local authority housing powers unrelated to stock ownership are those forming part of the land-use planning regime. However, while the past decade has seen a continuing trend towards strengthening such powers, council influence on social housing provision through direct funding has, in general, been in decline.

Growing affordability problems in certain areas have highlighted the inescapable potential for local authority/housing association tensions where the former retains a legal duty to rehouse certain homeless households, but can do so only through an essentially negotiated approach. Contracting out homelessness assessment functions to successor landlords only conceals this tension without solving it.

The shift of social housing out of local authority ownership creates a situation where social landlord activity appears much less susceptible to hierarchical direction by the state, at least in its local guise. Instead, a system is created where local authorities and other stakeholder organizations exert influence much more through partnerships, contracts and the planning system. In the longer term, as transfer landlords increasingly integrate within the wider housing association sector it seems likely that local specificity will be lost and with it the typical closeness characterizing council/transfer landlord relationships in the first 5–10 years after the end of council housing.

Chapter 10

Conclusions

Britain's social rented sector continues to account for almost a fifth of all homes and remains relatively large by international standards (Fitzpatrick and Stephens 2007, Whitehead and Scanlon 2007). By 2009, however, the sector was considerably smaller than at its 1980 zenith when it encompassed almost a third of all dwellings. More dramatically, while defying predictions of total extinction, the number of council owned-and-managed homes had, over this period, contracted to less than a quarter of the 1980 total.

As the measure mainly responsible for these developments, the Right to Buy for sitting tenants would be identified by most British commentators as the single most important housing policy of the late twentieth century (Jones and Murie 2006). Arguably of a similar order, however, has been the profound internal restructuring of the sector effected through stock transfer. Indeed, while Right to Buy was the main contributor to shrinking council housing until 1997, after this date it was overtaken by stock transfer and ALMO delegations. Whereas sales to sitting tenants 1998–2007 totalled 700,000, this was hugely outnumbered by both stock transfers and management delegation to ALMOs – each of these accounting for around 1 million homes over the same period. Whereas sales were dominant under Thatcher and Major, transfer and management outsourcing have been the main event in the New Labour era.

Particularly in England, 20 years of stock transfers have decisively ended the former supremacy of municipal landlordism. In place of state ownership and management, social housing in almost half of all localities is entirely in the hands of third sector organizations regulated but not controlled by government. In many other areas, local authority owned housing remains a reality but management decision-making has been distanced to 'arms length' from locally elected representatives.

Although 'voluntary' in origins, this reshaping of social housing has been largely willed by Ministers. Particularly since

1997, the process has been substantially 'top-down' in nature. Although it had been initially envisaged that the transfer process (as prefigured by Tenants' Choice) would be led by dissatisfied tenants this has proved far from true. Nevertheless, as we have argued, the phenomenon has been much more than a simple case of Ministerial diktat. The emerging story has featured complex central-local relations, as well as interactions between key stakeholder interests at the local scale. The policy itself has also evolved in a substantially incremental way.

This book has explored how these processes unfolded, the nature of the organizations created and the housing system impacts that have resulted. In this final chapter we reflect on the factors underlying the stock transfer experience, we discuss some of the longer-term implications and where the process might go from here. We also identify some of the as yet unanswered research questions arising from our analysis. Finally, we return to the question of whether stock transfer can be fairly seen as 'transformational'. Before moving to this discussion, however, we first revisit our title to reconsider exactly who are Britain's new social landlords and what is new about them.

Who are Britain's new social landlords?

Including the crop of English ALMOs, more than 300 new social landlords have come into being through the post-1988 restructuring of Britain's non-market rented sector. A few of the housing associations newly created in the early 1990s as freestanding bodies have been subsequently absorbed by larger counterpart landlords through mergers (see Table 5.1). A larger number, while continuing to exist as registered entities, have allied alongside other associations within group structures. In doing so, such associations will necessarily have sacrificed some or all of their autonomy. Potentially, such 'group subsidiary' organizations may continue to exist as little more than local 'brand names' for larger, remotely based conglomerates, or may in time become fully integrated into national or regionally homogeneous organizations, perhaps with functional rather than geographical structures. For the time being, however, the vast majority of the new bodies established through stock transfers and arms length housing management delegation since

1989 remained in existence twenty years into this process. These organizations constitute Britain's most clearly identifiable new social landlords.

Certainly the most vocal criticism of stock transfer – and, by extension, the establishment of ALMOs – has been the allegation that this represents privatization, inimical to tenants' interests. As discussed in Chapter 4, this perspective highlights what is seen as the fundamental divide between politically accountable council housing and the emerging forms of landlordism. A contrasting perspective has been that divestment of ownership and/or management of council housing to specially created bodies is no more than a cynical manoeuvre to evade public spending rules or exploit the opportunity to access additional government funding. Allied to this analysis is the view that stock transfer is little more than the preservation of 'unreformed' former housing departments within a new guise. Accordingly, the notion that stock transfer housing associations and ALMOs are, in any real sense, a new form of organization is seen as a misrepresentation. As we read it, however, the research evidence firmly refutes this contention. In particular, as reported in Chapter 6, it is clear that the evolution of transfer landlords over their initial 5–10 years of existence has tended to give rise to organizations distinctly more inclusive, more cohesive, more businesslike and, at least initially, less hierarchical than their local authority landlord predecessors.

Although the research evidence is much less complete, it seems highly likely that the above observations also apply in large measure to ALMOs. Perhaps to an even greater degree than has typically been true of stock transfer housing associations, the ALMO model incorporates a tenant empowerment dynamic. At least as portrayed by their trade body, recorded service improvements under arms length management reflect a 'commitment from all ALMOs to involve tenants much more closely in their work than was the case before ALMOs were established' (NFA 2009: 5). Taken at face value, this represents a fundamental challenge to any suggestion that ALMOs are no more than re-branded local authority housing departments. It is also significant that, as yet, while some ALMOs have completed Decent Homes stock improvement programmes, none has been dismantled to permit the recovery of full council control. Nevertheless, it has been reported that a number of local authorities with ALMOs have contemplated proceeding to stock transfer (as predicted in the 'slippery slope' argument advanced by defenders of council housing), and that in one case the local authority envisages the invitation of private sector organizations to bid for contracts to manage the 18,000 homes for which the ALMO is currently responsible (Stothart 2009). In a number of instances, follow-on five-year contractual terms have been signed to preserve existing arms length arrangements. This, too, is consistent with the contention that ALMOs have evolved into organizations distinct from their housing department predecessors and, consequently, not easily re-incorporated within local authority structures.

Beyond this it would, of course, be a mistake to imply that either (continuing) landlord local authorities or traditional housing associations have been entirely immune to reform. Especially as a result of the Best Value regime, through exposure to regulatory inspection and through financial accounting requirements (e.g. post-2001 Housing Revenue Account Business Planning), remaining council housing departments have certainly been subject to many reform pressures of the top-down kind. An early evaluation of Best Value impacts found more than a third of English local authorities asserting that the framework had substantially increased their engagement with tenants (Aldbourne Associates 2001). In response to regulatory stimuli of these kinds, municipal landlords have undoubtedly introduced many other innovations in recent years (see, for example, ARCH 2008). Also relevant here is the research evidence of steady year-on-year local authority performance improvement across a range of traditional housing management service indicators through much of the first decade of the new millennium (Pawson 2009a, Pawson and Jacobs 2010, forthcoming).

A number of the 'top-down influences' cited above had also impacted on long-established – as well as recently-created – housing associations. Perhaps of greater significance, as bodies outside the public sector since 1989, the need for commercial, market-orientated thinking has triggered far-reaching changes in the structures and operation of most larger associations, particularly reflecting 'institutional logics' of scale and efficiency (Mullins 2006). A key aspect of this has been the tendency towards organizational agglomeration which, in England, contributed to a 50 per cent increase in associations' average size in the six years to 2007 (Pawson and Sosenko 2008). There is also a case for arguing that transfer housing association practice has provided a sector-wide impetus for both tenant involvement and business planning.

There have also been continued 'bottom-up' drivers evident in parts of the transfer process and emerging sector, reflecting a competing 'institutional logic' of local accountability (Mullins 2006). These models build on the heritage of the earliest transfers to community-based associations in Scotland (Clapham and Kintrea 1994, 2000) and the voluntaristic 'bottom-up' (from the perspective of senior staff and local authority members if not from residents' perspectives) nature of the first whole stock transfers in England. Some landmarks along the path of more localist transfer models were the local housing company framework devised to encourage urban transfers in the mid-1990s and the Estates Renewal Challenge Fund estate-based transfers of the same era. In the early 2000s, the stock options process was legitimized by the mantra 'tenants at the heart' of the decision process, and support from the Community Housing Task Force encouraged some authorities to make a reality of this both in the process and the outcome of transfer. Stronger emphasis on bottom-up drivers was provided by the community gateway model devised by the Confederation of Co-operative Housing with support from the Chartered Institute of Housing (CIH 2002b), and the Welsh community mutual model (Bromiley et al. 2004). The first community gateway stock transfer was completed in Preston in 2005. Under its standard tri-partite board, the Preston Gateway Association has established an elected Gateway Tenants Committee charged with representing tenants to the board and electing tenant board members. All board reports are first considered by this Committee. The association's localist ethic is reflected in its definition of ten 'local community areas' as its managerial and participative framework. By 2009, three other community gateway-style transfer landlords had been established elsewhere in England and others had incorporated elements of the model.

These models stimulated debates about what constituted a 'true' gateway approach. The Confederation of Co-operative Housing advocated considerable investment in community empowerment, as happened in Preston, but in other cases the approach could be described as more 'gateway style' than true gateway, recognizing that without significant investment in capacity building, tenants are unlikely to be in a position to manage or even own the stock. Critics may argue that such models have often been more about constitutional rules than about investing in empowerment. Nevertheless, the gateway and mutual models have provided a clear alternative to the top-down model and to the migration of decision-making away from local communities within the restructuring social housing sector.

Given the arguments outlined above it would clearly be wrong to characterize stock transfer landlords and ALMOs as holding any monopoly on reform and innovation. Arguably, therefore, rather than being seen exclusively as 'transfer impacts, some of the developments discussed in this book are probably indicative of sector-wide changes affecting social housing since 1989.

Interpreting stock transfer and longer-term impacts

Stakeholder motivations for initiating, supporting or promoting stock transfer were reviewed in Chapter 3. What broader points can be made about the underlying drivers of the phenomenon? Relevant here is Kemeny's concept of the emerging 'maturity' of social housing systems with property portfolios largely developed in the middle of the twentieth century (Kemeny 1995). Key attributes of the maturation process are the twin effects of growing equity tied up in the stock, alongside growing requirements for re-investment in component replacement, repair and modernization. In these circumstances, the scope provided by stock transfer for property overhaul funded through equity release seems retrospectively obvious.

To the extent that transfer represents a (limited) form of privatization, it might be contended that the re-financing benefits of the process come at a price. However, we need to ask what – in the absence of the transfer process as seen – might have been the alternative scenario. Arguably, the process has represented a middle way between, on the one hand, continued deterioration of cash-starved council housing, and on the other, full-blooded privatization of a profit-orientated, and potentially asset-stripping, kind.

Nevertheless, while contesting the portrayal of stock transfer as naked privatization, we certainly accept that shifting ownership into the hands of commercial (if not profit-making) organizations brings risks. One of the clearest is the possibility that, over time, transfer associations will lose their geographical focus and, with that, the close identification with localities which was inherent within council housing.

To some extent, this has already occurred. Two mechanisms have been involved. Firstly, among 'first generation' transfer landlords, many made use of their fundamentally strong financial position to exploit opportunities to develop new social housing across authorities remote from their 'home base' (see Chapter 7).

Secondly, many transfer associations – not solely confined to those established through 'first generation' transactions – have entered into broader, geographically dispersed, organizational alliances. As noted above, such instances have generally involved transfer landlords accepting 'group subsidiary' status rather than full merger. While no longer fully 'independent', such organizations retain their status as a legal entity. However, given the recent sector-wide trend towards 'group consolidation' (Pawson and Sosenko 2008), it would seem highly likely that many such arrangements will morph into full mergers in coming years, potentially leading to full integration within larger, remotely-based, organizational structures. This opens up the potential for 'loss of local focus' to take place far more rapidly than through the 'out of borough' development of new social housing in which some first generation transfer associations became so heavily involved in the early 1990s. Such transactions may be seen as according with financial strength and efficiency through large scale procurement. At the same time, however, they raise major questions about local connectedness and the continuing viability of accountability relationships with tenants, local authorities and other stakeholders (Mullins 2006).

While we have argued that some 'privatization' critiques of stock transfer have been unconvincing and overblown, the scenario depicted above is probably not inconsistent with that foreseen in Ginsburg's (2005) characterization of transfer as representing a staged form of privatization, or Malpass and Victory's (2010, forthcoming) depiction of a 'modernisation process' with the potential for a variety of steps and eventual outcomes (see Chapter 1). While the initial step does not, in itself, represent decisive change from public to private, the resulting process may well result in a gradual dilution of public control and accountability and exposure to growing commercial influences. Relevant here is the changing regulatory landscape following from the Cave recommendations (Cave 2007) for regulated competition between a range of types of provider (Mullins and Sacranie 2008). Similarly, the growing presence of profit distributing organizations within the field, following the opening up of public development subsidy to private developers in 2004, is likely to have implications for the culture and practice of existing housing associations including stock transfer landlords. Mullins and Walker (2009) have begun to explore the impacts of this process in creating a mixed economy of providers and how this may affect the behaviour of both non-profit and for-profit actors and whether this may lead to organizational forms that blur distinctions between them. This seems likely to involve housing associations adopting hybrid commercial identities as they engage in activities similar to those of private developers, such as construction for market renting, for sale at market prices, and land banking. Housing association hybridity to cross-subsidize social housing provision through commercial activities was increasing until the credit crunch hit the housing market in 2008. Then, reduced availability of mortgage finance and consequentially decreasing sales reduced associations' ability to cross-subsidize grants for rented housing, and unsold stock and unused land caused further problems for association accounts, potential breaches of loan terms and higher long-term borrowing costs. This market situation strained the business models of hybrid housing associations and private developers alike. However, the impact of unsold and devalued assets on the annual accounts of housing associations, reflected in so called 'impairment charges', did not approach the scale of impact on the larger commercial developers. Analysis of annual accounts for 2008/9 indicated that 94 housing associations were required to post 'impairment charges' showing a combined loss in asset values of £174 million. However, the industry regulator pointed out that these impairment charges were equivalent to just 0.5 per cent of total assets (compared to write-downs of up to 35 per cent of value by some commercial builders) (TSA 2009b). Furthermore, these write-downs had not resulted in any breaches of covenants with lenders (which could have resulted in significant increases in interest costs).

Meanwhile, Mullins and Pawson (2010, forthcoming) have related housing association hybridity to resource dependence on public funding and private finance secured on commercial terms; housing associations have embraced the mixed economy of welfare to such an extent that they have themselves become hybrids. Hybridity is particularly associated with the 'growing pains' of increasing organizational scale. Very large associations appear to be emerging as a sector in their own right for which new forms of organization and governance are required (Appleyard 2006). These are associated with cuts in the numbers of regulated entities, reductions in the numbers of non-executives, payment of non-executives and appointment of more executive directors to boards. All of this is transforming the governance of these organizations in the interests of government-defined notions of business efficiency and enhanced flexibility to do commercial deals. In the process, traditional advantages claimed by associations of engagement with communities and local accountability have been called into question. As stock transfer organizations have been absorbed into regional and national groupings through combinations with traditional associations these questions have been writ large.

Policy evaluation

In evaluating the success of stock transfer as a policy, attention must focus primarily on its contribution to property upgrading as the main stated objective post-1997. As reported in Chapter 7, in England, transfer has contributed to a wider set of measures which are expected to have reduced the incidence of 'unsatisfactory' (i.e. 'non-Decent') social housing from 38 per cent in 2002 to around 10 per cent in 2010. After decades of disinvestment in council housing, the scale of this achievement should not be understated. The modest – though steady – improvement in tenant satisfaction recorded across English social housing in recent years (Pawson and Jacobs 2010, forthcoming, CLG 2009c), is probably testament to the impact of stock transfer and ALMO policy in facilitating progress towards Decent Homes Standard compliance, as well as the improvement of day-to-day service delivery.

At the same time, while transfer has been presented by government as a central element in a 'choice agenda' this must be seen as a questionable claim. The requirement that local authorities aspiring to transfer must secure majority tenant support has proved an important incentive to 'strike a good deal' in negotiations over valuations and to recognize tenant priorities in planning post-transfer services. It is also important to recognize the significance of efforts to empower residents in the options appraisal process after 2002, building on the earlier role of 'tenants' friend' consultants in supporting residents' groups in influencing the process of constructing ballot offer documents as well as simply providing advice. Even so, as a device to 'enhance tenants' choices' transfer clearly has significant shortcomings. Ultimately, the ballot 'choice' offered to tenants has usually consisted of no more than an opportunity to endorse or reject a single option, with rejection potentially incurring a heavy penalty in the form of debarred access to capital investment (at least in the short term). If this can be said to represent choice, it is certainly of the highly loaded variety. On this logic there is a certain resonance in the Defend Council Housing portrayal of stock transfer ballots as tantamount to 'blackmail', and the absence of a genuine 'fourth option' proved a long-running embarrassment to a government that had emphasized community engagement and customer choice but which resisted options out of line with its own agenda until the fundamental review of HRA reported in Chapter 8 and further discussed below. Associated with this is the concern about the perceived injustice of a situation where, thanks to their principled rejection of 'privatization', council tenants deny themselves the possibility of 'decent homes'. In practice, however, as discussed in Chapter 4, there are documented instances of councils faced with these circumstances and claiming to have subsequently found other means of complying with quality standards.

Nevertheless, whether council tenants are afforded genuine 'choice' on whether to endorse a transfer proposal remains highly arguable. What is, however, certain is that (except in Glasgow – see below) housing association tenants enjoy *no comparable right* of veto over any proposal for a 'change of landlord'. This 'discrepancy' might be seen as most pointed where a stock transfer association set up as an independent entity subsequently opts for an organizational merger with a remotely-based counterpart RSL.

Drawing attention to this inconsistency, Black (2006) noted that the 2001 Housing (Scotland) Act appeared to make provision for just such a choice where 'a disposal by ...a registered social landlord would result in a change of landlord...' (18). Taken together with other clauses in the legislation, this seemed to require tenant ballot endorsement for housing association merger proposals, just as for local authority stock transfers. However, while it has been conventionally accepted that Second Stage Transfers from Glasgow Housing Association can proceed only with such acceptance, government and regulator have denied that this obligation is more broadly applicable. Legally, they argue, the situation remains as it does in England and Wales – i.e. that (short of a 'marriage' forced by regulatory powers) a merger proposal needs only the endorsement of the paid-up members of the relevant associations. (See Chapter 5 for an explanation of 'association membership' under *Industrial and Provident Society* and *Company Limited by Guarantee* legal formats.) However, from 2005 English housing associations seeking regulatory approval for merger were required to develop a business case including the identification of benefits to residents.

As recognized by Black, official acceptance that association mergers could proceed only with tenant backing would be 'inconvenient' for the organizations involved and practicalities could present substantial logistical challenges for larger associations. Partly addressing his concern, however, with the establishment of the community gateway and community mutual models in England and Wales (see Chapter 5) we are, in any case, seeing some examples of mass membership transfer associations where it would seem that any subsequent merger proposal would, in fact, need to command widespread tenant support.

Prospects for stock transfer policy

Transfer trajectories

A separate question about future prospects concerns the transfer process itself. While the process had cut deep into local authority housing by 2009, just over half of all authorities retained stock ownership at this point (albeit that over 60 in England had delegated management to ALMOs). Consequently, there is clearly scope for the transfer process to continue.

In terms of the incidence of transfer activity, recent national trajectories were highly varied at the time of writing (2009). In Wales, a post-2005 upturn in transfer activity triggered by the imposition of the Welsh Housing Quality Standard appeared still in full swing. In England, however, there had been a marked downturn in transfer activity since 2007, while in Scotland divestment by local authorities had come to an abrupt halt in the same year.

The recent trend in England can be largely explained as a consequence of the policy cycle. As discussed in Chapter 3, the impetus for the post-2000 surge in transfers stemmed largely from the establishment of the Decent Homes Standard and the target for eliminating non-decent social housing by 2010.As noted in Chapter 2, stock options appraisals were stipulated for completion by 2005 and, even by then, time to complete a stock overhaul within the Decent Homes Standard deadline was beginning to run short. It is, therefore, probably unsurprising that whole stock transfers completed in 2008 were half those of the previous year, and that 2009 saw a reduction.

Fundamental reform of council housing finance in England

Whether this will be the end of the story is not clear. As the Decent Homes deadline approached, and many social landlords achieved compliance (or became more confident that this would be accomplished) attention shifted towards the longer-term sustainability of 'decent' standards. For the vast majority of remaining stockholding councils, sobering outputs were generated by associated financial modelling within the context of the existing Housing Revenue Account subsidy system. A national study to project future council housing income and expenditure demonstrated that under the current subsidy system, most stock-retaining local authorities would lack the HRA resources to sustain decent standards in the medium and long term (Dowler 2009a). 'We are talking about the Major Repairs Allowance across the country being 40 per cent short of what most people would estimate is a minimum investment need over 30 years' (Steve Partridge, Housing Quality Network consultant supporting the review group, *Inside Housing*, 14 March 2009).

However, as noted in Chapter 8 (see penultimate section), 2009 finally saw the emergence of fundamental reform proposals interpreted as holding out the possibility of a financially sustainable future for council housing in England (CLG 2009b). The proposals aimed to establish the basis for local authority landlords to become entirely self-financing and subsidy-free. Crucially, therefore, they would end the reviled practice under which most authorities had found a proportion of their rental income being 'creamed off' into government coffers – a system which had led, by 2008/09, to some £200 million being extracted from the sector entirely (CIH 2009). The existing system has also been criticized as undermining local accountability as well as preventing long-term financial planning.

The reform plan would involve the outstanding housing debt held by the 37 most indebted landlord authorities being redistributed across the 144 remaining landlord councils with below average or nil debt. This would leave every authority carrying debt equivalent to the group-wide norm, £8,500 per dwelling. According to *Social Housing* (September 2009), the resulting settlement would be likely to leave virtually all authorities on a sustainable 'self-financing' footing in terms of being able to balance their books without any further ongoing subsidy. The associated plan to end Treasury debt write-off as a means of facilitating stock transfer (see Chapter 3) seems quite logical within this context. What is less clear is whether such a facility would remain open (at least in theory) to highly indebted authorities in Scotland or Wales and seeing transfer as their only route to compliance with national property quality standards.

The CLG proposals have been seen as greatly eroding – possibly even eliminating – the financially advantaged status of housing associations *vis-à-vis* local authorities and, in this way, 'could bring to an end over two decades of whole stock transfers' (CIH 2009: 12). This assumes that, as enacted, the proposed settlement will effectively provide – for all authorities having reached the Decent Homes Standard – the capacity to invest in ongoing maintenance and renewals to retain DHS compliance. The CIH conclusion also assumes, probably rightly, that financial considerations remain the key driver for transfers (but see Chapter 3 for discussion of other transfer motivations).

The CIH prediction that the proposals could spell a complete end to transfers for the foreseeable future may well be borne out. Nevertheless, such an outcome does not seem entirely certain at the time of writing. For one thing, in terms of debt redistribution, the proposed HRA settlement could be interpreted as creating a relatively small number of clear 'winners' (admittedly, some of them big winners) and a much larger number of 'losers'. Whether it will be possible to secure universal acceptance of the plan therefore remains to be seen. Many other uncertainties also remain to be resolved – e.g. the extent to which landlord authorities would, under the proposals, enjoy scope to take on new debt (for investment) via prudential borrowing to place them on an equal footing with housing associations. One final factor to be borne in mind is the fact that, even under the 2009 reform proposals as announced, stockholding local authorities would remain dependent on the future availability of central government capital allocations. This represents a retreat from earlier and more radical proposals which envisaged a larger uplift in Major Repairs Allowances to be reflected in the debt redistribution and no subsequent dependence on capital grants.

Without question, it appears that full enactment of the reform proposals would greatly dampen existing financial incentives for remaining English landlord councils to terminate this role. Nevertheless, even assuming that the plans are fully operationalized, there are scenarios under which some transfers might still occur, post-2009. One of these would be where low debt authorities faced with the prospect of taking on a large share of liabilities from their heavily-indebted counterparts (under the proposed settlement) are thus incentivized to 'race for transfer' before this happens. For others with an urgent need for a solution to financial pressures resulting from the existing HRA system, it may be judged that any salvation via the proposed national debt restructure could not come soon enough to justify deferring a transfer ballot. Stothart (2009) reported there were 'several' authorities projecting unavoidable (and unlawful) HRA deficits in the near term (and before any reformed system could reasonably be expected to kick in). Moreover, the proposed debt restructure, even if tenable for most, may be insufficiently generous to create financial sustainability for all authorities (*Social Housing*, September 2009). Further, as acknowledged by the CLG consultation paper itself, the proposals would not be expected to end regeneration-inspired estate transfers. A final possibility is that further transfers might follow from local decisions that Decent Homes (and equivalent) quality thresholds were too low and where transfer might be judged the only practical route to the substantial investment required to achieve a more acceptable standard.

Scottish prospects

As to Scotland, following a wave of activity, 2003–07, no further local authority transfers were in prospect in 2009. In part, this reflects the policy cycle. Authorities recognizing the financial need for transfer to fund compliance with the Scottish Housing Quality Standard proceeded to ballot by 2006, with transfers endorsed by tenants being completed by 2007. However, it remains uncertain whether all authorities opting for stock retention are, in fact, capable of financing compliance with the Standard (see, for example, recently expressed doubts on the robustness of plans on the part of Dundee City Council – Scottish Housing Regulator 2009). Although the pro-transfer stance on the part of Scottish Ministers ended with the election of the Scottish National Party administration in 2007, it could even be the case that some authorities may need to reconsider this option to achieve Scottish Homes Quality Standard compliance. Some 'retention strategies' incorporate assumptions of substantial real-terms rent increases and/or large-scale asset sales. Nonetheless, without the continued availability of local authority housing debt write-off, re-visitation of the transfer option would certainly be impossible. And on this point – as noted above – uncertainty currently remains.

Beyond this, in advance of any HRA reform similar to that envisaged in England, there may well be questions about authorities' longer-term capacity to sustain Quality Standard compliance while restraining rent increases consistent with retaining 'affordability'.

In the more immediate future, the main ongoing stock transfer story in Scotland concerns Glasgow Housing Association which, in 2009, completed the first six of its second stage transfers involving 2,000 of Glasgow Housing Association's 70,000 remaining homes. Beyond this, GHA anticipated a further round of SSTs involving up to 20,000 dwellings being handed to LHOs as successor landlords. This activity, expected to be complete by 2011, was seen as the marking the outer limit of financial feasibility (GHA 2008). Glasgow City Council, however, has continued to press the association to make good a 2003 commitment to ballot all remaining Glasgow Housing Association tenants on their aspirations as to second stage transfers (Glasgow City Council 2009).

The big picture – England, Wales and Scotland

Standing back from the detail here, it would seem likely that 2009 may, indeed, mark end of the mass stock transfer era – a scenario already clear in Scotland by 2007. Council housing, while much reduced in scale and spread, looks set to remain extant in about half of the country for the foreseeable future. Within the council-owned sector, rather than being subject to termination through stock transfer, some ALMOs may remain intact, with some possibly coming more to resemble tenant management organizations (TMOs) as pre-figured by the Kensington and Chelsea TMO which adopted ALMO status, non-stockholding housing associations or even for-profit housing management contractors.

These predictions, of course, assume both that the 2009 HRA reform proposals are capable of achieving their stated objectives, and that the plans will be fully operationalized without undue delay. Particularly given the possible change of government at the UK level in 2010, this second assumption must be hedged with an element of doubt. If, for any reason, the planned HRA restructure does not proceed, remaining landlord local authorities in England would be thrown back into a situation where many would be likely to see transfer as their only salvation.

Implications of the broader economic climate

Irrespective of the English HRA reforms it must be recognized that the radically changed post-2007 economic – and public finance – climate has created a very different context for the transfer policy. Some informed commentators have suggested that hard-pressed governments eager to cash in state assets will seek new ways of facilitating transfers of 'positive value' local authority housing portfolios (Social Housing, 2009b; Johnson, 2009). Relevant to transfers in prospect in coming years is that, with the market for social housing having become much less competitive rising loan margins have increased the 'cost of money' for borrowers and created a climate where lenders enjoy greater freedom to stipulate more restrictive loan covenants which, if breached, lead to loan re-pricing.

In the medium term, there are concerns that a second order effect of the 2008 banking crisis – tougher regulation of bank lending – will further jeopardize access to affordable loan finance. Under new lending rules being proposed by the Financial Services Authority banks will be placed under greater restrictions as to the levels of capital and liquid assets to be held in reserve (Dowler 2009b). This could create additional upward pressure on interest rate margins for existing, as well as new, loans. Similarly, proposed new controls on banks 'borrowing short and lending long' could eliminate availability of the long-term loans which have been standard in association borrowing. This would increase associations' re-financing risk – the possibility of needing to re-finance at a time of high interest rates.

A final point relevant to any consideration of future prospects for the transfer policy is the continuing possibility that the increasingly regulated status of housing associations could lead to their being officially re-designated as public bodies for the purposes of national accounts (see Chapter 3). At a stroke, such a change could remove any remaining advantages enjoyed by housing associations over local authorities in terms of their respective financial regimes.

The logic of the 'modernisation' thesis (Malpass and Victory 2010, forthcoming) seems to suggest that the full marketization of social housing in Britain remains just a matter of time. While this interpretation may well be accurate, it has become more difficult to see any future extinction of council housing via continuing stock transfers to third sector providers as constituting the main mechanism in such a process.

International implications

While this book is squarely focused on stock transfer and the recent evolution of Britain's social rented sector, Chapter 1 established that transactions analogous to ownership handovers of public housing to other social landlords have also taken place or been seriously discussed in other countries. In part, this reflects the sweeping impact of new approaches to public sector management since the early 1980s in a variety of developed countries. Pollitt and Bouckaert's (2004) typology of some of these approaches is shown in Table 10.1. Governments tend to follow one of the four broad approaches at any particular time. However, over time, policy and political changes may lead to the switch to a different approach. Britain, the US and Australia have all used *marketization* since the mid-1980s with some use of *modernization* (in the US, and Britain after 1999) and *minimization* (Australia, and Britain since 1988). Stock transfers tend to have been most associated with the fourth minimization strategy. In this context we may distinguish between the British experience of contracting out to third sector non-profit organizations or ALMOs under highly regulated conditions from more full blown privatization.

The variety of contexts, motivations, models and barriers to stock transfer illustrated by these international examples indicates the need for careful consideration of the objectives, process and outcomes of transfer before any comparative conclusions can be drawn. It is hoped that the detailed analysis of these factors in relation to the English, Scottish and Welsh cases in this book provides a first step in this endeavour. Frameworks such as that presented in Table 10.1 could provide

TABLE 10.1 *Public sector reform approaches*

Approach	Description	Housing examples
Maintain	Tighten up traditional controls, reduce waste and corruption, restrict expenditure	Public housing stock residualized and access restricted to those with high and/or special needs; Restrict grants to most cost-efficient associations
Modernize	Professionalise the public sector, often using private sector management techniques	Risk based regulation; Use of key performance indicators Housing association mergers for scale economies
Marketize	Introduce market forces to public sector to increase efficiency through competition	Public-private-non-profit (i.e. hybrid) partnerships; Use of private finance – debt or equity Private and non-profit competition for tax credits
Minimize	Privatize or contract-out services to private or non-profit organizations – 'hollowing out' the state	Public housing stock transfers; Arms length management of social housing

Source: Gilmour (2009b: 20), based on approaches from Pollitt and Bouckaert (2004: 183–94). Cited with author permission.

the basis for comparative research that enables policy makers to avoid the perils of uncritical policy transfer (Hantrais 2009).

The research agenda

In this book we have attempted to draw together existing research on social housing transformation in Britain. However, while a considerable body of evidence exists, we see a number of significant gaps calling for new work. A key area of interest is the governance, accountability and organizational culture implications of transfer associations entering group structures, engaging in full mergers with others, and subsequently stream-lining structures so that links with pre-transfer local authorities become much less direct. What will be the impact of such developments for relationships between local authorities and such landlords? How effectively will acquiring landlords maintain routes of influence for local tenants and other stakeholders?

Other related research agendas ripe for future attention would include the longer-term development of relations between transfer associations and their local authority counterparts, particularly around regeneration issues. The extent to which the Community Gateway or Community Housing Mutual models provide real alternatives to dominant top-down models and deliver 'added value' – and whether any trade-offs are involved – is a further emerging area of interest.

Then, too, there is a need to track the relatively recent expectations that transfer organizations will play a wider neighbourhood regeneration role. Chapter 7 began to harvest data emerging from the increasing measurement of such activities from the National Housing Federation's (2008) audit of associations' activity beyond housing. It will be important to keep track of the increasing measurement of these activities as transfer organizations seek to re-invest efficiency savings into social investment activities (Mullins et al. 2010).

Network relationships with other third sector and community-based organizations as well as with local democratic bodies are likely to become increasingly important, for example in response to local area agreements and the place-shaping agenda. The ways in which transfer landlords exploit their 'local anchorage' or act as 'community bedrock organisations' (Wadhams 2006, 2009) to take a lead role in local strategic partnerships and support the development of a thriving third sector in their core neighbourhoods is also worthy of further research. Relevant research questions being developed within network governance research concerning for example democratic anchorage (Klijn and Skelcher 2007, Sørensen and Torfing 2005, 2007, van Bortel and Mullins 2009) should form part of the future housing transfer research agenda.

Arguably, a more substantial 'research deficit' concerns ALMOs which – as noted in Chapter 8 – have been subject to remarkably little independent or academic scrutiny (but see Reid et al. 2007). Again, particular areas of interest would be governance and accountability issues, with a specific focus on the nature of relationships between ALMOs and 'parent' local authorities, as well as on tenant involvement structures and techniques. The growing proliferation of social landlord organizational forms also call for comparative research to draw out strengths and weaknesses of different models – e.g. in terms of efficiency and effectiveness. A city-region case study approach would be one way of taking forward such an investigation (Gilmour 2009b).

There has also been surprisingly little research on the short- and medium-term outcomes of 'no votes'. While these have not been particularly numerous, there are dozens of local authorities across Britain where, despite proposed transfers having been voted down, Elected Members and officials will have needed to revisit previously rejected options for accessing investment. There is a clear case for investigation of how such authorities have sought to upgrade housing in the absence of private finance, and the outcomes for tenants in terms of the quality of works undertaken, rents, service quality and tenant empowerment.

Stock transfer: a transformative phenomenon?

Transforming social housing?

In Chapter 1 we discussed the extent to which stock transfer can be said to have made a 'real difference'. As noted earlier in this chapter, we see the research evidence as clearly refuting the argument that transfer has been nothing more than a case of 'the emperor's new clothes'. While many transfers may have been 'sold' to tenants with the strapline 'vote for change to stay (more or less) the same', we would agree with the privatization critics that proposals receiving tenant backing lead to more than a technical reclassification of landlord bodies. To what extent can transfer be fairly portrayed as 'transformational'?

As noted above, transfers have played a major role in ensuring that almost all social sector tenants live in homes satisfactory at least in their condition and basic facilities. However, the value of this achievement would be highly compromised if there were any doubt of its longer-term sustainability. Even more important than enabling compliance with defined property quality standards within (or close to) a set timescale, is the effect of the process in handing ownership of social housing to bodies with an embedded asset-management ethos and a business plan which make provision for enduring upkeep. Critically, therefore, the housing association financial model incorporates incentives for long-term thinking which have traditionally been denied to local authority housing and are arguably also absent from ALMOs who do not own the assets.

Nevertheless, whether the elimination of disrepair backlogs and the implementation of sustainable asset management policies can be properly termed a 'transformation' of social housing may well be questioned. Somerville (2004), for example, pointed out that the Westminster government's Decent Homes Standard is, in fact, a very unambitious yardstick and that compliance with the DHS is hardly synonymous with 'transformation'. To qualify for such a characterization, physical works would need to involve the re-modelling of built forms and estate layouts in ways which are more fundamental than what is commonly achieved through transfers.

One cohort of transfers, about which particular questions are raised on this score, is that which took place under the 1998–2000 Estates Renewal Challenge Fund (ERCF). Earlier research focusing on these projects cited practitioner concerns about longer-term sustainability (Pawson et al. 2005a). Part of the concern here was that the rather exclusive focus on property investment in the pre-transfer planning phase meant that many ERCF transfer business plans made only very limited provision for community investment and environmental improvements, both of which were subsequently recognized as being key to estates' long-term future. It was also clear from the research that most ERCF schemes had concentrated rather exclusively on renovating existing properties rather than considering whether longer-term sustainability of densely built estates overwhelmingly dominated by social housing demanded significant re-modelling and tenure diversification.

The significance of asset-management thinking among transfer housing associations has already been mentioned as a transformational impact of a positive kind. There is, nevertheless, evidence that transfer has brought about other significant cultural changes, not just in transfer landlords themselves, but more widely across the world of social housing. Within the housing association sector, in particular, transfer landlord thinking has influenced attitudes towards wider management and tenant involvement. This has occurred in two ways. Firstly, there has been a simple 'demonstration effect' whereby practices common to transfer HAs are being increasingly absorbed into mainstream thinking – either through direct observation or through incorporation in regulatory and other good practice advice. Secondly, some of the traditional housing associations which have been involved in partial transfers have been exposed to new ways of working (particularly in relation to tenant involvement) which have fed back into their practices as applied at an organizational level.

As suggested by Table 1.1, there is also scope for transfer to be credited with 'transformational' changes of a negative kind. Has it contributed to a more 'financially dominated' social housing sector? – probably yes. But, at least to the extent that effective management of resources is beneficial to all concerned, there is a positive side to this. Indeed, it is the ability to exploit the assets inherited through transfer that provide the basis for the longer-term sustainability and independence of transfer organizations.

Has transfer led to the downgrading of 'welfare promotion' as a key organizational objective? In a commercial organization – especially one with an overriding emphasis on maintaining asset values – there is certainly a risk of this. In the absence of a regulatory system requiring a continuing corporate focus on day-to-day service delivery, there would undoubtedly be a danger of transfer landlords – in common with other larger housing associations – becoming fixated on diversification and 'new business' development. At the same time, however, the recent burgeoning of community regeneration activity on the part of many associations operating in 'marginal areas' has often far exceeded pre-transfer expectations. That this stems partly from a recognition of commercial self-interest and sometimes from a strong value base committing these organizations to re-investing any surpluses in communities can be seen as a key strength of the hybrid model.

At this stage, there is no sign that transfer has transformed, for the worse, tenants' rights. Indeed, the creation of two-tier structures involving significantly weaker rights for new, post-transfer, tenants has become much less of a feature of the process than was true in the policy's early days. In Scotland, housing association tenants enjoy the same rights as council tenants by statute. In England and Wales, with all forms of landlord being regulated within a single framework under the Tenant Services Authority, the possibility of significant differences in rights in one part of the sector is in any case becoming even more limited.

As discussed earlier in this chapter, one area where transfer might – in the future – lead to a transformation of social housing in a negative sense is in landlord accountability to residents and local government. As yet, however, the scope for tenant influence on social landlord decision-making has generally been significantly increased as a result of the move from council to housing association landlords.

Transforming local governance

One way of looking at stock transfer is to see it as requiring the sacrifice of local authority influence as a quid pro quo for access to finance. As seen by Malpass (2005), however, the loss of the council role could be seen as 'the point of the exercise' rather than an incidental consequence of it. This links with Malpass's suggestion that, 'as the major responsibility of the lowest tier of local authorities it is possible that the demise of council housing might spell a similar fate for local government itself, at least across large areas of England' (ibid: 216). This refers to the fact that, across much of non-urban England, local government has remained split between shire county and district administrations, with the post-1974 division of functions between the two tiers placing housing at the latter level.

Although transfers have occurred in unitary authorities since 1998, the vast majority of those taking place over the past 20 years have involved former district council housing departments. Both in the 1990s, and again since 2005, local government re-organization has been progressively removing this tier of authorities. The hollowing-out of local government to which stock transfer contributes is particularly marked in this context and could be seen as having created the conditions ripe for what is a fairly major change in local governance going well beyond housing. In this context, however, some stock transfer organizations have, ironically, found themselves to be more locally accountable than local government, and as the key 'bedrock bodies' in the former district council areas. This is the case in some unitary counties where stock transfer landlords have remained anchored in the former district council areas from whence they originated, while local government has migrated up to the county level.

Stock transfers 1988–2009: their lasting significance

It has been widely assumed or asserted that ongoing stock transfer was an unstoppable process and that complete replacement of British council housing by housing associations was just a matter of time. As noted earlier in this chapter, however, the council housing finance reforms of 2009 might in fact come to be seen as marking the end of an era of mass stock transfers. Even if this is so, the process as it has unfolded over the past two decades will have left major impacts on the British housing system; impacts which will continue to reverberate and evolve for decades to come. Regardless of whether many further transfers occur, the stage has been set for a future for Britain's new social landlords, for policy-makers and for residents and communities that will differ substantially from the world before stock transfer. The extent to which the stock transfer and ALMO experience has been a staging post to a future social housing system that is altogether more embedded in the market, remains to be seen.

References

Aldbourne Associates (1996) *Vision into reality: The role of transfer authorities as enablers*. Swindon: Aldbourne Associates.

Aldbourne Associates (2001) *Implementing best value in housing and tenant participation compacts: The first year*. London: Department for Communities and Local Government (CLG).

Appleyard, R. (2006) *Growing up: A report of the Future of the Sector Commission*. London: L&Q Group.

ARCH (2008) Briefing on survey of ARCH (Association of Retained Council Housing) members. Available at www.arch-housing.org.uk.

Armstrong (1998) Cited by Daly, Mooney, Davis and Poole (2004) 'Whatever happened to stock transfer? A comparative study of Birmingham and Glasgow Councils' attempts to privatise their council housing stock.' Housing Studies Association Conference, Sheffield.

Ashby, J. (1999) *Learning from problem cases*. London: Housing Corporation.

Ashby, J. and Dudman, N. (2003) *Learning from problem cases 2*. London: Housing Corporation.

Audit Commission (2001) *Group dynamics: Group structures and registered social landlords*. London: Audit Commission.

Audit Commission (2002) *Housing after transfer: The local authority role*. London: Audit Commission.

Audit Commission (2003a) *ALMO inspections and the delivery of excellent housing management services*. London: Audit Commission.

Audit Commission (2003b) *Inspection report. Bolton at Home ALMO*. London: Audit Commission.

Audit Commission (2004a) District auditor issues final report in issues arising from housing stock transfer at Bath & North East Somerset. Audit Commission press notice 10 March 2004. Available at www.audit-commission.gov.uk.

Audit Commission (2004b) *Housing: Improving services through resident involvement*. London: Audit Commission.

Audit Commission (2004c) *Re-inspection report. Area housing service delivery, Salford City Council*. London: Audit Commission.

Audit Commission (2005) Inspection report: Bolton at home re-inspection. London: Audit Commission.

Audit Commission (2006) Inspection report: Ashfield Homes ALMO re-inspection. London: Audit Commission.

Audit Commission (2008) Website of the Audit Commission: www.audit-commission.gov.uk (accessed 31 October 2008).

Audit Scotland (2006) *Council Housing Transfers*. Edinburgh: Audit Scotland.

Ayton, A. (2004) *Board payment: The first year*. London: Housing Corporation.

Badcock, B. (2008). 'New Zealand.' In Cowans, J. and Maclennan, D. (eds), *Visions for social housing: International perspectives*. London: Smith Institute.

Barker, K. (2004) Review of housing supply – delivering stability: Securing our future housing needs. Final report – recommendations. London: The Stationery Office.

Beazley, M., Smith, M., Barrington, T., Curtis, J., Shaw, E., Spicer, S. and Stevens, T. (2004) 'A resident-led evaluation of community empowerment on Castle Vale Estate.' Birmingham: University of Birmingham, School of Public Policy.

Bennett, J. (2001) *Out of stock: Stock transfer, homelessness and access to housing.* London: Shelter.

Bisset, H. (2000) Social housing: Building a new foundation, Social Housing Innovations Project, consultants' report. Melbourne: Victorian Office of Housing.

Black, J. (2006) 'A vote for all?' *Roof,* May/June 2006: available at www.roofmagazine.org.uk.

Blair, T. (1999). 'Blazing the trail with the big switch.' Tameside Reporter. 14th October 1999: 2.

Bolton at Home (2008a) Annual report and financial statements for the year ended 31st March 2008. Bolton: Bolton at Home Limited.

Bolton at Home (2008b) Website of Bolton at Home: www.boltonathome. org.uk (accessed 27th October 2008).

Bradley, Q. (2008) 'Capturing the castle: Tenant governance in social housing companies.' *Housing Studies* 23(6): 879–97.

Braiden, G. (2009). 'Ambition knocked down.' *The Herald* (Glasgow). 27 March 2009.

Bramley, G. (1993). 'The enabling role for local authorities: A preliminary evaluation.' In Malpass, P. and Means, R. (eds), *Implementing housing policy.* Buckingham: Open University Press.

Bramley, G., Bartlett, W. and Lambert, C. (1995) *Planning, the market and private housebuilding.* London: UCL Press.

Bramley, G., Munro, M. and Pawson, H. (2004) *Key issues in housing: Policies and markets in 21st century Britain.* Basingstoke: Palgrave Macmillan.

Brandon, S. (2009) Here they stand. *Inside Housing,* 24 April 2009: available at www.insidehousing.co.uk.

Bromiley, R., Adamson, D. and Connolly, S. (2004) *Housing, mutuality and community renewal: A review of the evidence and its relevance to stock transfer in Wales.* Cardiff: Welsh Assembly Government.

Cabinet Office (2001) *A new commitment to neighbourhood renewal.* London: Cabinet Office.

Cadbury, A. (1992) *Report of the committee on the financial aspects of corporate governance.* London: Professional Publishing.

Cairncross, L. and Pearl, M. (2003) *Taking the lead: Report on a survey of housing association board members in 2003.* London: Housing Corporation.

Campbell Tickell (2005) *BME housing associations and stock transfers. Project report and good practice guidance.* London: Housing Corporation and ODPM.

Cave, M. (2007) *Every tenant matters: A review of social housing regulation.* London: CLG.

CCH (1999) *Tenants taking control: Housing cooperatives and tenant con-*

trolled housing. Manchester: Confederation of Co-operative Housing (CCH).

CDP (1977) Limits of the law. London: Community Development Project (CDP).

Centre for Public Services (2004) The case for the 4th option for council housing: a critique of Arms Length Management Organisations. Sheffield: Centre for Public Services.

CIH (2002a) *Empowering communities*. Coventry: Chartered Institute of Housing (CIH) with Confederation for Cooperative Housing and Cooperative Union.

CIH (2002b) *Growing confidence: Introducing the community gateway model*. CIH.

CIH (2002c) Memorandum of evidence on the Local Government Bill 2002. Available at www.parliament.uk.

CIH (2007) *Delivering housing strategy through local area agreements*. Coventry and London: CIH and IDeA.

CIH (2009) HRA reform: The really big issues. Available at the website of the Chartered Institute of Housing: www.cih.org (accessed 30 September 2009).

CIH in Scotland (2005) Section 5 referrals: Statistical examination of the use of the statutory referral process and an evaluation of its effectiveness. Available at www.cih.org/scotland/policy/resproject020.pdf.

Citizens Advice (2008) Possession actions: The last resort? Available at www.citizensadvice.org.uk.

City of Edinburgh Council (2006) Housing Transfer – Post-ballot Survey of Tenants. Report to Council 29 June 2006. Available at http://cpol.edinburgh.gov.uk/getdoc_ext.asp?DocID=84876.

City West Housing Trust (2008) Website of City West Housing Trust: www.citywesthousingtrust.org.uk (accessed 27 October 2008).

Clapham, D. and Kintrea, K. (1994) 'Community ownership and the break-up of council housing in Britain.' *Journal of Social Policy* 23(2): 219–45.

Clapham, D. and Kintrea, K. (2000) 'Community-based housing organisations and the local governance debate.' *Housing Studies* 15(4): 533–59.

Clapham, D., Kintrea, K. and Whitefield, L. (1991) *Community ownership in Glasgow: An evaluation*. Edinburgh: Scottish Office.

Clarke, J., Gerwutz, S. and McLaughlin, E. (2000) *New managerialism, new welfare?* London, Sage.

Clarke, J. and Newman, J. (1997) *The managerial state*. London: Sage.

CLG (2006a) *From decent homes to sustainable communities: a discussion paper*. London: CLG.

CLG (2006b) *Review of Arms Length Housing Management Organisations*. London: CLG.

CLG (2006c) *Strong and prosperous communities: The local government white paper*. London: CLG.

CLG (2006d) *Supplement to the guidance on arms length management*. London: CLG.

CLG (2007a) *Homes for the future: More affordable, more sustainable*. London: CLG.

CLG (2007b) *Housing Revenue Account manual, 2006–2007 edition*. London: CLG.

CLG (2008) *Housing statistics 2007*. London: Department for Communities and Local Government (CLG).

CLG (2009a) Local authority housing statistics, England 2007/08: Housing Strategy Staistical Appendix & Business Plan Statistical Appendix. Available at: http://www.communities.gov.uk/publications/corporate/statistics/lahousing200708 (accessed 16 June 2009).

CLG (2009b) *Reform of council housing financing: Consultation*. London: CLG.

CLG (2009c) Survey of English housing live tables – Table 817. Available at: www.communities.gov (accessed 16 June 2009).

CLG (2009d) Website of the Department of Communities and Local Government: www.communities.gov (accessed 16 June 2009).

Cluid Housing Association (2009) *A stock transfer and regeneration guide*. Dublin: Cluid Housing Association.

Cobbold, C. and Dean, J. (2000) *Views on the large scale voluntary transfer process*. London: Department of the Environment, Transport and the Regions (DETR).

Committee on Standards in Public Life (1996) *Second report: Local public spending bodies*. London: The Stationery Office.

Communities Scotland (2002) Homelessness arbitration: Note CSGN 2002/12, Regulation and Inspection Division. Edinburgh: Communities Scotland.

Communities Scotland (2005) *Research on governance within Registered Social Landlords: A response from Communities Scotland*. Edinburgh: Communities Scotland.

Communities Scotland (2007a) *Glasgow Housing Association inspection report*. Edinburgh: Communities Scotland.

Communities Scotland (2007b) *Scottish housing quality standard progress report*. Edinburgh: Communities Scotland.

Community Housing Task Force (2004) *Reviewing the strategic and enabling roles*. London: Office of the Deputy Prime Minister (ODPM).

Cope, H. F. (1999) *Housing associations: The policy and practice of registered social landlords*. Basingstoke: Palgrave Macmillan.

Cowan, D. and McDermont, M. (2006) *Regulating social housing. Governing decline*. London: Routledge Cavendish.

Crook, T., Currie, J., Jackson, A., Monk, S., Rowley, S., Smith, K. and Whitehead, C. (2002) *Planning gain and affordable housing: Making it count*. York: York Publishing Services.

Crook, T., Disson, J. and Darke, R. (1996) *A new lease of life? Housing association investment in local authority estates*. Bristol: Policy Press.

Daly, G., Mooney, G., Poole, L. and Davis, H. (2005) 'Housing stock transfer in Birmingham and Glasgow: the contrasting experiences of two UK cities.' *European Journal of Housing Policy* 5(3): 327–41.

Davis, H. and Spencer, K. (1995) *Housing associations and the governance debate*. Birmingham: University of Birmingham.

Davis, H. and Stewart, J. (1994) *The growth of government by appointment: Implications for local democracy*. Luton: Local Government Management Board.

DCH (2004a) *The case against ALMOs*. London: DCH.

DCH (2004b) *The case against transfer*. London: DCH.

DCH (2004c) *Choice or blackmail? Issues of democracy and fairness in the debate over the future of council housing*. London: Defend Council Housing (DCH).

DCH (2006) *The case for council housing in 21st century Britain*. London: DCH.

DCH (2009) Website of Defend Council Housing: www.defendcouncil-housing.org.uk (accessed 5 April 2009).

Deming, W. (1986) *Out of the crisis*. Cambridge: Cambridge University Press.

DETR (1998) *Modern local government: In touch with the people*. London: Department of the Environment, Transport and the Regions (DETR).

DETR (2000a) Arms length management of local authority housing: a discussion paper. London: DETR.

DETR (2000b) *The best value in housing framework*. London: DETR.

DETR (2000c) *Quality and choice – a decent home for all: The housing green paper*. London: DETR.

DiMaggio, P. J. and Powell, W. W. (1983) 'The iron cage revisited: Institutional isomorphism and collective rationality in organisational fields.' *American Sociological Review* 48(2), April 1983: 147–60.

DoE (1981) *Difficult to let investigations (Volumes 1 and 2)*. Housing Development Department Occasional Papers 4/80 and 5/80. London: Department of the Environment (DoE).

DoE (1987) *Housing: The Government's proposals*. London: DoE.

DoE (1992) Local authority housing in England: Voluntary transfers. Consultation paper. London: DoE.

Dowler, C. (2009a) 'HRA reforms crucial or councils could lose control.' *Inside Housing*, 22 May 2009: available at www.insidehousing.co.uk.

Dowler, C. (2009b) 'Tighter FSA rules could restrict loans.' *Inside Housing*, 13 July 2009: available at www.insidehousing.co.uk.

Duncan, T. (1991) *Local authority housing stock transfers*, Scottish Office Central Research Unit Paper. Edinburgh: Scottish Office.

Ellery, S. (2007) 'Disputed ALMO ballot sparks storm.' *Inside Housing*, 27 July 2007: available at www.insidehousing.co.uk.

Elton, L. (2006) *Review of regulatory and compliance requirements for RSLs. A report to the Housing Corporation by a review group chaired by Sir Les Elton*. London: Housing Corporation.

Ernst & Young (2002) *Sources of finance for housing stock transfers*. London: Office of the Deputy Prime Minister (ODPM).

Ferlie, E., Ashburner, L. and Fitzgerald, L. (1995) 'Corporate governance and the public sector: Some issues and evidence from the NHS.' *Public Administration* 73(3): 375–92.

Ferman, L. and Appleby, M. (2009) *Board members pay: Principles and practicalities*. London: NHF.

Fitzpatrick, S. and Stephens, M. (2007) *An international review of homelessness and social housing policy*. London: CLG.

Foucault, M. (1977) *Discipline and punish: the birth of the prison*. New York: Pantheon Books.

Friedman, R. and Alford, R. R. (1991). 'Bringing society back in. Symbols, practices and institutional contradictions.' In Powell, W. W. and DiMaggio, P. J. (eds), *The new institutionalism in organizational analysis*. Chicago: University of Chicago Press.

Gardiner, K., Hills, J. and Kleinmann, M. (1991) *Putting a price on council housing: Valuing voluntary transfers.* London: London School of Economics.

Garnett, D. and Perry, J. (2005) *Housing finance.* Coventry: CIH.

GHA (2003) *Stock transfer business plan.* Glasgow: Glasgow Housing Association (GHA).

GHA (2006) *GHA 30-year business plan 2006/07.* Glasgow: GHA.

GHA (2008) *Above and beyond: Shaping a new future for GHA – draft business plan 2009/10.* Glasgow: GHA.

Gibb, K. (2003) 'Transferring Glasgow's council housing: Financial, urban and housing policy implications.' *European Journal of Housing Policy* 3(1): 89–114.

Gibb, K., Kintrea, K., Nygaard, C. and Flint, J. (2005) *Review of the effectiveness and impact of transferring Scottish Homes houses into community ownership.* Edinburgh: Communities Scotland.

Gibb, K. and Trebeck, K. (2008) *Comparing models of social housing: a natural experiment.* Paper presented at the European Network of Housing Researchers conference, Dublin, 6–9 July 2008.

Gibney, J., Copeland, S. and Murie, A. (2009) 'Toward a new strategic leadership of place for the knowledge based economy.' *Leadership.* 5(1): 5–23.

Gilmour, T. (2009a) *Hierarchy or network? Transforming social housing in metropolitan Melbourne.* Paper presented at the Housing Researchers Conference, Sydney, 5–7 August 2009 (unpublished).

Gilmour, T. (2009b) *Network power: An international study of strengthening housing association capacity.* Available at: http://www.ahuri.edu.au/research_training/scholars/completed_scholars/anthonygilmour.html.

Gilmour, T. (2009c) Revolution? Transforming social housing in the Manchester city region. Paper presented at the ENHR Conference, Prague, 28 June–1 July 2009 (unpublished).

Ginsburg, N. (2005) 'The privatisation of council housing.' *Critical Social Policy* 25(1): 115–35.

Glasgow City Council (2007a) *Glasgow's strategic housing investment plan, 2008/09 to 2012/13.* Glasgow: Glasgow City Council.

Glasgow City Council (2007b) *Priority regeneration areas. A new approach to delivery, report by Director of Development and Regeneration Services to GCC Executive Committee, 30 March 2007.* Glasgow: Glasgow City Council.

Glasgow City Council (2009) *GHA 'above and beyond' draft business plan 2009/10, draft consultation response.* Glasgow: Glasgow City Council.

Glendinning, R., Allen, P. and Young, H. (1989) *The sale of local authority housing to the private sector.* London: HMSO.

Glynn, S. (2007). 'But we already have community ownership: Making council housing work.' In Cumbers, A. and Whittam, G. (eds) *Reclaiming the economy: Alternatives to market fundamentalism in Scotland.* Glasgow: Scottish Left Review Press.

Goodlad, R. and Scott, S. (1996) 'Housing and the Scottish New Towns: A case study of policy termination and quasi-markets.' *Urban Studies* 33(2): 317–35.

GoWell (2007) *The regeneration challenge in transformation areas: Glasgow.*

Glasgow: Glasgow Community Health and Wellbeing Research and Learning Programme.

Graham, T. (1999) *An evaluation of Scottish Homes large scale voluntary transfers*. Edinburgh: Scottish Homes.

Grant Thornton and Centre for Housing Research (2009) *Strategic review of the capital funding schemes for voluntary and co-operative housing*. Dublin: Centre for Housing Research.

Grayson, J. (2006) *Independent tenants movement in the case for council housing in 21st century Britain*. London: Defend Council Housing (DCH).

Greer, A. and Hoggett, P. (2000) 'Contemporary governance and local public spending bodies.' *Public Administration* 78(3): 513–29.

Gregory, R. and Hicks, C. (1999) 'Promoting public service integrity: A case for responsible accounting.' *Australian Journal of Public Administration* 58(4): 3–15.

Gruis, V. (2008) 'Organisational archetypes for Dutch housing associations.' *Environment and Planning C: Government and Policy* 26(6): 1077–92.

HACAS Consulting (2002) *Beyond bricks and mortar: Bringing regeneration into stock transfer*. Coventry: CIH.

Haffner, M. (2002) *Dutch social rented housing. The vote for housing associations?* Paper presented at the 9th European Real Estate Society Conference, Glasgow.

Handy, C. B. (1993) *Understanding organisations*. London: Penguin.

Hansard (2003) *Statement by the Minister for Housing and Planning, Keith Hill, 29 October 2003*. London: House of Commons.

Hansard (2004) *Information supplied by Keith Hill MP, 29 March 2004, Volume 419 column 1260*. London: House of Commons.

Hansard (2006) *Information supplied by Yvette Cooper MP, 25 May 2006, Column 2041W*. London: House of Commons.

Hantrais, l. (2009) *International comparative research: Theory, methods and practice*. Basingstoke: Palgrave Macmillan.

Hardman, I. (2009) 'Ealing to shut down arms length body.' *Inside Housing*, 16 September 2009: availbale at www.insidehousing.co.uk.

Hartley, J. and Rashman, L. (2002) *Organisational design in housing*. Community Housing Task Force discussion paper no.1. London: ODPM.

Hawkey, E. and Birch, J. (2004) 'Taking stock.' *Roof*, March/April 2004: available at www.roofmagazine.org.uk.

Hawksworth, J. and Wilcox, S. (1995a) *Challenging the conventions: Public borrowing rules and housing investment*. Coventry: CIH.

Hawksworth, J. and Wilcox, S. (1995b). 'The PSBR handicap.' In Wilcox, S. (eds), *Housing finance review 1995/96*. York: Joseph Rowntree Foundation.

HCCHG (2009) House of Commons Council House Group. Website www.support4councilhousing.org.uk/report/ (accessed 9th June 2009).

Heald, D. (1984). 'Privatisation and public money.' In Steel, D. and Heald, D. (eds), *Privatising public enterprises*. London: Royal Institute of Public Administration.

Higgs, D. (2003) *Review of the role and effectiveness of non-executive directors*. London: Department of Trade and Industry.

Hilditch, M. (2006) 'Leading ALMOs forced to make cuts.' *Inside Housing*, 8 December 2006: available at www.insidehousing.co.uk.

Hilditch, M. (2007) 'Transfers attract ALMO interest.' *Inside Housing*, 20 July 2007: available at www.insidehousing.co.uk.

Hilditch, M. (2008) 'Rapid turnover of arm's-length executives.' *Inside Housing*, 2 February 2008: available at www.insidehousing.co.uk.

HM Treasury (2003) *PFI: Meeting the investment challenge.* London: HMSO.

Hood, C. (1995) 'The "new public management" in the 1980s: variations on a theme.' *Accounting, Organisations and Society* 20: 93–109.

House of Commons (2003) *Delivering the Decent Homes Standard: social landlords' options and progress.* Research paper 03/65. London: House of Commons Library.

House of Commons (2004) *ODPM: Housing, Planning, Local Government & the Regions Committee. Report on decent homes, fifth report.* London: The Stationery Office.

House of Commons Library (2009) *The Decent Homes standard: Update.* Available at http://www.parliament.uk/commons/lib/research/briefings/snsp-03178.pdf.

Housemark (2007) *ALMOs tomorrow: a guide to ALMO business planning beyond Decent Homes.* Coventry: Tribal Consulting and Housemark.

Housing Corporation (1998) *Guidance for applicants seeking to become Registered Social Landlords: Stock transfer applicants.* London: Housing Corporation.

Housing Corporation (1999) *Regulating a diverse sector: Consultation paper.* London: The Housing Corporation.

Housing Corporation (2002) *The way forward: Our approach to regulation.* London: Housing Corporation.

Housing Corporation (2003) *Local authority nominations: Circular 02/03,* regulation. London: Housing Corporation.

Housing Corporation (2007) *Delivering affordable housing: meeting the challenges of growth and efficiency.* London: Housing Corporation.

Housing Quality Network (2005) *Best value in housing: what makes local authorities improve and sustain their performance?* ODPM Housing Research Summary No.217. Available at www.communities.gov.uk.

HUD (2009) Website of the US Department of Housing and Urban Development, public housing: www.hud.gov (accessed 21 January 2009).

Humphries, P. (2007) Council sends in its own team to help out ALMO. *Inside Housing*, 1 June 2007: available at www.insidehousing.co.uk.

Humphries, P. (2008) 'Arm's-length chief suspended amid health and safety fears.' *Inside Housing*, 22 August 2008: available at www.insidehousing.co.uk.

Hutton, W. (1995) *The state we're in.* London: Jonathan Cape.

Independent Commission of Enquiry (2002) *One size doesn't fit all. Community housing and flourishing neighbourhoods.* Birmingham: Independent Commission of Enquiry.

Insight (2008) *RSL board member remuneration, annual survey report 2008.* Lower Beeding, West Sussex: Insight Consultants.

Insight (2009) *Board member survey: A new horizon.* Lower Beeding, West Sussex: Insight Consultants.

Jacobs, K., Marston, G. and Darcy, M. (2004) '"Changing the mix":

Contestation surrounding the public housing stock transfer process in Victoria, New South Wales and Tasmania.' *Urban Policy and Research* 22(3): 249–63.

Johnson, D. (2009) Asset Realisation: Is there really any other choice? In Chartered Institute of Housing: *Investing in affordable housing: a radical rethink?*, 18 February 2010. Available at: www.cihscotland.org.

Johnson, G. and Scholes, K. (2002) *Exploring corporate strategy*. Harlow: Pearson Education.

Jones, C. and Murie, A. (2006) *The right to buy: Analysis and evolution of a housing policy*. Oxford: Blackwell.

Jones, P. (2009) *The evolution of tenants and community organisations: their relevance to policy and regulatory issues today*. Birmingham: University of Birmingham, Third Sector Research Centre.

Joseph, D. (2009) 'Boards' short-term sighs of relief set to give way to longer-lasting brow-furrowing.' *Social Housing* 21(7): 22.

Karn, V. (1991). 'Re-modelling a HAT.' In Malpass, P. and Means, R. (eds), *Implementing housing policy*. Buckingham: OUP.

Kearns, A. (1997). 'Housing association management committees: Dilemmas of composition.' In Malpass, P. (eds), *Ownership, control and accountability: The new governance of housing*. Coventry: CIH: 48–67.

Kearns, A. and Lawson, L. (2008) 'Housing stock transfer in Glasgow: The first five years. A study of policy implementation.' *Housing Studies* 23(6): 857–78.

Kearns, A. and Lawson, L. (2009) '(De)constructing a policy "failure": housing stock transfer in Glasgow'. *Evidence and Policy* 5(4): 449–70.

Kemeny, J. (1995) *From public housing to the social market: Rental policy strategies in comparative perspective*. London: Routledge.

Kintrea, K. (2006) 'Having it all? Housing reform under devolution.' *Housing Studies* 21(2): 187–207.

Klein, M. (1997) 'The risk premium for evaluating public projects.' *Oxford Review of Economic Policy* 13(4): 29–43.

Kleinman, M. (1993) 'Large-scale transfers of council housing to new landlords: Is British social housing becoming more like European?' *Housing Studies* 8(3): 163–78.

Klijn, E.-H. and Skelcher, C. (2007) 'Democracy and governance networks: compatible or not?' *Public Administration* 85(3): 587–608.

Lonsdale, C. (2005) 'Risk transfer and the UK Private Finance Initiative: A theoretical analysis.' *Policy & Politics* 33(2): 231–49.

Lowe, S. (2004) *Housing policy analysis. British housing in cultural and comparative context*. Basingstoke: Palgrave Macmillan.

MacKenzie, N. (2007) *Preparing for the renewal of your management agreement*. York: Housing Quality Network.

Malpass, P. (1997a). 'The local governance of housing.' In Malpass, P. (eds), *Ownership, control and accountability: the new governance of housing*. Coventry: Chartered Institute of Housing: 82–93.

Malpass, P. (1997b) *Ownership, control and accountability: The new governance of housing*. Coventry: CIH.

Malpass, P. (2000) *Housing associations and housing policy. A historical perspective*. Basingstoke: Palgrave Macmillan.

Malpass, P. (2001) 'The restructuring of social rented housing in Britain: Demunicipalization and the rise of "registered social landlords".' *European Journal of Housing Policy* 1(1). April 2001: 1–16.

Malpass, P. (2005) *Housing and the welfare state: the development of housing policy in Britain.* Basingstoke: Palgrave Macmillan.

Malpass, P. and Mullins, D. (2002) 'Local authority housing stock transfer in the UK. From local initiative to national policy.' *Housing Studies* 17(4): 673–86.

Malpass, P. and Murie, A. (1994) *Housing policy and practice.* London: Macmillan.

Malpass, P. and Victory, C. (2010, forthcoming) 'The modernisation of social housing in England.' *International Journal of Housing Policy.*

Maltby, P. (2003) *In the public interest? Assessing the potential for public interest companies.* London: Institute for Public Policy Research.

McDermont, M., Cowan, D. and Prendergrast, J. (2009) 'Structuring governance: A case study of the new organisational provision of public service delivery.' *Critical Social Policy* 29(4): 677–702.

McIntosh, A. (2002) 'Too much bumf.' *Inside Housing,* 27 September 2002: available at www.insidehousing.co.uk.

McIntosh, A. (2007) 'It's not a question of if, but when.' *Inside Housing,* 26 January 2007: available at www.insidehousing.co.uk.

McIntosh, A. and Bright, J. (2007) *Learning from success: What makes housing organisations improve?* York: Housing Quality Network.

McKee, K. (2009) 'Learning lessons from stock transfer: the challenges in delivering second stage transfer in Glasgow.' *People, Place & Policy Online* 3(1): 16–27.

McKee, K. and Cooper, V. (2008) 'The paradox of tenant empowerment: Regulatory and liberatory possibilities.' *Housing, Theory and Society* 25(2): 132–46.

Merrett, S. (1979) *State housing in Britain.* London: Routledge and Kegan Paul.

Meyer, J. W. and Rowan, B. (1977) 'Institutionalized organizations: formal structure as myth and ceremony.' *The American Journal of Sociology* 83(2), September 1977:.340–63.

Miles, R. E., Snow, C. C. and Meyer, A. D. (1978) *Organizational strategy, structure, and process.* New York: McGraw-Hill.

Mintzberg, H. (1993) *Structure in fives: Designing effective organisations.* New Jersey: Prentice-Hall.

Mintzberg, H. (1994) *The rise and fall of strategic planning.* London: Prentice-Hall.

Mitchell, A. (2009). 'Alan Walter, union activist and tireless campaigner for council housing'. *The Guardian* (London). 16 March 2009.

Monk, S., Crook, T., Lister, D., Rowley, S., Short, C. and Whitehead, C. (2005) *Land and finance for affordable housing: The complementary roles of Social Housing Grant and the provision of affordable housing through the planning system.* York: Joseph Rowntree Foundation.

Mooney, G. and Poole, L. (2005) 'Marginalised voices: Resisting the privatisation of council housing in Glasgow.' *Local Economy* 20(1): 27–39.

Morgan, P. (2006) Chief Executive report, Tenant Participation Advisory

Service, Executive Committee, 15 March 2006. Available at www.tpas.org.uk.

Mullen, T., Scott, S., Fitzpatrick, S. and Goodlad, R. (1997) *Tenancy rights and repossession rates: In theory and In practice*. Edinburgh: Scottish Homes.

Mullins, D. (1990) *Tenants choice. The role of the Housing Corporation*. Report by CURS for DoE. Birmingham: University of Birmingham.

Mullins, D. (1996) *Us and them: Report of a survey of housing enabling officers in local authorities which have transferred their housing stock under large scale voluntary transfers*. Birmingham: University of Birmingham.

Mullins, D. (1997) 'From regulatory capture to regulated competition: An interest group
analysis of the regulation of housing associations in England.' *Housing Studies* 12(3): 301–320.

Mullins, D. (1999) 'Managing ambiguity: Merger activity in the non-profit housing sector.' *International Journal of Nonprofit and Voluntary Sector Marketing* 4(4): 349–64.

Mullins, D. (2000) *Constitutional and structural partnerships: Who benefits? Housing Research at CURS No.8*. Birmingham: University of Birmingham.

Mullins, D. (2003). 'Involvement of users in governance, some experiences from the non-profit housing sector.' In Warburton, J. and Morris, A. (eds), *Charities, governance and the law: The way forward*. London: Key Haven Press: 95–118.

Mullins, D. (2004) 'Stock transfers: How is it for others?' *Cornerstone*, the magazine of the Homeless Agency. 20 July 2004: 9–11.

Mullins, D. (2006) 'Competing institutional logics? Local accountability and scale and efficiency in an expanding non-profit housing sector.' *Public Policy and Administration* 21(3), September 2001: 6–24.

Mullins, D., Beider, H. and Rowlands, R. (2004) *Empowering communities, improving housing: Involving black and minority ethnic tenants and communities*. London: ODPM.

Mullins, D. and Craig, L. (2005) *Testing the climate: mergers and alliances in the housing association sector*. Birmingham: University of Birmingham.

Mullins, D. and Murie, A. (2006) *Housing policy in the UK*. Basingstoke: Palgrave Macmillan.

Mullins, D. and Niner, P. (1996) *Common housing registers: An evaluation of current practice*. London: Housing Corporation.

Mullins, D., Niner, P. and Riseborough, M. (1992) *Evaluating large scale voluntary transfers of local authority housing. Interim report*. London: HMSO.

Mullins, D., Niner, P. and Riseborough, M. (1995) *Evaluating large scale voluntary transfers of local authority housing*. London: HMSO.

Mullins, D. and Pawson, H. (2009). 'The evolution of stock transfer: Privatisation or towards re-nationalisation?' In Malpass, P. and Mullins, D. (eds), *Housing, markets and policy*. London: Routledge.

Mullins, D. and Pawson, H. (2010, forthcoming). 'Hybrid organisations in social housing: Agents of policy or profits in disguise?' In Billis, D. (ed.) *Hybrid organisations in the third sector: Challenges of practice, policy and theory*. Basingstoke: Palgrave Macmillan.

Mullins, D., Reid, B. and Walker, R. M. (2001) 'Modernization and change in social housing. The case for an organisational perspective.' *Public Administration* 79(3), Autumn 2001: 599–623.

Mullins, D., Rhodes, M. L. and Williamson, A. (2003) *Non-profit housing organisations in Ireland, north and south: Changing forms and challenging futures*. Belfast: The Northern Ireland Housing Executive.

Mullins, D. and Riseborough, M. (1997) *Changing with the times. Critical interpretations of the re-positioning of housing associations*. Birmingham: University of Birmingham, School of Public Policy.

Mullins, D. and Riseborough, M. (2000). *What are housing associations becoming? Final report of Changing with the Times project*. Housing Research at CURS Number 7. Birmingham; University of Birmingham.

Mullins, D. and Sacranie, H. (2008) *Competing drivers of change in the regulation of housing associations in England: A multi-layered merging perspective*. Housing Studies Association conference, York, April 2008.

Mullins, D. and Sacranie, H. (2009) *Corporate social responsibility and the transformation of social housing organisations: Some puzzles and new directions*. Paper presented at the ENHR Conference, Prague, 28 June–1 July 2009 (unpublished).

Mullins, D. and Simmons, S. (2001) 'Taking stock – Transfer watch' *Roof*, July/August 2001: available at www.roofmagazine.org.uk.

Mullins D and Walker, B. (2009) 'Mixed motives? The impact of direct public funding for private developers on non-profit housing networks in England: Exploring a research agenda,' *European Journal of Housing Policy*, 9(2), 199–220.

Mullins, D., Watson, C. and Ham, Y.-J. (2010) *Social Investment Performance Management Toolkit for Housing Organizations*. Birmingham: University of Birmingham.

Munro, M., Pawson, H. and Monk, S. (2005) *Evaluation of English housing policy 1975–2000: Widening choice*. London: CLG.

Murie, A. (1993) 'Privatisation and restructuring public involvement in housing provision in Britain.' *Scandinavian Housing and Planning Research* 10: 145–57.

Murie, A. and Nevin, B. (2001) 'New Labour transfers.' In Cowan, D. and Marsh, A. (eds), *Two steps forward: Housing policy into the new millennium*. Bristol: Policy Press.

Murphy, L. (2006) 'Reflections on the impacts of the privatization of state housing in New Zealand.' *Housing Works, the Journal of the Australian Housing Institute*, May 2006.

NAO (2003) *The Decent Homes Programme*. London: NAO.

NAO (2010) *Improving social housing through transfer: Report by the Comptroller and Auditor General*. London: National Audit Office (NAO).

New Prospect (2008) Website of New Prospect: www.new-prospect.org (accessed 27 October 2008).

Newman, J. (2000). 'Beyond the new public management. Modernising public services.' In Clarke, J., Gerwutz, S. et al (eds), *New managerialism, new welfare?* London: Sage.

Newman, J. (2001) *Modernising governance. New Labour, policy and society*. London: Sage.

NFA (2008a) *ALMO governance: Empowering tenants*. York: National Federation of ALMOs (NFA).

NFA (2008b) *Annual review 07/08*. York: NFA.

NFA (2008c) *The future of ALMOs*. York: NFA.

NFA (2009) *A future for ALMOs – within local communities*. York: NFA.

NHF (2002a) Tenant satisfaction. Stock transfer briefing no.1. London: National Housing Federation (NHF).

NHF (2002b) *Why go to an existing housing association for transfer?* London: NHF.

NHF (2008a) Housing Bill puts half a million new affordable homes at risk: NHF press release, 14 January 2008. London: NHF.

NHF (2008b) *iN business for neighbourhoods: the evidence. The scale and scope of housing associations activity beyond housing*. London: NHF.

NHF (2008c) Neighbourhood audit report. London: NHF.

NHF (2009) The tools for success: The election manifest of the National Housing Federation. Available at https://www.housing.org.uk/Uploads/File/election_manifesto_09.pdf

Niner, P. and Rowlands, R. (2003) Involving Black and Minority Ethnic Tenants in decisions on housing investment options. Report on postal surveys. Birmingham: Birmingham University CURS.

NSW Department of Housing (2007) NSW planning for the future: community housing. Five year strategy for growth and sustainability 2007–2012, consultation draft. Ashfield: NSW Department of Housing.

Nygaard, C., Gibb, K. and Berry, M. (2007) 'Ownership transfer of social housing in the UK: A property rights approach.' *Housing, Theory and Society* 24(2): 89–110.

ODPM (2002) *A decent home: The revised definition and guidance for implementation*. London: ODPM.

ODPM (2003a) *Delivering decent homes: Option appraisal guidance for local authorities*. London: ODPM.

ODPM (2003b) *Guidance on arms length management of local authority housing*. London: ODPM.

ODPM (2003c) *Removing barriers in the transfer process to facilitate innovative private finance and deliver successful transfers: A consultation paper*. London: ODPM.

ODPM (2003d) *Review of the delivery of the decent homes target for social housing*. London: ODPM.

ODPM (2003e) *Stock transfer guidance*. London: ODPM.

ODPM (2003f) *Sustainable communities: Building for the future*. London: ODPM.

ODPM (2004a) *Effective co-operation in tackling homelessness: Nomination agreements and exclusions*. London: ODPM.

ODPM (2004b) *Guidance on arms length management of local authority housing, 2004 edition*. London: ODPM.

ODPM (2004c) *Housing transfer manual: 2005 programme*. London: ODPM.

ODPM (2005) *ODPM guidance on the payment of ALMO board members*. London: ODPM.

Orr, D. (2009) 'A major spanner in the works.' *Inside Housing*, 21 August 2009: available at www.insidehousing.co.uk.

Ounsted, D. (2007) *Tightrope or safety belt? Building board and council relationships at ALMOs and LSVTs*. York: Housing Quality Network.

Ouwehand, A. and van Daalen, G. (2002) *Dutch housing associations: A model for social housing?* Delft: DUP Satellite.

Oxley, M. (2001) 'Meaning, science, context and confusion in comparative housing research.' *Journal of Housing and the Built Environment*, 16(1): 89–106.

Page, D. (1993) *Building communities*. York: Joseph Rowntree Foundation.

Page, D. (1994) *Developing communities*. Teddington: Sutton Hastoe Housing Association.

Pawson, H. (2002) *Assessing stock transfer in Scotland*. York: Housing Quality Network.

Pawson, H. (2009a) *Analysis of local authority housing management performance, 2007/08*. York: Housing Quality Network.

Pawson, H. (2009b) 'Transfer on trial.' *Roof*, May/June 2009: available at www.roofmagazine.org.uk.

Pawson, H., Brown, C. and Lordon, M. (2008) Review of Wirralhomes choice-based letting service. Available at: www.wirral.gov.uk/LGCL/ 100007/200027/10060/Wirralhomes_report_V4_for__publication.pdf.

Pawson, H., Davidson, E., Morgan, J., Smith, R. and Edwards, R. (2009) *Second Generation: The impacts of housing stock transfers in urban Britain*. Coventry: CIH for the Joseph Rowntree Foundation.

Pawson, H., Donohoe, A., Jones, C., Watkins, D., Fancy, C. and Netto, G. (2006) *Monitoring the longer-term impact of choice-based lettings*. London: CLG.

Pawson, H. and Fancy, C. (2003) *Maturing assets: The evolution of stock transfer housing associations*. Bristol: Policy Press.

Pawson, H., Fancy, C., Morgan, J. and Munro, M. (2005a) *Learning lessons from the Estates Renewal Challenge Fund*. London: ODPM.

Pawson, H. and Jacobs, K. (2010, forthcoming) 'Policy intervention and its impact: New Labour's public service reform model as applied to local authority housing.' *Housing, Theory and Society*.

Pawson, H., Levison, D., Lawton, G., Parker, J. and Third, H. (2001) *Local authority policy and practice on allocations, transfers and homelessness*. London: DETR.

Pawson, H. and Mullins, D. (2003) *Changing places: Housing association policy and practice on nominations and lettings*. Abingdon: Policy Press.

Pawson, H., Mullins, D. and Rowlands, R. (2004) *Housing allocation, homelessness and stock transfer: A guide to key issues*. London: ODPM.

Pawson, H., Satsangi, M., Munro, M., Cairncross, L., Warren, F. and Lomax, D. (2005b) *Reviewing housing association governance*. Edinburgh: Communities Scotland.

Pawson, H. and Sosenko, F. (2008) *Sector restructuring. Housing Corporation sector study 61*. London: Housing Corporation.

Pawson, H., Sosenko, F., Cowan, D., Cole, M. and Hunter, C. (2010) *Investigating Housing Association policy and practice on rent arrears management*; London: Tenant Services Authority.

Perry, J. (2002) 'Taking stock: Partial transfers can play a key role in urban regeneration.' *Housing*, September 2002: 34–5.

PIEDA (1997) Evaluation of the performance of large scale voluntary transfer housing associations: Unpublished report to DETR by PIEDA plc.

Platt, S. (1988) 'Evasive action.' *Roof*, May/June 1988: available at www.roofmagazine.org.uk.

Pleace, N., Quilgars, D., Jones, A. and Rugg, J. (2008) *Tackling homelessness: Housing associations and local authorities working in partnership*. London: Housing Corporation.

Pollitt, C., Birchall, J. and Putnam, K. (1998) *Decentralising public service management*. London: Macmillan.

Pollitt, C. and Bouckaert, G. (2004) *Public management reform. A comparative analysis*. Oxford: Oxford University Press.

Pollock, A. M., Shaoul, J. and Vickers, N. (2002) 'Private finance and "value for money" in NHS hospitals: A policy in search of a rationale?' *British Medical Journal*, 18th May 2002: 1205–9.

Pomeroy, S. (2009) 'The devil's in the details: The ownership and management of social housing in Ontario, Canada.' Paper to Australian National Housing Conference, Melbourne 24–27 November.

Quirk, B. (2007) *Making assets work: The Quirk Review of community management and ownership of public assets*. Available at: www.communitymatters.org.uk (accessed 3 August 2009).

Randolph, B. (1993). 'The re-privatization of housing associations.' In Malpass, P. and Means, R. (eds), *Implementing housing policy*. Buckingham: Open University Press: 39–58.

Raynsford, N. (1991) 'Management at arms-length.' *Housing* 25(5): 13–17.

Rees-Mogg (2009). 'Good people + imossible task = collapse.' *The Times*. 2 March 2009.

Reid, B. (1995) 'Inter-organisational networks and the delivery of social housing.' *Housing Studies* 10(2), September 2001: 133–49.

Reid, B. and Hickman, P. (2002) 'Are housing organisations becoming learning organisations? Some lessons from the management of tenant participation.' *Housing Studies* 17(6). November 2002: 895–918.

Reid, B., Vickery, L., Bradburn, A. and Verster, B. (2007) *Learning from Arms Length Management Organisations. The experience of the first three rounds*. London: CLG.

Rhodes, R. A. W. (1997) *Understanding governance: Policy networks, governance, reflexivity, and accountability*. Buckingham: Open University Press.

Robertson, D. (2003) 'Glasgow's £2.3bn housing transfer "a fiasco".' Cited in Fraser, D., *The Herald*, 9 February 2003.

Robertson, D. (2009). 'Joint approach can knock GHA into shape.' *The Herald* (Glasgow). 27 March 2009.

Rochester, C. and Hutchison, R. (2002) *Board effectiveness in transfer organisations*. London: NHF.

Rogers, E. (2008) 'Sacked Citywest chair laments "incomprehensible" interference.' *Inside Housing*, 7 November 2008: available at www.insidehousing.co.uk.

Rollo, J. (2008) 'No vote' for stock transfer – what next for local authorities? Birmingham and Edinburgh as case study comparisons.' Unpublished MSc dissertation submitted to Heriot-Watt University.

Rosenberg, J. (1998) *Against the odds: Walterton and Elgin from campaign to control*. London: Walterton and Elgin Community Homes.

Rosenburg, L. (1995) 'Monitoring low cost housing initiatives. A longitudinal analysis of housing market trends within the privatised areas of four council-built estates in Scotland.' *Housing Studies* 10(3): 285–304.

Salix Homes (2008) Website of Salix Homes: www.salixhomes.org (accessed 27th October 2008).

Schein, E. (1992) *Organisational culture and leadership.* San Francisco: Jossey Bass.

Scottish Executive (2003) *Modernising Scotland's social housing: A consultation paper.* Edinburgh: Scottish Executive.

Scottish Executive (2004) *Community ownership review: Report of the expert group.* Edinburgh: Scottish Executive.

Scottish Government (2007) *Firm foundations: the future of housing in Scotland. A discussion document.* Edinburgh: Scottish Government.

Scottish Government (2008a) *Cash for councils to build housing.* News release, 25 November 2008. Available at www.scotland.gov.uk.

Scottish Government (2008b) *Housing statistics for Scotland: New housebuilding – local authority starts and completions.* Edinburgh: Scottish Government.

Scottish Housing Regulator (2009) *Dundee City Council inspection report.* Glasgow: Scottish Housing Regulator.

Scottish Office (1999) *Investing in modernisation: Housing green paper.* Edinburgh: Scottish Office.

Scottish Parliament (2003) Written answers 12 September 2003. Edinburgh: Scottish Parliament.

Simon, K. (2009) TBC. *The Independent*, 13 March 2009.

Skelcher, C. (1998) *The appointed state: Quasi-governmental organisations and democracy.* Basingstoke: Macmillan.

Social Housing (2003) 'Glasgow unlocks public-private funding for £2.25 billion works.' *Social Housing*, April 2003.

Social Housing (2009a) 'HCA makes bid to claw back transfers' gap funding cash.' *Social Housing*, August 2009.

Social Housing (2009b) 'Batten down the hatches, providers told, as sector anticipates harsh funding cuts.' December 2009: 5.

Somerville, P. (2004) 'Transforming council housing.' Paper to Housing Studies Association Spring Conference 2004. Available at http://www.york.ac.uk/inst/chp/hsa/papers/spring%2004/Peter%20Somerville.pdf.

Sørensen, E. and Torfing, J. (2005) 'The democratic anchorage of governance networks.' *Scandinavian Political Studies* 28(3): 195–218.

Sørensen, E. and Torfing, J. (eds) (2007) *Theories of democratic network governance.* Basingstoke: Palgrave Macmillan.

Spiller, M. and Lennon, M. (2009) 'Re-inventing social housing, a once in a generation chance.' *Housing Works, the Journal of the Australian Housing Institute*, April 2009.

Stephens, M., Elsinga, M. and Knorr-Siedow, T. (2008). 'The privatisation of social housing: three different pathways.' In Scanlon, K. and Whitehead, C. (eds), *Social housing in Europe II.* London: London School of Economics: 105–29.

Stockport Council (2006) Stockport Partnership Board, 14 September 2006. Investment implications of ALMO funding – report by Stockport Homes. Stockport: Stockport Council.

Story, C. (2008) 'Westminster sacks ALMO leader.' *Inside Housing*, 22 October 2008: available at www.insidehousing.co.uk.

Story, C. (2009) 'Stock transfer mooted for Northern Ireland.' *Inside Housing*, 10 April 2009: available at www.insidehousing.co.uk.

Stothart, C. (2009) 'Is stock transfer dead?' *Inside Housing*, 18 September 2009: available at www.insidehousing.co.uk.

Sullivan, H., Nevin, B. and Smith, M. (2000) *Evaluating succession in Castle Vale Housing Action Trust*. Birmingham: University of Birmingham, School of Public Policy.

Taper, T., Walker, S. and Skinner, G. (2003) *LSVTs: Staff impacts and implications*. London: ODPM.

Taylor, M. (1998) 'Ten years of stock transfer.' In Wilcox, S. (ed.), *Scottish housing review, 1988–1998*. Edinburgh: Scottish Homes.

Taylor, M. (1999) 'Unwrapping stock transfer: Applying discourse analysis to landlord communication strategies.' *Urban Studies* 36(1): 121–35.

Taylor, M. (2004) 'Policy emergence: Learning lessons from stock transfer.' In Sim, D. (ed.), *Housing and public policy in post-devolution Scotland*. Coventry: CIH.

Taylor, M. (2008) *Managing homelessness without housing*. Edinburgh: Scottish Council for Single Homelessness.

Terry, R., Doolittle, I. and Perry, J. (2005) *ALMOs – a new future for council housing*. Scarborough and Coventry: NFA and CIH.

Thorpe, C. (2006) 'Brixen case puts ALMOs on red alert over contracts.' *Inside Housing*, 17 February 2006: available at www.insidehousing.co.uk.

Tickell, J. and Phethan, N. (2006) *With the best of intentions. Learning from problem cases III*. London: Housing Corporation.

TSA (2009a) *Building a new regulatory framework discussion paper*. London: Tenant Services Authority (TSA).

TSA (2009b) *Quarterly survey of housing associations, July 2009*. Manchester: Tenant Services Authority (TSA).

Tulloch, D. (2000) *Tenants choice: Ten years on*. Stirling: University of Sterling, Housing Policy & Practice Unit.

Twinch, E. (2009) 'Second ALMO contract ends.' *Inside Housing*, 2 October 2009: available at www.insidehousing.co.uk.

Usher, D. (1988) *Council estate sales: Studies of local experiences and future prospects*. Bristol: School for Advanced Urban Studies.

van Bortel, G. and Mullins, D. (2009) 'Critical perspectives on network governance in urban regeneration, community involvement and integration.' *Journal of Housing and the Built Environment* 24(2): 203–19.

Varney, D. (2008) *Review of the competitiveness of Northern Ireland*. London: HM Treasury.

Wadhams, C. (2006) *An opportunity waiting to happen: housing associations as 'community anchors'*. London: National Housing Federation.

Wadhams, C. (2009) *Opportunity agenda: Supporting the first steps from capacity to community*. London: Housing Associations Charitable Trust.

Waite, A. (2008) *Housing stock transfer in Wales: The community housing mutual model*. Available at www.awics.co.uk/documents/briefing_papers/housing/Housing_Stock_Transfer_in_Wales__10-07-2008.pdf.

Walker, R. M. (1998) 'New public management and housing associations. From comfort to competition?' *Policy & Politics* 26(1): 71–87.

Walker, R. M. (2001) 'How to abolish public sector housing. Housing implications and lessons from public management reform.' *Housing Studies* 16(5), September 2001: 675–96.

Walsh, K. (1995) *Public services and market mechanisms: Competition, contracting and the new public management*. London: Macmillan.

Walter, A. (2007) 'Give us real choice.' *The Guardian*, 29 March 2007.

Walterton Estates (2008) The story of Walterton and Elgin Estates in Paddington. Available at www.locallocalhistory.co.uk/municipal-housing/walterton/index.htm (accessed 15 June 2009).

Wandsworth Borough Council (1993) *Report by Chairman of Housing Committee on stock transfer option*. London: Wandsworth Borough Council.

Warburton, J. (2008) *ALMOs and the new local government agenda: a briefing paper for ALMOs*. Coventry: Housemark.

Weaver, M. (2001). 'Call to use "homes for votes" cash for housing.' *The Guardian*. 14 December 2001.

Weaver, M. (2004) 'Shockwaves as tenants veto housing management switch.' *The Guardian*, 9 January 2004: available at www.guardian.co.uk.

Weaver, M. (2005) 'Limited choice.' *The Guardian*, 3 March 2005.

Webb, S. (2003) 'Dowry dilemmas.' *Inside Housing*, 29 August 2003: available at www.insidehousing.co.uk.

Welsh Assembly Government (2002) *The Welsh Housing Quality Standard: Guidance for local authorities on the assessment process and achievement of the standard*. Cardiff: Welsh Assembly Government.

Wheal, C. (2002) 'How to win at stock transfer.' *Housing Today*, 13 June 2002.

Whitehead, C. and Scanlon, K. (eds) (2007) *Social housing in Europe*. London: London School of Economics.

Wilcox, S. (1995) *Housing review 1995/96*. York: Joseph Rowntree Foundation.

Wilcox, S. (2003). 'Commentary: Housing expenditure plans.' in Wilcox, S. (ed.) *UK housing review 2003/2004*. Coventry and London: CIH and Council of Mortgage Lenders.

Wilcox, S. (2004). 'Housing expenditure plans.' in Wilcox, S. (ed.) *UK housing review 2004/2005*. Coventry and London: CIH and Council of Mortgage Lenders.

Wilcox, S. and Bramley, G. (1993) *Local housing companies: New opportunities for council housing*. York: Joseph Rowntree Foundation.

Williams, P. and Wilcox, S. (2001) 'Funding social housing: Changing times, changing markets.' *Housing Finance* 52(3): 398–45.

Wolch, J. P. (1990) *The shadow state: Government and the voluntary sector in transition*. New York: Foundation Centre.

Zitron, J. (1995) *Local housing companies: A good practice guide*. Coventry: CIH.

Zitron, J. (2004) *Stock transfers: Reflections on finance and government issues*. Paper presented to Housing Studies Association spring conference, Sheffield Hallam University, 15–16 April 2004 (unpublished).

Zitron, J., Terry, R. and Doolittle, I. (1999) *New structures for council housing*. Coventry and London: CIH and Local Government Association.

Index